ELITE ATTACK FORCES

AIRBORNE
AT WAR

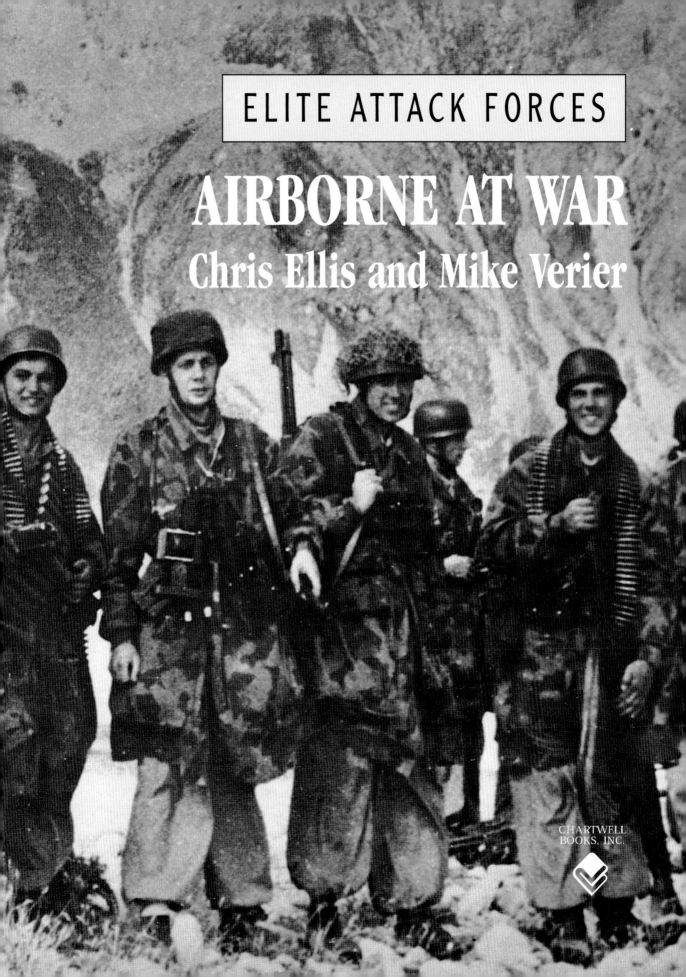

ELITE ATTACK FORCES

AIRBORNE AT WAR
Chris Ellis and Mike Verier

CHARTWELL
BOOKS, INC.

This edition published by 2007 by

CHARTWELL BOOKS, INC.
A Division of
BOOK SALES, INC.
114 Northfield Avenue
Edison, New Jersey 08837

ISBN 10: 0-7858-2324-7
ISBN 13: 978-0-7858-2324-7

Acknowledgements
All photos in the 7th Flieger section of this book
came from the author's collection unless otherwise
credited, while useful assistance with organisation
charts was provided by Peter Chamberlain, Simon
Forty, and George Forty. Information and many of
the illustrations in the 82nd Airborne section came
from Chris Ellis, George Forty, Simon Forty, and
Bruce Robertson. The maps on page 156 are based
on two in Robert Kershaw's *D-Day* (Ian Allan Ltd.
1985).

Previous page: Well-armed 7th Flieger paratroops
during the Gran Sasso raid.

Right: Fallschirmjäger at Cassino.
TRH Pictures

CONTENTS

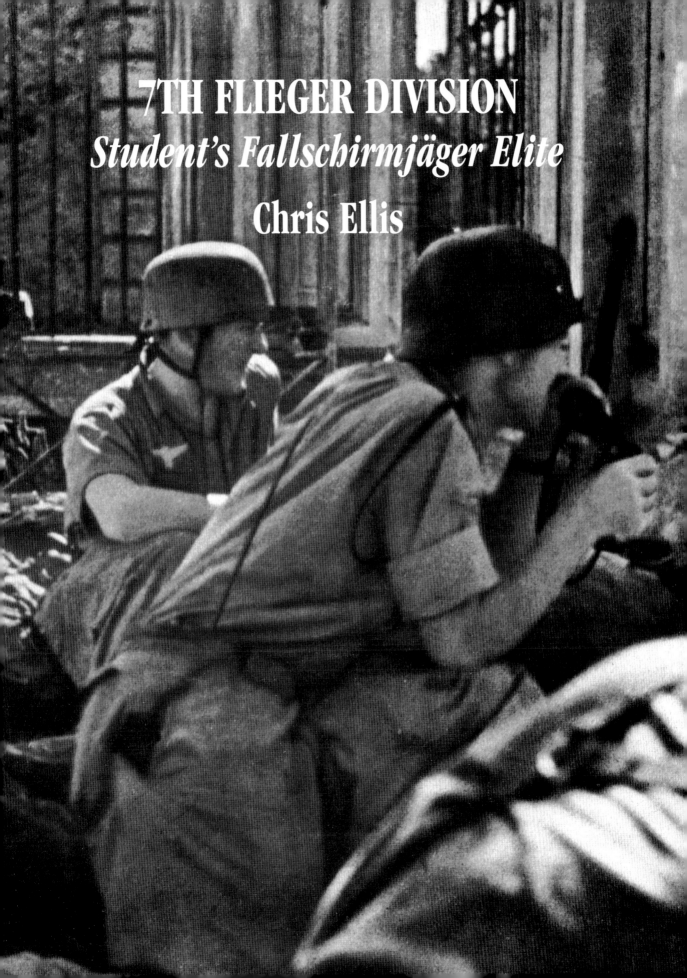

7TH FLIEGER DIVISION
Student's Fallschirmjäger Elite

Chris Ellis

ORIGINS & HISTORY

Wild notions of flying soldiers into battle were put forward as fantasies over the centuries, long before man had actually mastered the idea of flight. One of the ideas portrayed in patriotic French prints when Napoleon threatened to invade England in the early 1800s was a force of soldiers carried over the English Channel in hot air balloons to supplement the soldiers arriving by sea and through a hastily dug Channel Tunnel! Far fetched as these notions were – in this case assuming an adequate supply of balloons and an obliging wind – it is clear that utilising the sky and aerial transport as a means of carrying war to the enemy was occupying military minds from quite early times. When balloons became a practical possibility they were used by the military in, for example, the American Civil War and some colonial wars as an aid to military reconnaissance, even though they had no direct offensive capability.

By the time of World War I with its military airships and aeroplanes, however, the parachute had been perfected, as an escape aid from damaged aircraft and balloons, and the first real suggestion of using soldiers landed by parachute was almost certainly put forward by the ever-inventive Brigadier-General Billy Mitchell, one of the US Army's pioneer flyers. Noting the stalemate on the Western Front when the United States entered the war, he proposed that one way to make a breakthrough would be to land battalions by parachute behind enemy lines. The problem here was the fact that training a number of infantry battalions to land by parachute, and to get together enough parachutes to equip them and enough aircraft to carry them would be an immense logistic problem that would take a minimum of six months to achieve. But this was 1918 and the war ended in November of that year with no decisions being taken over this very prescient scheme.

In the 1920s the Italian Army carried out some trial drops with parachutists but did not pursue the idea. It was the Russians who developed the idea of military airborne operations in a big way. In the 1920s the Soviet government supported and funded sport parachuting, both from aircraft and from specially built jumping towers. It was popular and keenly followed, with the Osswiachim Parachute Club as national organiser. By 1940 there were over a thousand town and village parachute clubs affiliated to the national organisation. Against this background the first Red Army parachute units were formed experimentally in 1928. The first recorded use of parachute forces in the Red Army was in the military exercises of 1930 when a platoon commanded by a lieutenant dropped south of Moscow and 'captured' a divisional HQ with all its staff. The first Red Army parachute brigade was formed in 1932, 400 strong, and this force made demonstration drops at the Moscow Air Days of 1933 and 1934. By 1935 this force had been greatly expanded and in the summer exercises of that year, near Kiev, there was a drop by 1,000 parachute troops, followed by 5,000 airborne troops flown into the drop zone by transport aircraft. Official photographs and newsreel film of this spectacular event made some impact in the West as previous activities had not been publicised by the secretive Russians. A similar demonstration involving 6,000 airborne troops was staged in the 1936 summer exercises near Minsk in the Ukraine and this time military observers were invited from Britain, France and Czechoslovakia, and on this occasion they also witnessed the airborne forces going into action with conventional infantry weapons immediately after landing. Leading the British observers was Major-General Archibald Wavell, and his report of the event included the oft-quoted remark, 'If I had not seen it for myself, I should not have believed such a thing to be possible.'

By this time the Red Army was also experimenting with air drops of artillery and light vehicles, and was also looking at the use of gliders to land infantry and equipment. All this experience and development was dissipated, however, in 1937 when Stalin began his infamous purge of the army high command. Among the victims was Marshal Mikhail Tukhachevski, the dynamic C-in-C of the Red Army who had enthusiastically sanctioned and sponsored the establishment and growth of the airborne forces. The Parachute Command was disbanded and the troops dispersed to ordinary units. It was 1941 before the Red Army once again established airborne forces.

GERMAN INTEREST

The German high command was clearly aware of developments in Russia. Even before the Nazi Party came to power the old Weimar Republic's Reichswehr (armed forces) had a secret agreement with the Soviet government throughout the 1920s and early 1930s whereby weapons development and training was carried out covertly in Russia as a means of overcoming the strict conditions of the 1919 Versailles Treaty. One of a number of staff officers who travelled and worked in Russia in this period was Major Kurt Student who had been a flying ace and squadron commander in the Imperial Air Force of 1916–18. At this time Student was mainly concerned with engine and aircraft development but his brief covered all matters related to air operations.

Student was not the instigator of airborne operations in the German armed forces, however, being too junior in rank when the Nazi Party came to power in early 1933. A Reichs Aviation Ministry was set up in 1933 and Student, now an Oberstleutnant (lt-col) was appointed to take charge of technical training schools. Gliding and flying clubs were initially used to build up a cadre of trained personnel for the embryonic Luftwaffe (air force). Erhard Milch, a former director of Lufthansa, was appointed as aviation secretary to oversee the build up, with Hermann Göring in political control as Reichskommissar for Air. It was not until March 1935 that the Luftwaffe's formation was officially announced by which time it already had over 1,800 aircraft and 20,000 men, all in contravention of the terms of the Versailles Treaty. Göring now became formally commander of the Luftwaffe and the chief of staff was General Walther Wever (transferred from the Army) who was an astute and hard-working staff officer, though he was killed in an air accident in May 1936 and replaced by General Albert Kesselring. It was Wever who suggested to Göring – sceptical at first – that a battalion of parachute troops should be formed by the Luftwaffe, and it was Wever who kept the initial momentum going and ensured funding for training and equipment.

Above: The earliest use of parachutes was during WWI for escaping from damaged observation balloons.

The first men to become German parachute troops were not, however, Luftwaffe or even Army men; they were para-military policemen. This was due to Göring's influence and position of power. As Minister-President of Prussia, among his many offices, he was also the head of the Prussian Landespolizei. This was a para-military organisation of armed police which had been formed in Weimar days as a means of flouting the Versailles Treaty and putting more men under arms than was possible through the limited size permitted to the Heer (Army). At the time the Luftwaffe was formally announced in March 1935 other elements of re-organisation transferred all the para-military police units to the Army, and civilian policing was left to local forces of conventional type. Göring enjoyed sufficient power to retain direct control of one unit, Landespolizeigruppe *General Göring*, ostensibly to protect his own office and activities as a sort of private bodyguard. This was also transferred to the Army on 1 April 1935, and was renamed the Regiment *General Göring* while retaining its same duties. When General Wever persuaded Göring that a German parachute force was desirable to match Red Army progress, Göring selected his elite regiment to form the nucleus. In September 1935 he passed a formal order to Oberstleutnant Jakoby, the regimental commander stating that: 'The regiment will be transferred on 1 October 1935, intact, into the Luftwaffe. From volunteers of the Regiment you will organise a Paratroop Battalion as a cadre for the future German Parachute Troops.'

During October the regiment moved to the Altengrabow training area to familiarise themselves with aircraft and parachutes. From there they moved to the Döbritz training area and at Jüterbog airfield they lined up to watch a demonstration jump by a corporal with parachute experience. He made a heavy landing, due to misjudgement, and was carried away unconscious. However, this did not stop over 600 men coming forward next day when volunteers were called for to form the first parachute battalion. Named 1. Bataillon (1st Battalion), Regiment *General Göring*, the commander was Major Bruno Bräuer and the adjutant was Oberleutnant Vogel. The company commanders were Hauptmann Reinburger and Oberleutnants Kroh, Schulz, and Walther. All of them were soon promoted and all went on to important commands in World War II. Later the battalion was redesignated as the 4. Bataillon, Regiment *General Göring*, though it changed again to 1. Bataillon, Fallschirmjäger-Regiment 1 (1st Battalion, 1st Parachute Regiment), when the parachute forces were re-organised into 7. Flieger-Division in 1938.

Before then, however, there were more developments. Early in 1936 a Luftwaffe Parachute School was set up at Stendal, 60km north of Magdeburg, and this also became the official garrison town of the new parachute forces. Initially, of course, the 1st Battalion formed the entire establishment. They got down to serious training and the development of equipment, including the first standardised static-line parachute, designated RZ1. Techniques for delivering paratroops from the Junkers Ju 52 transport were tried and valuable work was done. However, there was a lull in expansion of the new force after its mentor, General Wever, was killed in an air crash. His successor, Kesselring, preferred to concentrate on expanding the air fleet and regarded paratroops as a sideline. However, by this time Kurt Student, now a colonel (Oberst), had been appointed Inspector General for Luftwaffe Training Schools, and the Stendal Parachute School came within his province.

The first official appearance of the Luftwaffe paratroops was in October 1936 when a platoon was dropped into simulated action during the autumn exercises that took place in Lower Saxony. By this time the German Army, too, was giving serious thought to paratroop formations and received permission to organise a

parachute company. This was formed early in 1937 and sent to Stendal to train since the Army had no parachute training facilities of its own. The company commander was Oberleutnant Zahn and his second-in-command was Oberleutnant Pelz, noted at the time as a leading pentathlon exponent. By the autumn of 1937 this company was considered fully trained and also had a full complement of heavy weapons. In the spring of 1937 the Luftwaffe parachute battalion and the new Army parachute company jumped in exercises at Mecklenburg observed by Hitler, who was said to be impressed by the spectacle. It was now decided to expand the Army parachute company to battalion strength and this was completed by the spring of 1938. The first battalion commander was Major Heidrich, an experienced infantry instructor who went to Stendal to qualify as a parachutist first despite being then aged 41. This followed the example set by Major Bruno Bräuer of the Regiment *General Göring* who also qualified as soon as he was appointed and had then made the first 'official' jump of the new German parachute arm two years earlier on 11 May 1936.

Above: Balloon parachutists during WWI. Parachutes were developed as aids to escape damaged aircraft and balloons. Observation balloons were extensively used by the military from the American Civil War onwards by all leading powers, including the Germans. This was an early appreciation of the value of airpower to further military operations, giving a third dimension to the land war.

7. FLIEGER IS FORMED

By the spring of 1938 Hitler's ambitions for expanding 'Greater Germany' were well under way, starting with a covert plan to annexe Czechoslovakia, finalised as Fall Grün (Case Green) in May. This necessitated some hasty military planning and the use of airborne troops was seen as a way of getting behind the strong Czech border defences. To organise the airborne arm from the forces already available, the experienced Kurt Student was appointed with the rank of Generalmajor and in the way the Luftwaffe had of designating their air combat commands, the Luftwaffe

Above: Detail showing the static line on an RZ1 parachute, the original German parachute that was superseded by the RZ20.

airborne forces became 7. Flieger-Division from 1 July 1938, and Student's command became effective from that date. However, he had to work fast because the division was required to be combat-ready by 15 September in time for Case Green to start. Student, enthusiastic and hard-working was up to the task, which was why he had been selected, but he also had the advantage of commanding Göring's respect and confidence which allowed him to plan, train, and organise in the way he thought best. This freedom of action was almost certainly helped by the fact that at the time nobody else of high rank knew anything about the subject!

Student set up his divisional HQ at Berlin-Tempelhof airfield with Hauptmann Heinz Trettner as chief of staff and a small planning team picked from trusted Luftwaffe colleagues. Such directives on airborne operations that had by then emanated from the Armed Forces High Command (OKW) saw the use of paratroops largely for securing airfields to allow the Luftwaffe to fly in troops, or sabotage or raiding operations in small units behind enemy lines. Student started planning afresh, however. His conception was that airborne operations would ideally take place in three phases. First would be the landing of shock troops by glider to take out key positions and defence posts. Secondly paratroops would secure airfields or areas big enough to land aircraft, or attack defence lines from the rear. Thirdly air landing troops would be brought in to the landing zones already secured by the paratroops to pave the way for the arrival of regualr infantry and heavy weapons. Student described these as shock tactics deliberately intended to cause 'surprise, fright and panic' combined with speed of events.

For the Case Green operations the Army parachute battalion was taken under command of 7. Flieger. At the time the division comprised Division HQ; 1st Battalion of 1. FJR (Oberstleutnant Bräuer), the Army Parachute Infantry Battalion (Major Heidrich), Air Landing Battalion 'Regiment *General Göring*' (Major Sydow), an infantry gun company (Oberleutnant Schram), a medical company and a signals company. Also included was a newly formed glider company commanded by Leutnant Weiss. This was equipped with the new DFS 230 glider which had been ordered in 1937 after a demonstration in front of Kesselring, Milch, Udet and other senior Luftwaffe officers. The famous test pilot Hanna Reitsch had flown the prototype on that occasion and impressed the watchers with her fast precise landing from a 1,000m cast-off by the towing Ju 52. Eight soldiers demonstrated a fast exit from the aircraft. All other tests were successful and a small initial order was placed.

The DFS 230 had been designed in 1933 for meteorological research but when the influential aviator Ernst Udet saw it he recognised its potential as a load or personnel carrier for military use and used his contacts to secure development of a sturdier military prototype. For Case Green six wings of Ju 52s were put under command, but the division was still short of men for the air landing component and the Army could not be persuaded to put more units under Luftwaffe control. To make up the numbers Student asked Göring if the Nazi Party's top SA unit, the Regiment *Feldherrenhalle*, could be assigned and quickly be given some field training. This was done, though its fighting value would have been doubtful had the invasion of Czechoslovakia gone ahead.

Göring, with his SA rank and connections, was honorary colonel of the *Feldherrenhalle* and during the military element of their training, some young members of this SA regiment were given parachute and airborne experience and the regiment was affiliated to the Luftwaffe to the extent that the men wore Luftwaffe field dress when on annual manoeuvres. By this connection the regiment became, in effect, a reserve Luftwaffe unit and as soon as the war started the *Feldherrenhalle* members were absorbed into the air landing assault battalion and the new 2nd Parachute Regiment of the expanding 7. Flieger-Division. Others went to the Army's *Feldherrenhalle* Battalion.

Student and his men worked hard and he was able to report 7. Flieger 'combat ready' on 1 September 1938, two weeks ahead of the deadline. These two weeks were used for intensive air landing exercises. However, as is well-known, Case Green never took place, for the crisis talks that led to the Munich Agreement at the end of September resulted in Hitler being allowed to take over the German-speaking Sudetenland area of Czechoslovakia in October 1938 and war was averted for another year. Göring was keen to show off the Luftwaffe's air landing capability, anyway, so as part of the Czech occupation he had 7. Flieger fly into the key area around Freudenthal (their Case Green objective in fact) using an impressive fleet of 242 Junkers 52s. This was actually more of a demonstration than a realistic exercise for there was no opposition and no critical time factor, and a good deal of showing off. But Göring liked what he saw and said afterwards, 'This business has a great future.'

This event gave a good deal of new impetus to the build-up of a Luftwaffe airborne force, and Student's stock was high. From 1 January 1939, the Army Parachute Battalion was transferred to the Luftwaffe (not without much arm-twisting by Göring) and it became the 2nd Battalion, FJR 1, still commanded by Major Heidrich. The Air Landing Battalion became the 3rd Battalion, FJR 1 (Mayor Sydow) and Bräuer now commanded the newly expanded regiment with the rank of Oberst (colonel). His place as 1st Battalion commander was taken by Major von Grazy. The Army agreed to commit the 22nd Infantry Division as the designated air landing component for future operations, essentially an ordinary infantry division which would be carried in by the Ju 52 transports and would train in this role. Moreover it agreed the division would come under 7. Flieger command in battle. During 1939 the establishment of 7. Flieger-Division expanded considerably with the addition of 7th Howitzer Battery, 7th Anti-Tank Company, 7th Intelligence Company, 7th Medical Company and smaller support and logistics units. Student was given extra responsibility by being appointed, additionally, as Inspector-General of Airborne Troops.

A highlight of 1939 was the appearance of 7. Flieger troops in Hitler's huge 50th birthday parade in Berlin under the command of Oberst Bräuer. They made a big visual impact, not only with the German people but with Germany's potential enemies. For, unlike all the units in parade dress, the parachute battalions wore full combat kit with their distinctive jump smocks, helmets, and slung rifles. They looked as though they meant business.

Above: Troops learning jumping posture on a training rig, showing splayed leg position (much like a modern skydiver).

Below: Awaiting their turn for practice, Fallschirmjäger at Stendal Parachute Training School.

READY FOR WAR

In March 1939, in defiance of the terms of the Munich Agreement, Hitler seized the remainder of Czechoslovakia by military force. For this 7. Flieger-Division was detailed to drop on and secure Kbely Airport near Prague and to seize Hradcany Castle, the seat of government. But a day-long blizzard prevented flying operations and fast moving Army units took these objectives instead. When the weather cleared 7. Flieger did no more than fly into the airport which was already in German hands.

POLAND

Hitler's next ambition was to take Poland and covert plans were made to mass the military units involved near the German–Polish border. Mobilisation was ordered on 26 August 1939. For its part 7. Flieger-Division was to move by road convoy from its base in Berlin to Breslau (then the capital of German Silesia but now Wroclaw in Poland). While the troops were on the move on 1 September 1939, the invasion of Poland started. The men of 7. Flieger heard the news during a meal break on the Autobahn. The division's units were ordered to airfields near Breslau there to await operational orders for deployment as the high command saw fit. However, no airborne operations were actually carried out in the campaign.

Britain and France had declared war on Germany on 3 September when Hitler ignored their ultimatum to withdraw his forces from Poland but they could give no direct military help to Poland and, if anything, their involvement caused the campaign to be hastened. Fast moving panzer divisions, using the *Blitzkrieg* tactics which made such an impact in World War II, seized several objectives that were earmarked to be taken by 7. Flieger. These included Graudenz and the Vistula Bridge near Pulawy, but in each case the troops were in their Ju 52s on the runway when the operations were called off. Morale among the men dropped in the circumstances, but in mid-September they actually saw action. However, this was in a motorised infantry role, not as paratroops.

Their task was to seize and secure airfields between the Vistula and Bug Rivers to deny their use to Polish units, many of which had been cut-off or outflanked in the fast moving ground war. First contact with the enemy was on 14 September when the 3rd Battalion clashed with Polish units. Student himself was nearly captured when his staff car inadvertently drove through a Polish position. And on 24 September the 2nd Battalion had a particularly tough engagement that brought the division's first casualties of the war at Wola-Gulowska. First of several men to die was Feldwebel (sergeant) Mensch, a

Above: Paratroops under training having their
parachute packs checked before a jump.

Below: German Fallschirmjäger dived from the
aircraft rather than jumped.

popular and experienced NCO. The dead
were buried in an old fort at Demblin.

Soon Poland capitulated and 7. Flieger
carried out 'occupation' duties, guarding
airfields and Luftwaffe HQs and sorting out
prisoners, before being ordered back to
Berlin in mid-October. The division's leaders
were disappointed that their skills in air-
landing were not needed, but on the other
hand this preserved the surprise factor
which would be better exploited in Hitler's
plan to conquer Western Europe in 1940.
This scheme, Fall Gelb (Case Yellow), was
already being developed.

TACTICS AND EQUIPMENT

During the winter months the men of 7. Flieger
trained hard, and in early 1940
they started specialist training for their key part in the campaign to come. By
then they had already long worked out their modes of operation and developed
the special equipment needed in parachute drops and air landings.

Very distinctive to the parachute troops was the combat dress which
comprised high boots, a long smock, and a rimless close-fitting helmet, plus
detachable knee-pads for wear when jumping. This general style of clothing was
adopted with detail variations by the parachute troops of other countries later
in the war.

In the very earliest days a conventional ripcord parachute was used, but this
had the disadvantage that jumping had to be done from a great height, well
above the minimum safe height of 200 metres (650ft) for this type of chute. A
much lower jump height was considered vital for military operations and very
quickly a static-line parachute was developed,
designated RZ1 which allowed a jump height of around
120 metres (400ft). With the RZ1 the static line was
hooked to a rail inside the aircraft and the parachute
was automatically pulled open at a safe distance from
the aircraft. Because the Germans adopted the old
Salvatore parachute design, which attached to the
harness above the small of the back, the parachutist
could not reach and manipulate the shroud lines.
Descent and direction were not controllable—unlike
their British and US counterparts. In these conditions
it was also difficult for German paras to 'spill' the wind
and after landing the man could be dragged along the
ground and injured if the chute was difficult to release.
The jerk of the static line also caused the chute to
swing in descent and the jumper could do virtually
nothing to control this. To reduce swing in the air the
German paratroops used a distinctive spread-eagled
'diving' position as they left the aircraft and
maintained this in descent. They were taught to land

face forward on all fours, hence the provision of the knee pads and also elbow pads, though not all men wore the latter. Winds stronger than 14mph meant the chutes were carried over a wide area and the preferred weather for a 'copybook' drop was light airs and calm which was an obvious operational limitation. Later parachute designs, such as the RZ16 of 1940 and RZ20 of 1941, were better-shaped and more stable, but never satisfactory.

Because of the parachutes' limitations the parachutists' side arms and ammunition were dropped separately in parachute containers, colour coded for each unit, and carried under the wings of the drop aircraft. The parachutist himself jumped carrying a pistol with 20 rounds, benzedrine tablets, field dressing, some food (chocolate, biscuits, etc.) and a knife, all carried in the pockets of the smock. The knife could be used to cut away the parachute lines if there was difficulty releasing the harness. The necessity of using the arms and equipment containers was another limitation. Even though they had smoke markers which activated when they hit the ground, these containers still had to be collected, opened and the contents distributed, before the troops could go into action effectively. If the containers fell far away, got stuck in trees, or fell into streams, etc., there were major problems.

Above: Landing training—the position accounts for the padding on uniform knee and elbow.

The standard paratroop carrier – and glider tug – was the slow but rugged tri-motor Junkers 52. It was designed as an airliner in 1930 and the first major user was, naturally, Lufthansa, though it was also sold abroad to other airlines such as Swissair, Air France and about 28 other airline customers. Militarised versions were ordered for the new Luftwaffe in 1934–35, mainly as transports. Though it was obsolescent by the late 1930s, with its fixed undercarriage, low top speed (270km/hr or 168mph), and limited capacity it remained in service through World War II. It was immensely tough and reliable and was popularly known to servicemen as 'Tante Ju' (Auntie Junkers). One aircraft could carry 13 paratroops sitting facing inwards on canvas seats. The exit door was in the port (left) side. A Staffel of 12 aircraft could carry a company of 156 men, and a Gruppe of four Staffeln could carry a battalion. This was 'rule of thumb' and in practice more aircraft were often used to carry support units or reinforcements, etc., and equipment such as light anti-tank guns and motorcycle combinations. Later it was found that these types of item could be carried under the fuselage between the wheel struts.

Parachute training lasted eight weeks and men were taught to pack their own parachutes. Much ground training was given in landing techniques and aircraft exit techniques using ground fuselage rigs and suitable jumping platforms and towers. Extensive physical training was given to make the soldier fit for the stress of jumping, landing and going into action and the German paratroops were some of the fittest and toughest fighting men of the war. This was aided by the fact that all were volunteers; any unfit or psychologically unsure men were weeded out early on in the training course. While Stendal remained the main training school for paratroops, further schools were opened during World War II at Wittstock, Braunschweig, and Châteaudun in France. This was necessary as the German parachute forces expanded greatly as the war progressed.

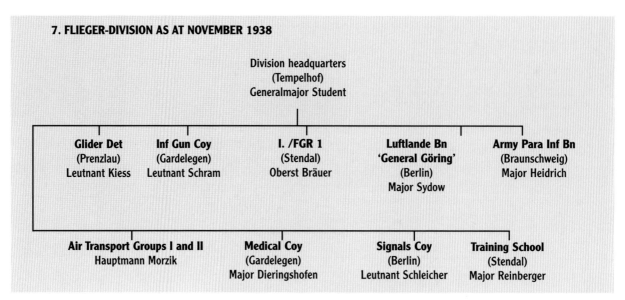

7. FLIEGER-DIVISION AS AT NOVEMBER 1938

Division headquarters
(Tempelhof)
Generalmajor Student

Glider Det	Inf Gun Coy	I. /FGR 1	Luftlande Bn	Army Para Inf Bn
(Prenzlau)	(Gardelegen)	(Stendal)	'General Göring'	(Braunschweig)
Leutnant Kiess	Leutnant Schram	Oberst Bräuer	(Berlin)	Major Heidrich
			Major Sydow	

Air Transport Groups I and II	Medical Coy	Signals Coy	Training School
Hauptmann Morzik	(Gardelegen)	(Berlin)	(Stendal)
	Major Dieringshofen	Leutnant Schleicher	Major Reinberger

Above: Order of battle of 7. Flieger Division at November 1938.

Right: Men of the 7. Flieger Division march past on Hitler's birthday parade, 20 April 1939.

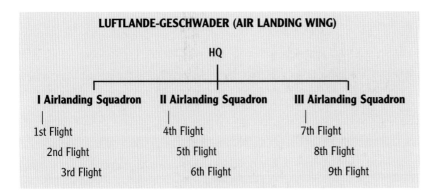

LUFTLANDE-GESCHWADER (AIR LANDING WING)

HQ

I Airlanding Squadron	II Airlanding Squadron	III Airlanding Squadron
1st Flight	4th Flight	7th Flight
2nd Flight	5th Flight	8th Flight
3rd Flight	6th Flight	9th Flight

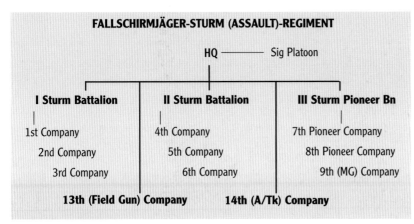

FALLSCHIRMJÄGER-STURM (ASSAULT)-REGIMENT

HQ ——— Sig Platoon

I Sturm Battalion	II Sturm Battalion	III Sturm Pioneer Bn
1st Company	4th Company	7th Pioneer Company
2nd Company	5th Company	8th Pioneer Company
3rd Company	6th Company	9th (MG) Company

13th (Field Gun) Company   **14th (A/Tk) Company**

Above left: Organisation of the Ju 52 Luftlande-Geschwader 1 used for para operations in 1940.

Left: German organisation chart dated September 1940 for the Fallschirmjäger-Sturmregiment. For the 1941 Crete operation a fourth battalion was added.

Below: Paratroop stick dropping from a Junkers Ju 52. This shows the correct intervals between jumpers in a stick.

IN ACTION

Above: Parachutes hanging up awaiting packing. The Fallschirmjäger packed his own parachute prior to jumping.

INVASION PLANS

Fall Gelb (Case Yellow), the invasion of France and Flanders, was decided upon by Hitler as soon as the Polish campaign was over. He issued orders on 9 October 1939 to commence the offensive in the West only a month later on 12 November, but the Army High Command was able to get it postponed, pointing out the logistic impossibility of moving the divisions from Poland to the West, then reorganising them for the new campaign, all against the background of worsening winter weather. Therefore the campaign was put back to spring 1940.

One of the uses for the airborne forces, already decided on, was the taking of key positions in the forthcoming offensive, and to prepare for this Student set up a unit under the 'camouflage' name of Test Section Friedrichshafen. This unit comprised the 1st Company of the 1st Battalion, FJR 1, and the Pioneer Platoon of the 2nd Battalion, plus a glider squadron, all under command of Hauptmann Koch. The force totalled 11 officers and 427 men. Their task was to perfect the technique of landing gliders in the smallest possible area with a dedicated assault force. Later this unit revealed its true purpose when it was renamed Assault Battalion *Koch* (Stürmabteilung *Koch*).

This was all part of the preparation for the deployment of 7. Flieger in the opening stages of the forthcoming offensive. The assault battalion would take the key Belgian frontier fort of Eben Emael, a commanding defence position, plus the key bridges along the Albert Canal. The rest of 7. Flieger, with 22nd Air Landing Division under command also, would take and secure the key airfields and river crossings in Holland. For this campaign 7. Flieger was put under the nominal control of Luftflotte 2 (commanded by Kesselring) which would be providing the air cover for the operation.

ACTION IN NORWAY AND DENMARK

The first parachute operation of the war took place not as part of the planned Case Yellow, but as part of Operation Weserübung (Weser Exercise), the occupation of Norway and Denmark. This operation had to be organised and staged hurriedly as the Germans got wind of a planned Anglo–French landing in Norway to block the shipping of iron ore to Germany from northern Sweden which was taken out from Narvik, down the Norwegian coast to the Baltic ports. To forestall Allied plans, German forces moved into Denmark and Norway on the morning of 9 April 1940.

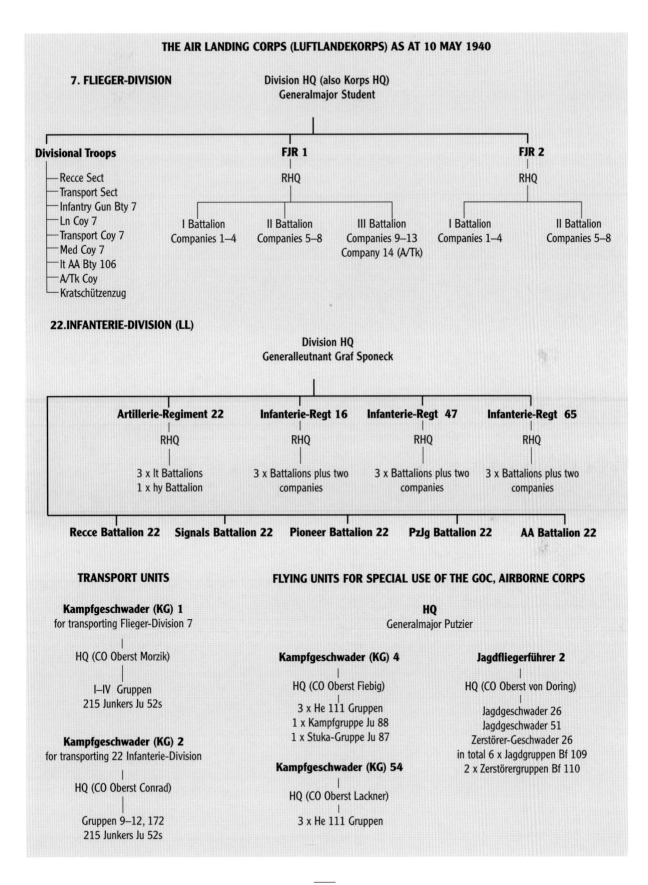

THE AIR LANDING CORPS (LUFTLANDEKORPS) AS AT 10 MAY 1940

7. FLIEGER-DIVISION

Division HQ (also Korps HQ)
Generalmajor Student

Divisional Troops
- Recce Sect
- Transport Sect
- Infantry Gun Bty 7
- Ln Coy 7
- Transport Coy 7
- Med Coy 7
- lt AA Bty 106
- A/Tk Coy
- Kratschützenzug

FJR 1
RHQ

I Battalion	II Battalion	III Battalion
Companies 1–4	Companies 5–8	Companies 9–13
		Company 14 (A/Tk)

FJR 2
RHQ

| I Battalion | II Battalion |
| Companies 1–4 | Companies 5–8 |

22.INFANTERIE-DIVISION (LL)

Division HQ
Generalleutnant Graf Sponeck

Artillerie-Regiment 22	**Infanterie-Regt 16**	**Infanterie-Regt 47**	**Infanterie-Regt 65**
RHQ	RHQ	RHQ	RHQ
3 x lt Battalions	3 x Battalions plus two	3 x Battalions plus two	3 x Battalions plus two
1 x hy Battalion	companies	companies	companies

Recce Battalion 22   **Signals Battalion 22**   **Pioneer Battalion 22**   **PzJg Battalion 22**   **AA Battalion 22**

TRANSPORT UNITS

Kampfgeschwader (KG) 1
for transporting Flieger-Division 7

HQ (CO Oberst Morzik)

I–IV Gruppen
215 Junkers Ju 52s

Kampfgeschwader (KG) 2
for transporting 22 Infanterie-Division

HQ (CO Oberst Conrad)

Gruppen 9–12, 172
215 Junkers Ju 52s

FLYING UNITS FOR SPECIAL USE OF THE GOC, AIRBORNE CORPS

HQ
Generalmajor Putzier

Kampfgeschwader (KG) 4

HQ (CO Oberst Fiebig)

3 x He 111 Gruppen
1 x Kampfgruppe Ju 88
1 x Stuka-Gruppe Ju 87

Kampfgeschwader (KG) 54

HQ (CO Oberst Lackner)

3 x He 111 Gruppen

Jagdfliegerführer 2

HQ (CO Oberst von Doring)

Jagdgeschwader 26
Jagdgeschwader 51
Zerstörer-Geschwader 26
in total 6 x Jagdgruppen Bf 109
2 x Zerstörergruppen Bf 110

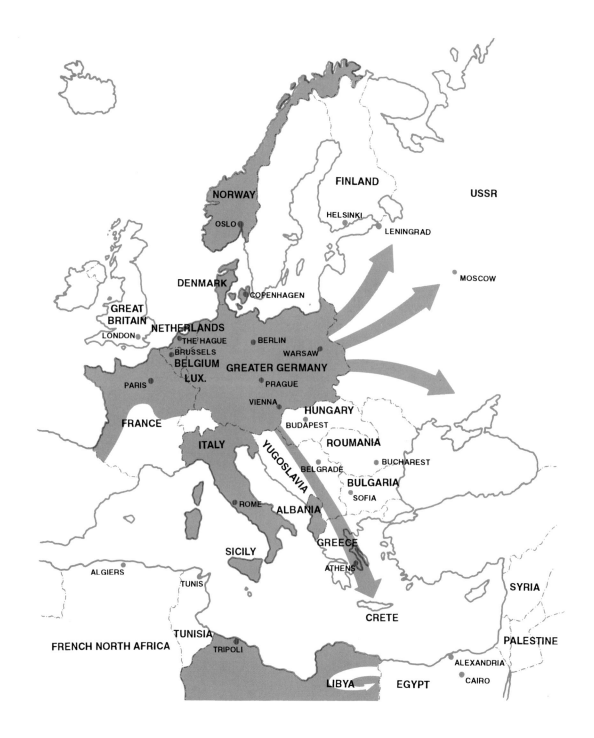

Map showing Fallschirmjäger deployments in the early war years, 1940–42.

Norway and Denmark: Parachute and air landings April 1940, including I./FJR 1 reinforcement of Narvik.

Holland: Airfields and bridges 10 May 1940.

Belgium: Fort Eben Emael and Albert Canal bridges 10 May 1940.

Corinth: Glider and paratroop landings on canal 27 April 1941.

Crete: Landings by 7. Flieger Division, 5. Gebirgs Division, Fallschirm Assault Regiment, Fallschirm-Pioneer-Bn, Corps Troops.

Eastern Front: 7. Flieger Division detachment and Div HQ.

Western Desert: Fallschirmjäger Brigade Ramcke November 1942.

Tunisia: Defensive ops 1942–43 by FJR 5 and Fallschirm-Pioneer-Bn 21.

Map showing Fallschirmjäger deployments in the later war years, 1943–45.

Leros: I./FJR 2, 12 November 1943.

Sicily: Defensive operations by 1. FJD, July 1943.

Italy, Anzio and Monte Cassino: Defensive operations by 1. FJD, 1943.

Italy, Rome: Defensive operations by 2. FJD, 1943.

Italy, Mt Rotondo: Capture of Italian Army HQ by II./FJR 6, September 1943.

Elba: Capture of island by II./FJR 7, 17 September 1943 .

Italy, Gran Sasso: Battlegroup Rescue of Mussolini, 12 September 1943.

Italy: Defensive operations in north by 4. FJD, 1944.

Western Front: Defence of Normandy and Brittany by 1. Fallschirm-Armee from July 1944.

Western Front: Defence of Maas and Waal rivers, September1944.

Western Front: Ardennes Offensive, December 1944/January 1945.

Western Front: Defence of the Rhineland, 1945.

Eastern Front: 2. FJD at Zhitomir and Kirovgrad.

Eastern Front: 'Hermann Göring' Fallschirm-Pz-Korps defence of Breslau, 1945.

Eastern Front: Defence of Austria 1945.

Eastern Front: Defence of Berlin 9.FJD, 1945.

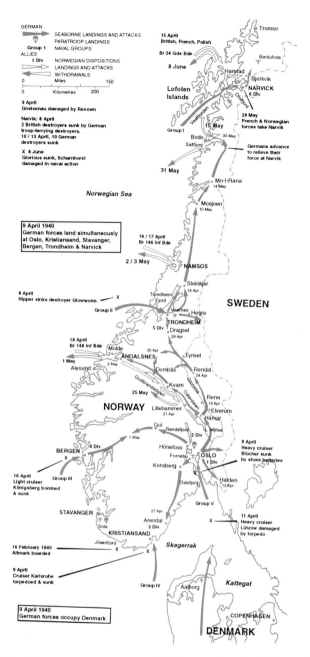

LEGEND

GERMAN
⬇ SEABORNE LANDINGS AND ATTACKS
PARATROOP LANDINGS
Group 1 NAVAL GROUPS
ALLIES
1 Div NORWEGIAN DISPOSITIONS
LANDINGS AND ATTACKS
WITHDRAWALS

0 Miles 150
0 Kilometres 200

9 April
Gneisenau damaged by Renown

Narvik: 8 April
2 British destroyers sunk by German
troop-ferrying destroyers.
10 / 13 April, 10 German
destroyers sunk

X 8 June
Glorious sunk, Scharnhorst
damaged in naval action

Norwegian Sea

9 April 1940
German forces land simultaneously
at Oslo, Kristiansand, Stavanger,
Bergen, Trondheim & Narvik.

8 April
Hipper sinks destroyer Glowworm

18 April
Br 148 Inf Bde

1 May
Alesund

10 April
Light cruiser
Königsberg bombed
& sunk

16 February 1940
Altmark boarded

9 April
Cruiser Karlsruhe
torpedoed & sunk

9 April 1940
German forces occupy Denmark

15 April
British, French, Polish
Br 24 Gds Bde
8 June
NARVICK
6 Div
28 May
French & Norwegian
forces take Narvik
Germans advance
to relieve their
force at Narvik

Mo-I-Rana
Mosjoen

16 / 17 April
Br 146 Inf Bde
2 / 3 May
NAMSOS
Steinkjer
Trondheim
Fjord
Vaernes Hegra
TRONDHEIM
Dragset
Molde
ÅNDALSNES
Dombås Rendal
Kvam
Gudbrandsdalen
Lillehammer
Hamar
L. Mjøsa
Gol
Randsfjord
Hönefoss
Fornebu OSLO
Konsberg 1 Div
Oslofjord
Halden

9 April
Heavy cruiser
Blücher sunk
by shore batteries

11 April
Heavy cruiser
Lützow damaged
by torpedo

BERGEN
4 Div
Group III

STAVANGER
Arendal
Sola
KRISTIANSAND
Jösenfjord
Skagerrak

Group IV
Aalborg *Kattegat*

COPENHAGEN
DENMARK

SWEDEN

NORWAY

Above: The Battle of Norway.

Above right: Men of the 7. Flieger Division march past on Hitler's birthday parade, 20 April 1939. The collar and tie plus full parachute harness were normal for ceremonial occasions. A Luftwaffe general in ceremonial dress stands second in the line of officers nearest the camera.

Below right: Muster of Fallschirmjäger at Bjornfjell Station near Narvik. The CO in the foreground, Fritz Becker, is addressing his men.

To spearhead the Denmark operation, 1st Battalion of 1st Parachute Regiment (I./FJR 1) was deployed, commanded by Major Erich Walther. The 4th Company (less one platoon) was dropped on the Storstrøm causeway and Vordingborg bridge linking Falster and Seeland with Copenhagen, charged with holding it until the invading German divisions arrived to cross it. This they did in a copybook landing, and the few Danish troops holding the bridge were so surprised by the novelty of the event that they surrendered at once. Notice of this operation was so short that Hauptmann Walther Gericke, the company commander, had only a road map and postcards as a planning guide. The detached platoon was dropped on two airfields at Ålborg in northern Denmark to secure them for the air-landing troops and covering fighters. The operation was completed in 30 minutes.

The Battalion HQ and 2nd Company (Hauptmann Walther) were to land directly by aircraft at Fornebu airport, near Oslo, and secure it for 163rd Infantry Division to be flown in. This mission was nearly a disaster. The airport was obscured by fog and there was brisk AA fire from the Norwegian defenders. The Junkers 52s carrying the paratroops were forced to hold off and two of them collided. The situation was saved by one of the Bf 109 escorting fighters that ran out of fuel and force-landed on the runway firing its guns as it came in. Meanwhile the main force of Ju 52s carrying the infantry division had arrived and, seeing a gap in the fog, followed the Messerschmitt in, only to come under fire on the ground. By now, however, the Ju 52s carrying the paratroops had landed under cover of this diversion, and in 30 minutes they secured the airfield, as the defenders began to run out of ammunition and were overwhelmed by superior numbers. By evening all of Oslo was in German hands.

The 3rd Company (Leutnant von Brandis) was to secure Sola airport at Stavanger and, again, it was lucky to succeed for very murky weather and high winds made the drop zone hard to find. At one point the cloud base was as low as 10 metres (30ft). However, just as the aircraft approached they found a calm and clear patch over the airfield and the men dropped in copybook manner. A foretaste

of future problems came when the defenders at the edge of the airfield put down accurate small arms fire and prevented the paratroops from recovering their small arms and ammunition containers for over 30 minutes. Only the diversion when the follow-up Ju 52s with the air-landing troops arrived over the airfield allowed the situation to be retrieved and the paratroops swiftly secured the perimeter.

The 1st Company (Leutnant Schmidt) was held in reserve on 9 April, but on 14 April it, too, was deployed. On that evening it was dropped at Dombås in the Gudbrandsdal valley about 90 miles north of Oslo; this was such a disastrous operation that it was not publicised afterwards. The object was to hold the Trondheim–Lillehammer road south of Åndalsnes to prevent a newly landed British infantry brigade from linking up with Norwegian troops retreating north from Oslo. One Ju 52 was shot down on its approach run up the valley, and the other aircraft were too low, finding height difficult to judge over deep snow. Many containers were lost in snow drifts and some men were injured, or even killed, by low hard landings. Norwegian troops, well concealed in the valley sides and familiar with the area, pinned down the company with fire. Only 61 men survived the jump and after five days hard fighting there were only 34 left when they ran out of food and ammunition and surrendered. Schmidt was badly injured early on by small arms fire but stayed in command throughout. For this he was awarded the Knight's Cross. The men were not in captivity for long because the Norwegians capitulated the following month. But this action demonstrated a problem that was to be repeated several more times in the years ahead – the limited period that paratroops could realistically hold a position before being relieved by the main force. Schmidt's tiny force did well to last as long as it did, blocking a key route.

Above: Men of Assault Group *Koch* after having been relieved at Eban Emael (note name on truck) leaving for Maastricht.

More tough fighting came in the far north at Narvik. Road links there were primitive at the best of times but in winter they were non-existent. General Dietl's 34. Gebirgs Division had landed by sea at Narvik but was now cut off by a successful British landing near the port, with good gunfire support from the strong Royal Navy force of ships in Narvik Fjord. The only way in was by air and all the surviving companies of I./FJR 1 were parachuted in as reinforcements in the last two weeks of May. This was done piecemeal over several days – the last drop as late as 29 May – since the Ju 52s had to fly the long haul north from Trondheim. This necessitated fitting long range tanks inside the fuselage so only a handful of paratroops could be carried at a time. In addition a number of mountain troops were given quick seven day courses at the parachute school at Stendal and were also parachuted in with the paratroops.

The fierce fighting at Narvik only ended when the British pulled out at the end of May 1940 due to the grave situation in France. On 8 June 1940, men of I./FJR 1 at last moved into Narvik against no opposition. At this moment the men of II./FJR 1 were en route to Trondheim from Oslo by train as further reinforcements for Narvik, but they were no longer needed. With operations in Norway at an end, all the FJR 1 men returned to Germany on the cruiser *Nürnberg*.

EBEN EMAEL

Fall Gelb (Case Yellow) – the invasion of France and Flanders scheduled for 10 May 1940 was an immense undertaking, and the German airborne forces had a key part in its launch. In the Army Group B sector, Sixth Army, commanded by Generaloberst von Reichenau, had to cross the River Maas and push back or penetrate the Belgian defenders while heading for Tirlemont and neutralising the well defended area around Louvain from the north. This section of the front was covered by 4th Panzer Division and 151st Infantry Regiment of XXVII Corps which were routed from Aachen, through Maastricht, and over the border into Belgium.

At this point the fortress of Eben Emael, between the River Maas and Albert Canal, dominated the approaches and would be a formidable obstacle for the invaders. It was on a 150ft high ridge, surrounded by anti-tank ditches, and bristled with guns. In addition to taking the fort it was vital to secure the bridges over the Albert Canal. It was for this key task – taking out Eben Emael and capturing the bridges intact – that Sturmabteilung *Koch* had been formed and highly trained at Hildesheim in conditions of great secrecy and security. Hitler took a close personal interest in all the planning for Fall Gelb and, according to Student, it was Hitler's idea to take Eben Emael by a glider landing on the roof. Student was at first dubious, but when he studied the detail he thought it was possible. Later he described it as the most original of Hitler's many ideas.

The biggest immediate problem was bringing a DFS 230 glider to an abrupt halt on the relatively small roof the fort. Trials were carried out by wrapping barbed wire round the landing skid but this made little difference. Eventually they settled on a serrated metal cladding on the skid that would dig in like a ploughshare as the glider landed. Many practice landings were needed, however, and rehearsals were carried out on former Czech defence bunkers on the Sudetenland borders. The Germans also managed to get plans of the fort from pre-war building contractors, so the exact size of the fort could be replicated for landing practice, and they knew the internal layout.

Assault Group *Koch* comprised 11 officers and 427 men, plus 42 DFS 230 glider pilots. For the operation of 10 May it was divided into four groups, code named Granite, Iron, Steel and Concrete. Of these the key unit was Assault Group Granite (Oberleutnant Witzig) for it was to take the fort itself, the key to the whole invasion plan. In this group were two officers, and 83 NCOs and men, all trained as combat engineers, plus 11 gliders and pilots. On 9 May Assault Group *Koch* moved to Cologne-Ostheim and Cologne-Butzweilerhof airfields, and at 04.30 on 10 May it took off for its objectives.

Granite had a tough job. The fort was garrisoned by 1,200 men, had twelve 75mm howitzers in casements, four more in armoured cupolas, and two 120mm howitzers in armoured cupolas. There were also seven AA guns and numerous machine gun posts, all on top of a fort that was roughly diamond shaped and about 900m x 800m (980yd x 875yd) in size. To destroy the guns and emplacements, the men had two sizes of special hollow-charge grenades, conventional explosives, flamethrowers and machine guns. En route to the target two gliders were lost. One was cast off prematurely by mistake, but the glider with Oberleutnant Witzig snapped its tow rope and landed in a field. In his absence Leutnant Delica and the senior NCO, Oberfeldwebel Wenzel, took charge of the force when the gliders swooped out of the dawn sky and landed perfectly on the Eben Emael fort roof at 05.32. Meanwhile, Witzig had commandeered a car and gone for help. He got another Ju 52 to tow the glider out of the field in which it had landed, and his glider finally set down on the fort roof at 08.30, three hours late but there nonetheless.

The men of Granite, some 55 in all, had actually knocked out most of the enemy guns within ten minutes of

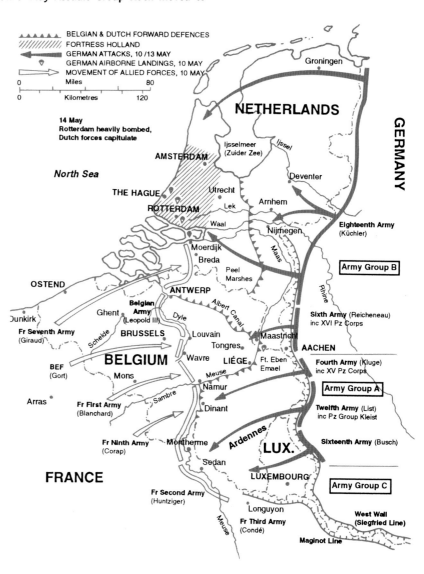

The German attack on the West.

landing and were then engaged in clearing the interior galleries and pinning down the defenders in a lively fire fight. Only one gun cupola had been ignored as it was thought to be ineffective. This was not the case, however, as the twin guns in it opened fire and pinned men down. Leutnant Delica called in a Stuka squadron by radio to bomb the cupola. They missed, but the intensity of the bombing caused the Belgians to cease using the cupola anyway. The fighting in the fort actually went on for a whole day, because it was full of tunnels, galleries and underground magazines, all of which had to be fought for. In addition Belgian troops made several unco-ordinated attacks on the fort from the north-west. It was not until 07.00 on 11 May that Group Granite was relieved. Out of the tiny force that landed, Granite had lost six men killed and 20 wounded, but had achieved a victory out of proportion to its tiny size.

The other assault groups had less dramatic but equally important objectives. Assault Group Steel (Oberleutnant Altmann and 112 men) landed its gliders near the Veldwezelt bridge right on time at 05.30, took the bridge in a brisk assault, and removed the explosives which had been set to blow it. They had a tough job holding the bridge, however, against heavy counter-attacks, and they called in Stukas to bomb the attackers. 4th Panzer Division was due to relieve them during the day, but did not arrive until the following afternoon on 11 May. Some relief came on the afternoon of 10 May, however, when men of 51st Engineer Battalion managed to cross the Maas and work their way up the banks of the canal towards the bridges.

Assault Group Concrete (Leutnant Schlacht and 134 men) landed at 05.15 and seized Vroenhoven bridge quickly, despite superior Belgian numbers. The Belgians had not stood to, thinking that the gliders were merely crashing aircraft. The bridge was saved from demolition by the initiative of Gefreiter (corporal) Stenzel who pulled the wires from the charge just as a Belgian engineer was about to detonate it. Numerous Belgian counter-attacks were beaten back and an artillery barrage which attempted to destroy the bridge proved ineffective. The group was finally relieved at 21.40 that evening when an infantry battalion arrived on the approach march from Maastricht. In the day's fighting, Concrete lost seven killed and 24 wounded.

The only failure was at the objective of Assault Group Iron (Leutnant Schächter and 114 men). The Canne bridge was near the Eben Emael fort and could be seen from there. As the force landed at 05.35 it was spotted by the fort commander who immediately blew the bridge. The men could be enfiladed from the fort and suffered heavy casualties of 22 dead and 26 injured. Schächter was killed and his deputy Leutnant Meissner took command. It was 23.30 before the bridgehead was relieved after tough fighting.

HOLLAND

The Army Group B plan for Fall Gelb also recognised the need for the swift neutralisation of Holland. The number of waterways meant that bridges could be blown and flood defences opened as an effective means of delaying a military advance into the country. In addition, von Bock, the Army Group B commander, thought a British force might be put ashore at Antwerp to reinforce the Dutch Army. To prevent all these possibilities it was decided to use 7. Flieger-Division to spearhead the invasion. The division would seize key bridges at Dordrecht, Rotterdam, Moerdijk, and over the Diep River. In addition it would land and secure

Left: Hitler inspecting the troops that took Eben Emael, one of a series of photographs of this event.

the main airfields in the west of Holland so that 22nd Air Landing Division could be brought in to take The Hague (and thereby the seat of government) and the approaches to Rotterdam.

All of 7. Flieger was involved. 1st and 2nd Battalions of 1st Parachute Regiment (I. and II./FJR 1) were to land on the Dordrecht and Moerdijk bridges. 3rd Battalion (III./FJR 1) was to land at Waalhaven, and six companies of 2nd Parachute Regiment (FJR 2) were to take Valkenburg and two smaller airfields nearby, backed up by 47th Infantry Regiment of 22nd Air Landing Division which would be air-landed quickly behind them.

These units moved to Münster, Paderborn, and Dortmund airports ready for the jump on Holland which was timed to take place 30 minutes after the jumps in Belgium. The first drop was III./FJR 1 (Hauptmann Schulz) at Waalhaven. This

Below: Hitler meeting Oberleutnant Meissner and Hauptmann Witzig at the award ceremony for the Eben Emael and Albert Canal missions.

Right: Hitler posing with the assault leaders of the raid on Eben Emael. Major Koch (promoted for his part in the mission) is to Hitler's right, Witzig next to Koch; to Hitler's left is Oberleutnant Meissner.

Right: Hitler posing with the assault leaders of the raid on Eben Emael. Major Koch (promoted for his part in the mission) is to Hitler's right, Witzig next to Koch; to Hitler's left is Oberleutnant Meissner.

airfield was well defended by AA and ground troops but was quickly captured by the paratroops after a determined fight to take the control tower. They also took out an AA position that failed to surrender. Two regiments of 22nd Air Landing Division (Generalmajor Graf von Sponeck), 16th and 25th Infantry Regiments, came in as scheduled with the second wave, as did Generalleutnant Student and staff who set up 7. Flieger-Division HQ on the airfield.

II./FJR 1 (Hauptmann Prager) jumped north and south of the two long bridges (road and rail) over the Maas at Moerdijk and secured them safely even though the Dutch already had them wired for demolition. Leutnant Tietjen played a key part in storming the road bridge defences and its concrete pillboxes and was awarded the Knight's Cross for this. Actually II./FJR 1 had to hold these bridges for four days, much longer than anticipated, against sturdy Dutch assaults, including attacks by the crack Dutch Light Division which was falling back from the east. On 14 May the German perimeter round the bridges had still not been relieved. Student got together two paratroop companies from Waalhaven, together with the divisional artillery support (infantry gun and anti-tank gun companies) which had flown in with the second wave, and lorried them to the bridges where they engaged the Dutch attackers and gave much needed support until the SS *Leibstandarte Adolf Hitler* Regiment arrived, much delayed, to take over the positions.

The Dordrecht bridge was secured by I./FJR 1 (Hauptmann Walther), though the 3. Kompanie commander, Leutnant von Brandis, who had led the assault at Sola in Norway, was killed. The bridge was held for two days, again longer than had been anticipated, until the leading units of Eighteenth Army arrived. The paratroops suffered relatively heavy casualties.

The attack at Valkenburg was the least successful part of the whole operation. The drop by companies of FJR 2 on the airfield went according to plan, but the incoming Ju 52s found the ground too soft and sank into it on landing. Immobilised, they were an easy target for the defenders and many of the 47th Infantry's men were killed. Following aircraft had to be diverted, but the two small airfields nearby, Ypenburg and Ockenburg, had not been secured as the companies designated to take them had been wrongly positioned. One company landed at the Hook of Holland by mistake and had to make its way back, and many of the containers were lost or scattered. Ju 52s landing on these small unsecured airfields therefore ran into heavy defensive fire and 17 were destroyed, blocking these also. Remaining aircraft landed where they could, some on beaches near The Hague and ten on the main Hague–Rotterdam road, but even some of these veered off the road in cross-winds and were damaged. The final wave of aircraft was diverted to Waalhaven, the only safely held place to land.

The result of all this was heavy casualties and scrappy and confused fighting by the surviving paratroops and men of 22nd Division. The prime object of 47th Infantry Regiment had been to seize The Hague, and with it the Dutch government, high command, and royal family. None of this was achieved and the royal family and senior military staff were able to escape to England to continue the war in exile. Kesselring blamed Student for this fiasco, since he had landed with his troops too early, and at Waalhaven he was cut off from news of Valkenburg. However, in the general euphoria of victory, and the perceived success of the parachute operations, Student's reputation did not suffer.

Surrender in Holland came on 14 May, only four days after the invasion. It culminated in a savage bombing attack on Rotterdam which, owing to faulty communications, proceeded after Dutch surrender talks had already started. General Schmidt of XLIX Corps, who had become the area commander, ordered Generalleutnant Student to drive into Rotterdam and take charge of the surrender talks on the German side. Dutch and German troops were still clashing in the area. Hearing shooting outside the building where negotiations were taking place, Student went to the window to see what was happening. A stray German bullet hit him in the right forehead just behind his eye. His sight and life were saved by a skilled Dutch surgeon in a nearby hospital but he was hospitalised in Berlin until

Below: Men of Assault Group Koch, in full combat dress. The NCO on the left wears an Army eagle on his smock, but a Luftwaffe tunic and collar patches. This was not unusual in 1940 since a number of the troops involved were former members of the Army Fallschirm-Infanterie-Bataillon. Photo taken shortly after the unit had been relieved.

August 1940, and convalescent until January 1941. His speech was affected, but he did not lose his energy, determination or mental ability.

In Student's absence Generalmajor Richard Putzier took temporary command of 7. Flieger-Division. Because of the overall success of the invasion in the West, and the propaganda impact of the parachute landings, many of the shortcomings and limitations of the operation were overlooked, Hitler gave a well publicised reception to the men who captured Eben Emael and presented their bravery awards personally. Plans were approved to enlarge the airborne forces and open a second parachute training school. Göring basked in the publicity and praise his Luftwaffe paratroops received, and feted Student's leadership.

In reality losses had been high. Thanks mainly to the errors at Valkenburg some 40% of the officers and 28% of the men of 22nd Air Landing Division had been killed. Some of the parachute drops had also sustained high casualty rates and, of 430 Ju 52s in use, about 65% were destroyed or damaged beyond repair. The units engaged in the Valkenburg landings lost 90% of their aircraft. These high losses might well have limited airborne operations in the near future, had any been planned to take place.

OPERATION SEA LION

Though Operation Sea Lion (Seelöwe), the German invasion of Britain, was never to happen, it was planned in some considerable detail and, indeed, was altered in some aspects as time went by, particularly in respect of the proposed use of airborne troops.

The speed of the German campaign in the West surprised even the German high command and there was no immediate prospect of an invasion immediately following the Dunkirk withdrawal and the fall of France in June 1940. Not only would the forces need to be reorganised for an invasion, but it was necessary to have air superiority over the Channel and southern England (leading to the Battle of Britain in summer 1940) to keep the Royal Navy at bay, and time was required to assemble a large invasion fleet of barges to carry men, tanks and equipment across the Channel.

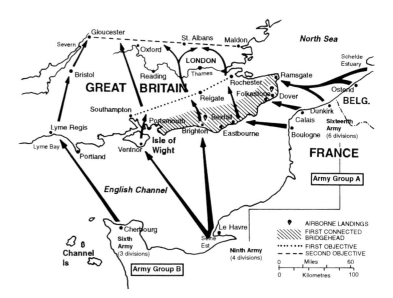

Operation Sea Lion—the projected invasion of Great Britain.

Clearly, with the perceived success of airborne forces in Belgium and Holland, they would also have a key role to play in an invasion of Britain. The impact and imagery of the May operations made German paratroops a powerful propaganda tool and there was a genuine 'parachute scare' in Britain through the rest of 1940, with German paratroops expected daily. German paratroops dropping disguised as nuns started as a serious rumour – one of many – before ending up as a joke. One of the major duties of the newly raised Home Guard (or LDV as it was first officially known) was to defend against parachute landings and one of the early nicknames for them was 'Parashots'.

To prevent glider and Ju 52 landings all flat fields and parklands were strewn with posts or old cars, and straight wide roads were provided with obstructions or bars which could be put in place quickly to prevent aircraft landings. Road signposts and even station names were removed to confuse the expected invaders, and church bells were banned, only to be rung as a warning in the event of air or sea invasion.

One result of the successful Eben Emael operation was a decision to expand Assault Group *Koch* into a full strength assault regiment (Fallschirmjäger-Sturmregiment) under command of Oberst Meindl, specifically for deployment in the proposed invasion. At one stage in the planning the new regiment was to land on the Dover coast-gun batteries and immobilise them in similar style to the guns of Eben Emael. Hitler, at first, had no fixed ideas about the deployment of the airborne forces and in his initial directive on 16 July 1940 he merely asked for suggestions, or whether they should be used as a mobile reserve. The first scheme put forward, however, was that paratroops would be dropped at Brighton and on the hills inland behind Dover to guard the west and east flanks of the sea landing, but 7. Flieger's acting commander, Putzier, was unhappy with this. Potential drop zones in these areas were well obstructed by the British and the lightly armed airborne troops would be very vulnerable to counter-attacks.

On 12 September the plans were changed, under the influence of Kesselring, and it was now proposed to take out the coastal gun batteries at Dover, as noted above, and land also north-west of Folkestone to secure the canal crossing at Hythe. Alternatives considered were dropping paratroops along the line Dymchurch–Bonnington–Kingsnorth–Woodchurch–New Romney to secure the Military Canal, and making another landing at Canterbury to cut off the great Stour sector. It was also proposed to land on Lympne airfield to secure it and fly in 22nd Air Landing Division in a copy of the Waalhaven/Valkenburg landings in Holland.

The most finalised plan along these lines went into great detail with the following deployments:

1. Kampfgruppe *Meindl* to land at Hythe, secure the Military Canal crossings and move along the line from Hythe rail station to Saltwood to prevent any outflanking moves by the British.

Above: German parachute troops jumping over Holland. 10 May 1940.

Above: Fallschirmjäger and Army infantry link up outside Rotterdam, May 1940, they are wearing full combat dress.

Right: A Fallschirmjäger during the 1940 advance on the west.

Opposite, Above: Crashed German Ju 52 transport, one of many that were lost in the invasion of Holland.

Opposite, Below: Fallschirmjäger dropping over Northern France, training jump, 23 November 1940.

Above: German parachute troops jumping over Holland, 10 May 1940.

2. Kampfgruppe *Stentzler* to drop and seize the heights at Paddlesworth and hold off any counter-attacks.

These two groups would be timed to drop as the landing craft carrying 17th Infantry Division hit the beach near Folkestone.

3. Kampfgruppe *Bräuer* to drop one hour later south of Postling. This enlarged group would consist of a complete parachute battalion, a parachute engineer battalion, the anti-tank company of FJR 1, all of FJR 2 and FJR 3, and an extra battalion as divisional reserve.

Once landed Kampfgruppe *Bräuer* was to take *Stentzler* under command and the combined force was to take Sandgate and the high ground west of Paddlesworth. FJR 2 was to move north of Postling and guard against attack from the north while FJR 3 was to secure the western flank with one battalion detached to capture and hold Lympe airfield for a later fly-in by 22nd Air Landing Division, possibly as late as S plus 5.

Because of the postponements and eventual cancellation of Operation Sea Lion all this became academic, but early in September 1940 the 7. Flieger-Division staff got as far as selecting the airfields in France and Flanders that would used as departure points, and organising the logistics for getting the units into place, and the Kampfgruppen (assault groups) were set up as outlined in the plans. Student, still on sick leave, took an outside interest in all this and was personally opposed to concentrating the bulk of the airborne forces in the Folkestone area. He had other ideas, too, such as fitting Ju 52s with long range tanks so that 7. Flieger could later be used in the invasion of Northern Ireland. Hitler himself suggested parachute landings to seize Plymouth and Cornwall in later stages of the invasion, but by the time these matters were discussed in January 1941 the whole invasion idea was little more than fantasy.

OPERATION ATTILA

Another scheme which came to nothing was the plan to neutralise the French fleet at Toulon, should it attempt to leave harbour and defect to the Allied side. Under the terms of the Vichy Agreement, the fleet was supposed to remain inactive and southern France was not occupied, so any defection would take time to rectify. Hitler asked Student, in December 1940, for a contingency plan should the French fleet start to leave port. Student's first task on returning to duty on 1 January 1941, was to work this out. After sending a staff officer in disguise to visit the port area, and studying reconnaissance photographs, Student suggested that while the fleet was still raising steam, 7. Flieger assault troops would land by glider on the adjacent jetties alongside the ships in Eben Emael style, while a parachute drop secured the rest of the port area. He suggested that some naval men fly in with the gliders to deal with scuttling attempts and close down engine rooms, etc. Some naval personnel were selected for this. The project was named Operation Attila but the need to activate it never arose.

XI. FLIEGERKORPS IS FORMED

While Student was recuperating in the autumn of 1940, the decision was taken by OKH to increase the German airborne forces from divisional to corps strength. Student was promoted to General der Flieger and became corps commander. He took most of his 7. Flieger-Division staff with him, so Student's successor as divisional commander, Generalleutnant Süssmann, had to appoint a new staff. The corps was vested as XI. Fliegerkorps in January 1941. The chief of staff was Generalmajor Schlemm and the chief operations officer (1a) was Oberstleutnant Trettner.

XI. Fliegerkorps initially comprised Corps HQ, 7. Flieger-Division, 22nd Air Landing Division, plus the newly expanded Fallschirmjäger-Sturmregiment (Oberst Meindl) as corps troops, along with a flak battalion, a medical Abteilung, the parachute training schools, and various small transport and logistic units.

THE CORINTH CANAL

Bulgaria had intended to remain a neutral state but events in the Balkans in 1940/early 1941, including the Italian invasion of Greece, made Hitler decide to

Below: Men of FJR 2 drop to link up with the force at the bridge over the Corinth Canal.

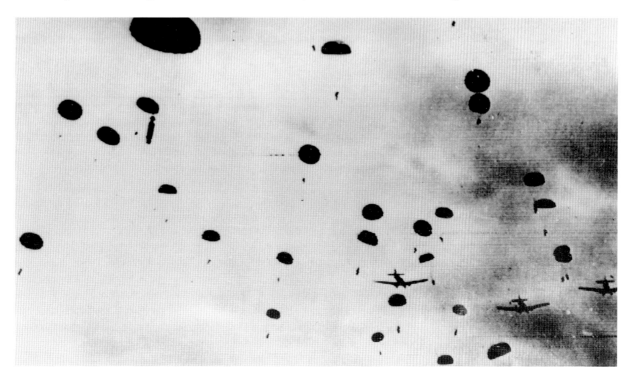

bring Bulgaria under the Axis sphere of influence. Following heavy pressure, the Bulgarian prime minister signed a co-operation pact with the Axis on 1 March 1941, and German forces moved in at once. OKW considered that airborne forces would be useful in expelling the British from Greece and the Aegean islands in the offensive called Operation Marita which was to start on 6 April 1941. British troops from Libya and Egypt had been sent to aid the Greeks when Italy launched its flagging invasion of that country.

Early in March 1941 a brigade group, essentially a strengthened 2nd Parachute Regiment (FJR 2) under command of Generalleutnant Süssmann was sent to Plovdiv in Bulgaria. The initial intention was for it to drop on the island of Lemnos which commanded the entrance to the Dardanelles and was strategically important for possible future air operations, against the Romanian oil fields for example. But Lemnos was only lightly defended by the British, as it turned out, and it fell at once to a small German force landing by boat, so the paratroops were not required.

The Greek campaign was fast moving once Operation Marita started. The Yugoslav Army surrendered on 17 April, forcing the British under General Wilson to withdraw quickly south. Then Greek forces in Epirus were cut off and forced to surrender on 23 April, and complete withdrawal of British troops to Crete and Egypt was considered essential to avoid a similar fate. Greek harbours were now under Luftwaffe air attack and the small ports of the Peloponnese had to be used. The only route there was the bridge over the Corinth Canal and, if this could be taken, the British would be severely disrupted and certainly curtailed in their plans.

FJR 2 was moved to Larissa in Greece for the attack on the morning of 26 April, having under command I. and II./FJR 2 plus an assault engineer company, a signal company, a medical company, and an artillery company. The assault engineers were to land by the bridge in gliders at 07.00, seize it, and remove any demolition devices. The rest were to drop by parachute each side of the bridge to form a bridgehead. It was considered a hazardous mission, not least because of the stream of British troops crossing the bridge and moving south. But the surprise factor was thought to outweigh this. The glider landing was made by 6. Kompanie of II./FJR 2 (Leutnant Hans Teusen) and went to plan. But the bridge was blown just as the assault engineers removed the charges, the explosion being caused it is thought by either a stray British AA shell hitting the explosives or canny British troops firing at them. Some of the assault engineers were killed as the bridge went down. By now the Ju 52s carrying the paratroops had arrived overhead and dropped I. Bataillon to the north and II. Bataillon to the south of the bridge. Despite the mayhem of the explosion, and much British small arms fire, casualties were few but one Ju 52 flew into the mountain side killing all but two aboard, and some paratroops landed in the deeply gorged canal and were drowned.

Teusen's men moved south after the withdrawing British troops. They took the Corinth airfield and next day moved on, taking the surrender of about 900 British and 1,500 Greek troops after Teusen made out they were part of a much larger German invasion force. For this enterprise, Teusen was awarded the Knight's Cross. I. Bataillon to the north held out in the bridgehead for two days until German ground troops arrived on 28 April. By then the assault engineers had built a new temporary bridge over the canal. One feature of the operation which aided the paratroops was a plentiful supply of British Army vehicles which were captured and used to give much needed mobility.

While the Corinth Canal operation was successful as far as it went, it would have been much more useful had it been staged two days earlier, for then virtually all the British troops would have been bottled up on the Greek mainland and might

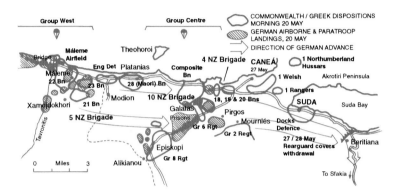

Left: Maps showing the Crete operation. The top one shows the landings of 20 May; the bottom the battle in the north of the island.

Below: Fallschirmjäger jumping over Crete during the second-wave landings on Heraklion during the afternoon of 20 May 1941.

never have been able to withdraw to Crete or Egypt. Student was very displeased since the operation was mounted at very short notice with no reference to, or consultation with, XI. Fliegerkorps HQ in Berlin, even though it had been sanctioned by Hitler. By this time planning was under way for the much more ambitious Operation Mercury (*Merkur*) to capture Crete and in Student's view the use of paratroops at Corinth compromised security in the Aegean area by prematurely revealing the presence of the airborne forces which would be so vital in that battle.

CRETE

Student considered the taking of Crete to be a logical conclusion to the Operation Marita campaign. It could have several advantages. First it would remove the British forces from the Aegean area and prevent it being used by them as an air base for bombing the Ploesti oil-fields in Romania. Then it could provide a useful staging post for further airborne operations against the Suez Canal, Cyprus, Malta, or even Syria. He put his ideas to Hitler, via the good offices of Göring, on 20 April 1941.

Hitler was dismissive of the further objectives like Suez and Malta, but he approved of the idea of taking Crete itself. Hitler appreciated the idea of having the island in German hands to remove the chances of it being used as an air base by the British, but he also saw it as a good diversion from Operation Barbarossa, the invasion of Russia due to begin in early summer and in the advanced planning stage. His approval for what was designated Operation Mercury came in a directive of 25 April with the proviso that it should be carried out as soon as possible, and should not conflict with the launch of Barbarossa. Some units, such as the air component, might be needed for Barbarossa afterwards.

Below: Pioneer with a standard light flamethrower in action on Crete.

The soonest possible date was 17 May which left just over three weeks for planning and positioning of the troops, a very tight schedule indeed. In the pace of developments both sides suffered from either making the wrong assumptions or faulty interpretation of intelligence. Student correctly assumed the Luftwaffe would have air superiority, for he could count on fighter cover and dive bombers from the nearby Greek bases, and the transports and gliders, too, had only a short hop from Greece. The RAF had only a few fighters on Crete, and there were just a few old tanks and small numbers of field and AA guns, too, for Crete had been low priority in defence terms, garrisoned by just three battalions to defend the naval base at Suda Bay. Student assumed that the bulk of the British and Commonwealth forces evacuated from Greece had been taken to Egypt, leaving only token numbers in Crete, but many men had, in fact, moved only as far as Crete and there were over 25,000 men there.

Ultra intercepts gave the British an awareness that something was planned in the Aegean area, but the exact nature of what was intended was not clear at first. It was known in April that Ju 52s of XI. Fliegerkorps had moved to the Balkans and that 22. Luftlande-Division (Air Landing

Above: Fallschirmjäger in action on Crete during the tough fighting that followed the landings.

Division) was to move to Yugoslavia. Also that General Süssmann of 7. Flieger-Division was in the area receiving signals. But this did not necessarily point to Crete, as the Corinth Canal landing (Operation Hannibal to the Germans) showed on 26 April. However, intensive air reconnaissance sorties took place over Crete on 24–25 April, and signals were intercepted concerning extra aviation supplies and orders not to bomb airfields on Crete or mine Suda Bay. Crete was clearly high on the list for invasion and General Wavell, C-in-C Middle East, ordered the tough dynamic New Zealander General Bernard Freyberg to the island on 30 April to organise the defence. Though depleted, and short of equipment due to losses in Greece, there were three infantry brigades, New Zealand, Australian, and British, which Freyberg deployed west, centre, and east of the island respectively.

On 6 May Ultra intercepted an important signal which gave virtually the entire schedule and order of battle for the forthcoming Crete invasion, complete with all landing areas and objectives. It also revealed there would be a follow-up of more troops, equipment, and supplies brought in by sea, all to be ready for 17 May. This was one of the most complete revelations of plans that Ultra came up with in the whole war and Freyberg was one of the first recipients of intelligence on this scale. In the circumstances he made the best possible use of it by having his men ready and waiting at all the drop zones and objectives and able to give the paratroops a hard fight. Intercepts picked up that the operation was delayed, largely due to late arrival of aviation fuel, first to 18 May then to 20 May. The defenders over-estimated the importance of the sea landings and slightly under-estimated the strength of the air landings, particularly at Maleme, but overall the valuable knowledge was exploited to the full. The biggest surprise for the Germans was finding how well the British and Commonwealth forces were disposed to meet them, for they were of course unaware that Ultra had intercepted their plans.

For the landing on Crete, XI. Fliegerkorps was greatly augmented. The original Fallschirmjäger-Sturmregiment had been re-designated as the Luftlande-Sturmregiment (air landing assault regiment – LLStR) with four battalions as part

Above: Ramcke handing out medals to survivors of the Crete operation, summer 1941.

of the corps troops. It was virtually a small division in its own right, reflected in the promotion of its commander, Meindl, to Generalmajor. 7. Flieger had three three-battalion regiments and strong divisional troops including a machine-gun, anti-tank, and pioneer battalions and artillery batteries. The 5. Gebirgs Division (5. Gebirgs-Division – Generalmajor Ringel) had replaced the 22nd Division as air landing division, partly to save moving the 22nd Division which had been moved to Romania to protect the oil-fields, and partly because a mountain division was thought more suited to the rugged Crete terrain. Student had initial misgivings about this change, partly because he did not get on with Ringel, but also because the division had no previous air landing experience. However, 5. Gebirgs Division was considered a crack unit and certainly proved invaluable in Crete.

The logistical problems of getting all the units and equipment to Greece were considerable. The gliders, for example, had to be shipped in components by rail, sheeted over for security, and all air and rail movements had to be dovetailed into the movements readying forces for Barbarossa which would begin soon, and Barbarossa movements had priority. The logistical task was so complex it had its own code name, Operation Flying Dutchman.

There proved to be a shortage of Ju 52s which meant the landing had to be made in two waves with the same aircraft used twice. There were four landing zones to be attacked by three groups. Group West was to take and secure the important Maleme airfield. Group Centre was to take the island capital Canea, Suda Bay and Retimo airfield. Group East was to take the town and airfield of Heraklion. The first wave was to go in early in the morning to take Maleme, Canea and Suda Bay, and the same aircraft would return at 13.00 with the second wave to take Retimo and Heraklion airfields.

VIII. Fliegerkorps aircraft had started attacking targets in Crete on 14 May, concentrating on the AA defences of the airfields and Suda Bay. Just before the landing on 20 May, VIII. Fliegerkorps carried out intensive bombing of defence positions to the west of the island. As the bombing run ended, I./LLStR landed in gliders to take Maleme airfield and AA positions near Canea and Suda Bay. One mission was to secure the bridge over the Tavronitis River. The other LLStR battalions dropped west and east of Maleme. II./LLStR (Major Stentzler) was charged with taking Hill 107, the high ground dominating Maleme airfield, but this took until next day due to stubborn resistance by 22nd New Zealand Battalion which even withstood Stuka attacks on its positions. FJR 3 parachuted on to the plain southwest of Canea.

III./LLStR took particularly heavy casualties when the men jumped. They were widely scattered, as were their containers, and so many were killed or wounded that the unit was no longer battle-worthy. II./FJR 3 suffered a similar fate. LLStR's commander, Meindl, was among the early casualties and Major Stentzler of II./LLStR took over command. 7. Flieger's commander, Generalleutnant Süssmann died when his glider crashed on landing.

The first-wave landings, in short, were a failure with only minor objectives taken, and too many men landing in the wrong place. The second wave fared even worse. It was delayed by late returning aircraft, slow refuelling by hand from jerricans, and huge dust clouds which slowed the take-off rate. Thus the second-wave drops were late and staggered and were no longer synchronised with the scheduled bombing runs which preceded them. FJR 2 dropped at Retimo but was pinned down by the defenders and failed to take the airfield. FJR 1 and II./FJR 2 landed at Heraklion but took heavy casualties as they jumped, had two companies decimated, and were scattered so widely it took all night to round up the survivors. They failed to take the airfield as intended.

The first day of operations had been close to disastrous, though little of this was known until evening by General Student back at HQ in Greece. Fortunately for the Germans there were only a few minor unco-ordinated Allied counter-attacks during the night, for a really concentrated counter-attack could well have wiped them out. The plans called for 5. Gebirgs Division to land on Retimo and Heraklion airfield on 21 May, but as there was no certainty these would be secured in time, concentration was switched to Maleme where there was at least a foothold. Even so Maleme airfield was not finally taken until 14.00 on 21 May after more Stuka attacks and the dropping of the two last LLStR companies. Student now sent in Oberst Ramcke, one of his staff officers who had been teaching 5. Gebirgs Division air landing skills, to take over command from the injured Meindl. Ramcke dropped at Maleme soon after it was secured, bringing with him a reserve battalion to make up the numbers after the heavy casualties. At 15.00 the first Ju 52s landed bringing in the mountain troops, a welcome sight to the hard pressed paratroops. Congestion on the small airfield as Ju 52s crowded in caused a few collisions and wrecks, however.

The sea landings, in two convoys largely composed of commandeered Greek caiques, were also disastrous. Two mountain division battalions, some 7. Flieger divisional troops, guns and supplies, were almost all lost when both convoys were virtually wiped out by powerful Royal Navy forces, though this was at some expense to the Royal Navy who lost two destroyers (one of them the famous *Kelly*) and a cruiser to Luftwaffe air attack. Prospects still looked bleak for the invaders.

A counter-attack at Maleme airfield was beaten back on the night of 21–22 May and Student and the divisional HQ flew in on the evening of 22 May. By this time three battalions of 5. Gebirgs Division were in place. That evening General Ringel took command of the western part of the island and moved his men south-east into the mountains to turn the New Zealand flank just west of Canea. The

Below: All the drops over Crete were made at low level. Here the technique is practised at a training school.

Above: DFS 230 glider of I./LLStR alongside Tavronitis Bridge, between Maleme and Suda Bay, one of the objectives successfully captured by the Fallschirmjäger.

Left: This Ju 52 has been hit by anti-aircraft fire and is about to fall from the sky. Only five paras have got out so far.

Opposite, Above: II./LLStR after taking the vital Hill 107 on 21 May. The flag is to show attacking aircraft that the location is in German hands.

Opposite, Below: Matilda knocked out by II./FJR 1 near Heraklion airfield.

Above: Paras drop over Crete. This action convinced the Allies there was a future for airborne troops; it convinced Hitler that airborne operations were too costly in manpower and munitions.

Opposite, Above: Men of 7. FJD in action in Russia during the late autumn of 1941.

Opposite, Below: MG 42 team in winter camouflage in Russia.

reorganised survivors of the Luftlande-Sturmregiment, now commanded by Ramcke, plus 100. Gebirgs Regiment, made a frontal attack near the coast road and captured Canea on 26–27 May. Ringel's men pushed on east to relieve the paratroops still stuck at Retimo and Heraklion, and Freyberg decided to evacuate his troops from the island on 27 May, ordering all remaining British and Commonwealth troops south to Sfakia where Royal Navy ships took them off. 100. Gebirgs Regiment (Oberst Utz) had a good campaign. They set off in hot pursuit of the retreating troops and captured 10,000 of them, leaving only 17,000 to be evacuated. The last of them had gone by 31 May and Crete was now wholly in German hands after a very short but bloody campaign. Freyberg's withdrawal was largely due to lack of equipment and reinforcements, not due to lack of courage, intelligence or fighting qualities. He was short of radios, guns and tanks for so much had been lost in Greece, and the lack of resources at Middle East Command meant he was left to do the best he could with the under-equipped forces available. Air support was virtually non-existent.

British and Commonwealth casualties were about 2,500 dead and wounded and over 10,000 captured, and 2,011 naval men were lost in the sea actions. In XI. Fliegerkorps, losses were 3,352 dead and missing, and 3,400 wounded out of a force of 22,000. The XI. Fliegerkorps' men moved back to Germany in mid-July 1941 when relieved by occupation troops. The losses and carnage of the Crete campaign had a deep effect on Hitler and the high command. Essentially it saw the end of full scale airborne operations by the Luftwaffe. At a gallantry awards ceremony for men of the campaign on 19 August 1941, Hitler said to Student: 'Crete has shown that the days of paratroopers are finished. The parachute force is purely and simply a weapon of surprise. The factor of surprise has now been used up.'

Crete was, indeed, the last set-piece airborne operation by the Germans. They were costly in fuel, aircraft, resources, and men. From mid-1941 onwards the paratroops fought mainly as elite ground troops, though there were a few occasions when small airborne operations were mounted.

THE RUSSIAN FRONT

From June 1941 most German high command concentration was on Operation Barbarossa, the invasion of Russia. In that month there was a small scale air drop when paratroopers were used to seize intact bridges over the River Dvina to let the Brandenburg Division pass through. In September 1941 II./LLStR was sent by air direct from its base at Goslar to attack a Russian bridgehead over the Neva near Petruschino on the Leningrad front. Though they succeeded in pushing back the Russians, they suffered heavy casualties including the death of the commander, Major Stentzler. Later that month FJR 1, FJR 3, and 7. Flieger-Division HQ and divisional troops also went to the Leningrad front, now under command of Generalmajor Petersen. By 17 November, 7. Flieger had repulsed 146 Russian attacks in 46 days, destroyed 41 Soviet tanks and taken 3,400 prisoners, though sustaining over 3,000 killed or wounded itself. The commander of Sixteenth Army paid a special tribute to the division's fine fighting record over this period.

FJR 2 was sent to Mius in winter 1941–42 and saw hard fighting as part of the resistance to the attempted breakout from Leningrad. I./LLStR (Major Koch) was used to defend the key Anisowo-Gorodishche airfield near Moscow in winter 1941–42, repulsing heavy attacks, while sometimes cut off, in severe winter weather.

XI. FLIEGERKORPS AS AT 20 MAY 1941 (THE BATTLE OF CRETE)

XI. FLIEGERKORPS HQ

CO General der Flieger Student
Chief of Staff Generalmajor Schlemm
Ia Oberstleutnant i.G. Trettner
QM Oberstleutnant Seibt
Ic Hauptmann Mors
IW (weather) Regierungsrat Dr Brand
IIa Oberst v. Fichte
IIb Oberstleutnant Ehrlich
Signals officer Oberstleutnant Dr Weyland
Engineer staff officer Oberstleutnant Barenthin
Weapons and equipment Major Käthler
IVa Oberregierungsrat Hopf
IVb Oberfeldarzt Dr Höfer
Field reporting Kriegsgerichtsrat Rüdel

XI. FLIEGERKORPS TROOPS

Corps Reconnaissance Flight

Transport Flight XI

Transport Company

Ln Section 41 (mot)

Fallschirm lt AA Battalion

Fallschirm Medical Section

Luftlande-Sturm (Assault)-Regiment

HQ (CO Generalmajor Meindl)

I Battalion (CO Major Koch)
II Battalion (CO Major Stentzler)
III Battalion (CO Major Scherber)
IV Battalion (CO Hauptmann Gericke)

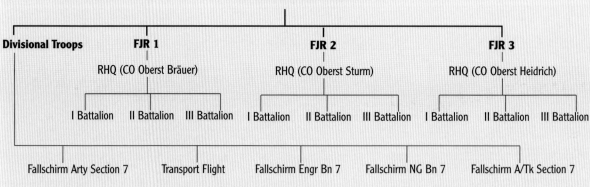

7. FLIEGER-DIVISION

Division HQ
Generalleutnant Süssmann

Divisional Troops — FJR 1 — FJR 2 — FJR 3

FJR 1: RHQ (CO Oberst Bräuer) — I Battalion, II Battalion, III Battalion
FJR 2: RHQ (CO Oberst Sturm) — I Battalion, II Battalion, III Battalion
FJR 3: RHQ (CO Oberst Heidrich) — I Battalion, II Battalion, III Battalion

Fallschirm Arty Section 7 — Transport Flight — Fallschirm Engr Bn 7 — Fallschirm NG Bn 7 — Fallschirm A/Tk Section 7

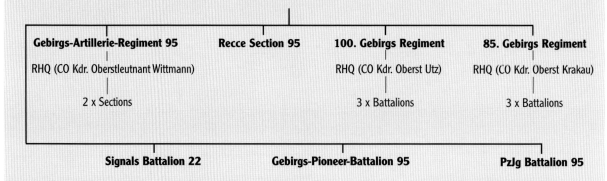

5. GEBIRGS-DIVISION

Division HQ
Generalmajor Ringel

Gebirgs-Artillerie-Regiment 95 — Recce Section 95 — 100. Gebirgs Regiment — 85. Gebirgs Regiment

Gebirgs-Artillerie-Regiment 95: RHQ (CO Kdr. Oberstleutnant Wittmann) — 2 x Sections
100. Gebirgs Regiment: RHQ (CO Kdr. Oberst Utz) — 3 x Battalions
85. Gebirgs Regiment: RHQ (CO Kdr. Oberst Krakau) — 3 x Battalions

Signals Battalion 22 — Gebirgs-Pioneer-Battalion 95 — PzJg Battalion 95

1. FALLSCHIRMJÄGER DIVISION AT THE SECOND BATTLE OF CASSINO

Div HQ (CO Generalleutnant Heidrich)

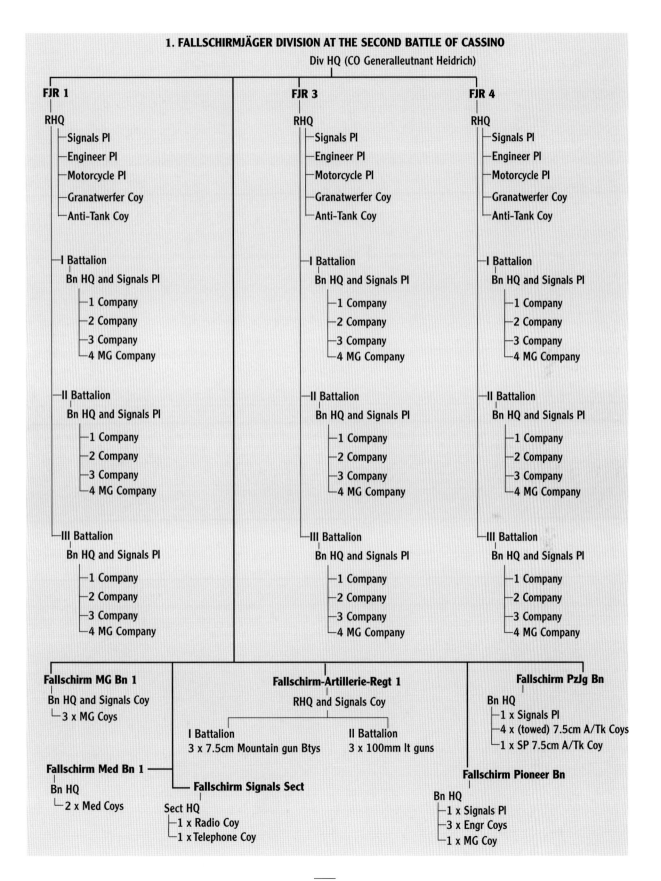

FJR 1

RHQ
- Signals Pl
- Engineer Pl
- Motorcycle Pl
- Granatwerfer Coy
- Anti-Tank Coy

I Battalion
Bn HQ and Signals Pl
- 1 Company
- 2 Company
- 3 Company
- 4 MG Company

II Battalion
Bn HQ and Signals Pl
- 1 Company
- 2 Company
- 3 Company
- 4 MG Company

III Battalion
Bn HQ and Signals Pl
- 1 Company
- 2 Company
- 3 Company
- 4 MG Company

FJR 3

RHQ
- Signals Pl
- Engineer Pl
- Motorcycle Pl
- Granatwerfer Coy
- Anti-Tank Coy

I Battalion
Bn HQ and Signals Pl
- 1 Company
- 2 Company
- 3 Company
- 4 MG Company

II Battalion
Bn HQ and Signals Pl
- 1 Company
- 2 Company
- 3 Company
- 4 MG Company

III Battalion
Bn HQ and Signals Pl
- 1 Company
- 2 Company
- 3 Company
- 4 MG Company

FJR 4

RHQ
- Signals Pl
- Engineer Pl
- Motorcycle Pl
- Granatwerfer Coy
- Anti-Tank Coy

I Battalion
Bn HQ and Signals Pl
- 1 Company
- 2 Company
- 3 Company
- 4 MG Company

II Battalion
Bn HQ and Signals Pl
- 1 Company
- 2 Company
- 3 Company
- 4 MG Company

III Battalion
Bn HQ and Signals Pl
- 1 Company
- 2 Company
- 3 Company
- 4 MG Company

Fallschirm MG Bn 1
Bn HQ and Signals Coy
- 3 x MG Coys

Fallschirm-Artillerie-Regt 1
RHQ and Signals Coy

I Battalion
3 x 7.5cm Mountain gun Btys

II Battalion
3 x 100mm lt guns

Fallschirm PzJg Bn
Bn HQ
- 1 x Signals Pl
- 4 x (towed) 7.5cm A/Tk Coys
- 1 x SP 7.5cm A/Tk Coy

Fallschirm Med Bn 1
Bn HQ
- 2 x Med Coys

Fallschirm Signals Sect
Sect HQ
- 1 x Radio Coy
- 1 x Telephone Coy

Fallschirm Pioneer Bn
Bn HQ
- 1 x Signals Pl
- 3 x Engr Coys
- 1 x MG Coy

Right: Unusual provisions—airdropping a goat as food for paras on Crete.

Below : Tunisia, 1942. BMW RI2 and sidecar (or other equivalent motorcycles) were the largest vehicles airdropped or carried in the Ju 52. They were used to tow light guns and trailers and by recce units.

In late summer 1942, Hitler suggested a parachute operation to take the key passes in the Caucasus for a mountain division offensive, but this was cancelled after further study showed it to be of doubtful tactical value, so 7. Flieger-Division moved out of Russia, first to France, then back to Germany. However, in October 1942 the division was sent to Smolensk to hold a 90km (56-mile) front extending north to Velizh. This proved a quiet front, however, and FJR 1 was used temporarily to reinforce the defence of Orel while FJR 3 took part in an attack to relieve a surrounded garrison at Velikiye Luki. In November 1942 7. Flieger-Division was renamed 1. Fallschirmjäger Division (1. FJD), and was now commanded by Generalmajor Heidrich. A new 2. Fallschirmjäger Division (2. FJD) was also formed, commanded by Generalmajor Ramcke. In spring 1943 both divisions were sent to France as reserve forces, 1. FJD to Avignon and 2. FJD to Nîmes.

NORTH AFRICA

In spring 1942, British forces based on Malta were causing severe problems to the supply routes across the Mediterranean to sustain Rommel's *Afrika Korps*. Hitler and Mussolini agreed with Kesselring, now the Mediterranean Luftwaffe commander, that Malta should be taken in the summer of that year – Operation Hercules. This would involve a drop by 30,000 German and Italian paratroops, the latter being available because Generalmajor Ramcke had been heading a training mission in Italy to create the *Folgore* Parachute Division. Six Italian Army divisions would simultaneously invade by sea supported by the Italian Navy. Planning by Student's staff started in April 1942 with Ramcke designated as the airborne force commander. Planning was at an advanced stage when Hitler had second thoughts

Below: FJR 3 en route to Sicily to reinforce German troops after the Allied invasion, 12 July 1943.

Above: German Fallschirmjäger during the defence of Cassino, dug in after the aerial bombing.

Opposite, Above: Mussolini at Gran Sasso, 12 September 1943. Skorzeny is to his right. Note the Fallschirmjäger behind Mussolini is wearing a standard German helmet rather than a para one, an increasingly common occurrence towards the end of the war.

Opposite, Below: On of the DFS 230 gliders on the Italian, Gran Sasso, 12 September 1943.

and cancelled the operation, swayed by a low opinion of the Italian contribution on which success depended.

Ramcke's men, already assembling in Italy in brigade strength, were sent instead as an independent brigade group, Fallschirmjäger Brigade *Ramcke*, to reinforce Rommel's hard-pressed *Afrika Korps*. In August 1942 they arrived at Alamein. In the main battle at Alamein the brigade was forced into a fighting withdrawal on 2 November at the height of Eighth Army's onslaught. In the confusion the paratroops lost most of their transport and supplies, and communication, too, but on 6 November they ambushed a complete British armoured brigade supply column with all its stores and with this captured transport and booty they pulled back with relative ease until they caught up with the rest of the *Afrika Korps* west of Mersa Matruh. For this initiative Ramcke was awarded the Oak Leaves to his Iron Cross, and returned to Europe to give further distinguished service.

After Operation Torch, the North Africa landings, Tunisia was under threat and FJR 5, a newly raised regiment commanded by Major Koch, was sent out in December 1942, together with 21st Parachute Engineer Battalion (Major Witzig) Both commanders were veterans of Eben Emael. They had to cover a 500km (300-mile) front and took part in hard fighting including the offensive that took Bou Arada. The units stayed in Tunisia until the German forces there surrendered on 12 May 1943.

ITALY

When the Allies landed in Sicily on 10 July 1943 1. Fallschirmjäger Division was airlifted from its Avignon base to Rome, for onward transit to Sicily. FJR 3

(Oberstleutnant Heilmann) made a parachute jump into Catania, Sicily, on 12 July to secure the airport for the rest of the division to fly in. But the Allied bridgehead was already well established and the German forces could do little to stem the tide. With the Luftwaffe *Hermann Göring* Panzer-Division 1. FJD made a fighting withdrawal to Messina from where German forces were being evacuated. 1. FJD acted as a rearguard and was the last to leave on 17 August. In one notable incident of the campaign, on 15 July, FJR 3 was cut off by British forces near Cantania but escaped to join the others by creeping away quietly in single file during the night under an unguarded bridge.

When Marshal Badoglio's government ousted Mussolini on 25 July Il Duce was taken to the island of Ponza, then on to La Maddalena in Sardinia. XI. Fliegerkorps under Student was now sent to Rome, taking also 2. FJD under command when it was flown in from its Nîmes base. 3. Panzergrenadier-Division was also taken under corps command. 2. FJD came from the north and 3. Panzergrenadier-Division from the south to secure Rome and keep open lines of communication to the south. The government and Italian royal family were forced to leave.

In Italy Eighth Army troops landed in Calabria on 3 September, and FJR 3 was in action again. Italy surrendered and the new Badoglio government joined the Allies. The US Fifth Army landed at Salerno where FJR 4 and the *Hermann Göring* Division were the main defenders, the battle for the Salerno beachhead lasting until 17 September. All the regiments of 1. FJD now came together under divisional command and took part in the fighting withdrawal north.

Several parachute operations followed. When the Italian army surrendered, II./FJR 6 (formerly IV./LLStR, Major Gericke) flew from Foggia to drop on Monte Rotondo, near Rome, to capture the Italian Army chief, General Roatta. After fighting into his HQ they found he and his staff had already fled to Pescara. Next came the rescue of Mussolini, which was entrusted to SS-Hauptsturmführer Skorzeny who was assigned the Paratroop Demonstration Battalion under Major

Left: Cassino—Fallschirmjäger counter-attacking the New Zealanders.

Opposite, Above: Well-armed Fallschirmjäger— several carrying the FG42 parachute assault rifle which was being troop-tested at the time of the Gran-Sasso raid. It proved unsatisfactory but further development lead to the StuG 44, used in the last year of the war.

Opposite, Below: Anti-tank gunners man a 2.8cm PaK 41 near a roadblock in Rome (see caption on page 56). Both men wear helmet netting. An open ammunition box lies ready behind the gun. The gunlayer sports a field dressing on his right arm.

KORPS-FALLSCHIRM-PIONEER BATTALION, 1942

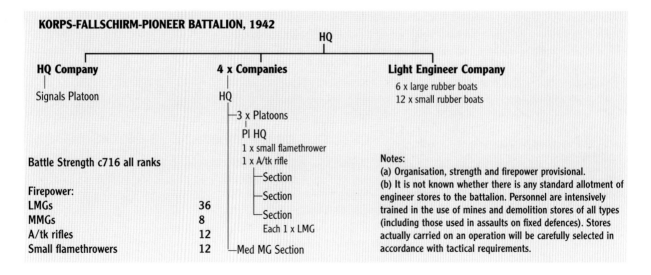

HQ

HQ Company

Signals Platoon

Battle Strength c716 all ranks

Firepower:
LMGs	36
MMGs	8
A/tk rifles	12
Small flamethrowers	12

4 x Companies

HQ

⊢3 x Platoons
│ Pl HQ
│ 1 x small flamethrower
│ 1 x A/tk rifle
│ ⊢Section
│ ⊢Section
│ ⊢Section
│ Each 1 x LMG
└Med MG Section

Light Engineer Company

6 x large rubber boats
12 x small rubber boats

Notes:
(a) Organisation, strength and firepower provisional.
(b) It is not known whether there is any standard allotment of engineer stores to the battalion. Personnel are intensively trained in the use of mines and demolition stores of all types (including those used in assaults on fixed defences). Stores actually carried on an operation will be carefully selected in accordance with tactical requirements.

FALLSCHIRM-ARTILLERIE-ABTEILUNG, 1942-43

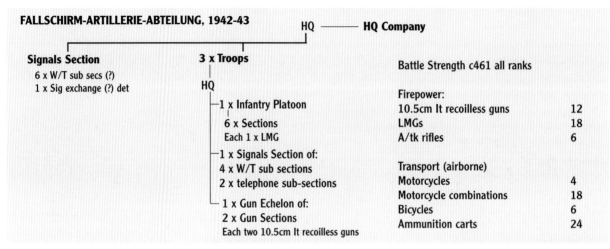

HQ ——— HQ Company

Signals Section
6 x W/T sub secs (?)
1 x Sig exchange (?) det

3 x Troops

HQ

⊢1 x Infantry Platoon
│ 6 x Sections
│ Each 1 x LMG
⊢1 x Signals Section of:
│ 4 x W/T sub sections
│ 2 x telephone sub-sections
└ 1 x Gun Echelon of:
  2 x Gun Sections
  Each two 10.5cm lt recoilless guns

Battle Strength c461 all ranks

Firepower:
10.5cm lt recoilless guns	12
LMGs	18
A/tk rifles	6

Transport (airborne)
Motorcycles	4
Motorcycle combinations	18
Bicycles	6
Ammunition carts	24

Right: Paras in Holland, 1940. The MG34 team has recovered the weapon from its container and is readying it for action. By 1942–43 the Fallschirmjäger had become ground troops in all but name.

IX. FLIEGERKORPS, 1941–42

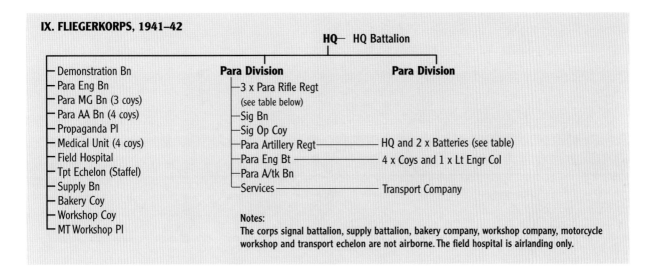

HQ — HQ Battalion

- Demonstration Bn
- Para Eng Bn
- Para MG Bn (3 coys)
- Para AA Bn (4 coys)
- Propaganda Pl
- Medical Unit (4 coys)
- Field Hospital
- Tpt Echelon (Staffel)
- Supply Bn
- Bakery Coy
- Workshop Coy
- MT Workshop Pl

Para Division
- 3 x Para Rifle Regt
  (see table below)
- Sig Bn
- Sig Op Coy
- Para Artillery Regt —————— HQ and 2 x Batteries (see table)
- Para Eng Bt ————————— 4 x Coys and 1 x Lt Engr Col
- Para A/tk Bn
- Services ————————— Transport Company

Para Division

Notes:
The corps signal battalion, supply battalion, bakery company, workshop company, motorcycle workshop and transport echelon are not airborne. The field hospital is airlanding only.

FALLSCHIRMJÄGER-REGIMENT, 1942-43

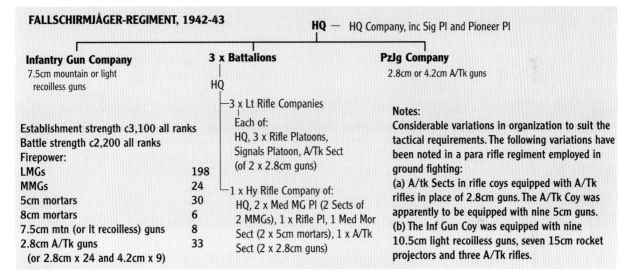

HQ — HQ Company, inc Sig Pl and Pioneer Pl

Infantry Gun Company
7.5cm mountain or light
recoilless guns

Establishment strength c3,100 all ranks
Battle strength c2,200 all ranks
Firepower:

LMGs	198
MMGs	24
5cm mortars	30
8cm mortars	6
7.5cm mtn (or lt recoilless) guns	8
2.8cm A/Tk guns	33
(or 2.8cm x 24 and 4.2cm x 9)	

3 x Battalions

HQ
- 3 x Lt Rifle Companies
  Each of:
  HQ, 3 x Rifle Platoons,
  Signals Platoon, A/Tk Sect
  (of 2 x 2.8cm guns)
- 1 x Hy Rifle Company of:
  HQ, 2 x Med MG Pl (2 Sects of
  2 MMGs), 1 x Rifle Pl, 1 Med Mor
  Sect (2 x 5cm mortars), 1 x A/Tk
  Sect (2 x 2.8cm guns)

PzJg Company
2.8cm or 4.2cm A/Tk guns

Notes:
Considerable variations in organization to suit the tactical requirements. The following variations have been noted in a para rifle regiment employed in ground fighting:
(a) A/tk Sects in rifle coys equipped with A/Tk rifles in place of 2.8cm guns. The A/Tk Coy was apparently to be equipped with nine 5cm guns.
(b) The Inf Gun Coy was equipped with nine 10.5cm light recoilless guns, seven 15cm rocket projectors and three A/Tk rifles.

Left: Para and motorcycle in Belgium. Solo and sidecar combos were dropped with the troops and were used for reconnaissance and transport.

Above: Units of 2. FJD were airlifted to the south of Rome in July 1943 to hold the city against a possible Italian coup. Here the unit attacks Italian forces commanded by General Carboni who were protecting Rome and the King's palace.

Opposite, Above: Flak Vierling in Normandy. The Quad version was only used in ground fighting since it could not be carried in a Junkers Ju 52.

Opposite, Below left: Generalleutnant Meindl, commander of II. Fallschirmkorps (3. FJD and 5. FJD) with Rommel, commander in chief Army Group B.

Opposite, Below right: Hermann Göring in early 1945 with Generalleutnant Schmalz, the commander of the eponymous 'Hermann Göring' Fallschirm-Pz-Korps.

Mors for the task. It was discovered that Mussolini had been secretly taken from La Maddalena to a mountain hotel on the Gran Sasso, Abruzzi. On 12 September a paratroop company landed by glider alongside the hotel, freed Mussolini, and flew him out in a Fieseler Storch which Hauptmann Gerlach had landed expertly in front of the hotel. They took him to Rome, then on to Rastenburg to meet Hitler.

A week later, on the night of 17 September, II./FJR 7 of 2. FJD dropped near Portoferraio on the island of Elba with the task of taking the city and the west side of the island. The next morning II./FJR 7 dropped on the southwest of the island, and Army troops landed by boat to secure the whole island and capture the Italian garrison. Allied troops recaptured most of the Aegean islands, but on 12 November, in a final fling, I./FJR 2, veterans of Crete and Corinth, dropped on Leros (in combination with a boat landing) and recaptured the island from the British.

The toughest battle in Italy was at Monte Cassino which was a major defence point on the Gustav Line blocking the way to Rome. The ad hoc Parachute Group *Schulz* (from FJR 1 and FJR 3) was among the original defenders from January 1944, but in March 1944 1. FJD took over the full defence responsibility, holding out in the rubble to which the monastery was largely reduced in the January–June 1944 period when it was under Allied attack. When Monte Cassino was first taken over, men of the *Hermann Göring* Division spent three weeks collecting up the archives and treasures from the monastery and moving them to safety at the Vatican and La Spoleta. Huge Allied efforts were needed to dislodge the defenders and outflank the position. Most of 1. FJD got away safely when the position was abandoned, and the depth of the walls and network of tunnels and dugouts in the ruins contributed to their survival from intense shelling and bombing.

The Anzio landing in January 1944 saw the first engagement of a new formation, 4. FJD which had been vested at Perugia in December from new regiments FJR 10, 11, and 12. This was made up of core personnel from 2. FJD, LLStR, and various Italian volunteers and men transferred from Luftwaffe field units. The commander was Oberst, later Generalmajor, Heinz Trettner. One battalion from each 4. FJD regiment joined with the *Hermann Göring* Panzer-Division and they held the beach head until Fourteenth Army arrived in strength. Fierce fighting ensued with 4. FJD in the thick of it until the Cassino battle flared up again in May.

THE FINAL YEARS

On paper the German airborne forces expanded considerably in the final 18 months of the war. Much of this was achieved by the decision to disband Luftwaffe field divisions and incorporate them into the airborne forces. In addition some other Luftwaffe personnel became available as the air element was reduced in size by attrition. Very little attempt was made at airborne training, for the new divisions were essentially ground fighting troops, but most of the new formations were leavened by veterans from the old days in core positions. They ensured that the airborne traditions were carried on by the new units. However, as the war came closer to its end some grandly named divisions were little more than scratch formations, often well under strength and sometimes reduced to a few battle groups.

In October 1943 3. Fallschirmjäger Division (3. FJD) was formed in France comprising FJR 5, 8, and 9. There were now four airborne divisions and in January 1944 they were organised into I. Fliegerkorps (1. and 4. FJD) based in Italy and II. Fliegerkorps (2. and 3. FJD) based in France. There was also the former Luftwaffe-manned *Hermann Göring* Panzer-Division which became in the new scheme of things the *Hermann Göring* Fallschirm Panzer-Division. Later a second Panzer division was formed and the two divisions formed the *Hermann Göring* Fallschirm Panzerkorps and were transferred to the Eastern Front in 1945.

Right: From a well-known sequence of photos, taken during a 1944 exercise in France; note the man on the left wears the standard ammunition bandolier.

Opposite, Above: Another scene from the same Normandy exercise.

Opposite, Below: Flak 88 next to a Marder II—a 7.5cm PaK on a Panzer II chassis.

Above: 9. FJD surrenders to the Russians in Berlin, May 1945. Note the Su-122 at left.

Left: Ramcke surrendering to the US Army at Brest on 20 September 1944.

Opposite, Above: The 'Hermann Göring' Fallschirm Panzerkorps attacking Soviet armour south of Bautzen on 22 April 1945—the last German victory on the Eastern Front.

Opposite, Below: Panthers of the Fallschirm Panzerkorps were attached to FJR 2 for a counter-attack near Kirovgrad in December 1943. Oberst Kroh, the regimental commander, is second from right.

In March 1944, Student, now a Generaloberst, was told to form all these elements into 1. Fallschirm-Armee, under control of C-in-C West. In September 1944 it came under control of Army Group B and was responsible for defence of the Low Countries. 5. FJD was formed at Rheims in March 1944, comprising FJR 13, 14 and 15 and fought in Normandy at St Lô and Caen but was largely wiped out in the Falaise Pocket. 6. FJD, comprising FJR 17 and 18, was a low strength division formed in Normandy in June 1944 and almost wiped out soon after. 7. FJD was a scratch formation got together hastily by Generalleutnant Erdmann, Student's chief of staff, largely to defend the line of the Albert Canal in September 1944, but some units were thrown into the Arnhem battle with some success. 8. FJD was another scratch division, much under strength, from assorted units which fought in defence of the homeland in the January–April 1945 period.

9. FJD was formed near Stettin in January 1945, with newly raised FJR 25, 26 and 27 and disparate units for service on the Eastern Front. It fought at Breslau and on the Oder and was involved in the defence of Berlin where it surrendered to the Russians in May 1945. 10. FJD was formed in February 1945 with some men pulled out of Italy before the surrender there. It was intended to go to the Dutch–German border with 1. Fallschirm-Armee, but then was switched to Austria instead, later moving into Moravia where it surrendered to the Russians. 11. FJD existed only on paper except for a few staff officers and its designated commander, Oberst Gericke. New regiments FJR 37, 38 and 39 were to be raised for service in Holland

Above and Right: Realistic training kept the Fallschirmjäger as a credible fighting force until well into 1945. These photos show various equipment and locations, including: Normandy 1944 (Above), MG34 in the LMG (bipod) role (right); manning a roadblock (centre right), and with an MP40 SMG (Bottom right).

Top right: Early war (note white canopies) training exercise.

in March 1945 but in the chaotic last few weeks of the war this never happened.

In the spring of 1944 two independent assault gun brigades, equipped with the Sturmgeschütz (StuG) III, were formed at Melun in France from airborne personnel, StuG-Brigade XI and StuG-Brigade XII. The former was transferred to the Eastern Front in the closing weeks of the war, but in 1944 they both acted in support of various airborne divisions fighting in the west including 5. FJD in the Ardennes and 7. FJD in defence of the Reich.

1. FJD and 4. FJD fought on in Italy until the final surrender of the forces there in April 1945. 2. FJD, under Ramcke, fought with distinction in Normandy, countering the US airborne divisions around Carentan, then in Brittany, and finally holding out at 'Fortress Brest' until September 1944. FJR 6 survived the surrender of 2. FJD, fought at Arnhem, and made the last German airborne drop of the war as part of the Ardennes Offensive in December 1944, though this was not a success and missed its objectives. The various 1. Fallschirm-Armee divisions fought at Arnhem and Nijmegen, took part in the defence of the Maas and the Waal, the Reichswald battle, the withdrawal to the Rhine, defence of the Rhinelands and the Ems and Weser withdrawal. The *Hermann Göring* Fallschirm Panzerkorps ended the war on the Eastern Front, mainly in East Saxony and lower Silesia. They were among the forces achieving the last German victory of the war, the recapture of Bautzen, and finally surrendering to the Russians near Dresden.

Above: MG.34 used in the heavy machine-gun role on a tripod, the carrying straps are clearly visible. The gun commander on the left carries the map case of an officer.

Left: A weapons container being carried out to a waiting aircraft. The concertina-like cylinder on the end is designed to take the impact on landing.

Right: The 27mm *Leuchtpistole* manufactured by Walther was used for signalling purposes. The four types of ammunition available were high explosive, smoke, indicator (ie signal flare) and single illuminating parachute flare. The man is wearing a flare cartridge bandolier. Note rank badge on right arm of camouflage smock.

CONSTITUENT UNITS OF THE FALLSCHIRMJÄGER DIVISIONS, APRIL 1943–APRIL 1945

1st Fallschirmjäger Division
Created out of 7. Flieger-Division April
  1943 (CO Generalmajor Heidrich
  promoted Generalleutnant during
  1944)
FJR 1 (CO Oberst Schulz)
FJR 3 (CO Oberst Heilmann)
FJR 4 (CO Oberst Walther)
Fallschirm Artillery Regiment 1 (CO Major
  Schram)
Fallschirm PzJg Battalion I
Fallschirm Pioneer Battalion I
Fallschirm Signals Battalion I
Fallschirm MG Battalion I
Fallschirm Medical Battalion I

2nd Fallschirmjäger Division
Raised Brittany 1943
  (CO Generalleutnant Ramcke)
FJR 2 (CO Oberst Kroh)
FJR 6 (CO Major Liebach)
FJR 7 (CO Oberst Straub)
Fallschirm Artillery Regiment 2
Fallschirm PzJg Battalion II
Fallschirm Engineer Battalion II
Fallschirm Signals Battalion II
Fallschirm Medical Battalion II
Fallschirm Services Units
Fallschirm AA Bn II, Fallschirm Mortar Bn
  II and Replacement Bn II raised Jan
  1944

3nd Fallschirmjäger Division
Raised France 1943
  (CO Generalmajor Schimpf)
FJR 5* (CO Major Becker)
FJR 8 (CO Major Liebach)
FJR 9 (CO Major Stephani)
Fallschirm Artillery Regiment 3
Fallschirm PzJg Battalion III
Fallschirm Pioneer Battalion III
Fallschirm AA Battalion III
Fallschirm Mortar Battalion III
Fallschirm Signals Battalion III

* FJR 5 lost in Africa (reconstituted it
  became part of 3. FJD in March 1944

4th Fallschirmjäger Division
Raised Italy during Nov/Dec 1943
  (CO Generalmajor Trettner)
FJR 10 (CO Oberst Fuchs)
FJR 11 (CO Major Gericke)

FJR 12 (CO Major Timm)
Fallschirm Artillery Regiment 4
Fallschirm PzJg Battalion IV
Fallschirm Pioneer Battalion IV
Fallschirm Signals Battalion IV
Also units from the Italian Divisions
  'Folgore' and 'Demgo'

5th Fallschirmjäger Division
Rraised France April 1944
  (CO Generalleutnant Wilke)
FJR 13 (CO Major von der Schulenburg)
FJR 14 (CO Major Noster)
FJR 15 (CO Major Groschke)
Fallschirm Artillery Regiment 5
Fallschirm PzJg Battalion V
Fallschirm Pioneer Battalion V
Fallschirm Mortar Battalion V
Fallschirm AA Battalion V
Fallschirm Signals Battalion V

6th Fallschirmjäger Division*
Raised Metz and Nancy April 1944
  (CO Generalmajor von Heyking)
FJR 16 (CO Oberstleutnant Schirmer)
FJR 17
FJR 18
Fallschirm Artillery Regiment 6
Fallschirm PzJg Battalion VI
Fallschirm Mortar Battalion VI
Fallschirm AA Battalion VI
Fallschirm Pioneer Battalion VI
Fallschirm Signals Battalion No VI
Replacement Battalion
Reconnaissance Company

* Division re-raised around Kleve in the
  Rhineland, end 1944, following
  decimation in France and Belgium

  (CO Generalmajor Plocher)
FJR 16 (CO Oberst Dorn (2 x battalions)
FJR 17 (CO Oberst Vetter)
FJR 18 (CO Major Witzig)
Fallschirm Artillery Regiment 6
Fallschirm PzJg Battalion VI
Fallschirm Mortar Battalion VI
Fallschirm AA Battalion VI
Fallschirm Pioneer Battalion VI
Fallschirm Signals Battalion No VI
Replacement Battalion
Reconnaissance Company

7th Fallschirmjäger Division
Raised Belgium September 1944
  (CO Generalleutnant Erdmann)
FJR 19 (CO Oberst Menzel)
FJR 20 (CO Oberstleutnant Grassmel)
FJR 21 (CO Oberst Loytweg-Hardegg)
Fallschirm Artillery Regiment 7
Fallschirm PzJg Battalion VII
Fallschirm Pioneer Battalion VII
Fallschirm Mortar Battalion VII
Fallschirm Signals Battalion VII
Divisional Units

8th Fallschirmjäger Division
Raised January 1945
  (CO Generalmajor Wadehan)
FJR 22 (CO Oberstleutnant von der
  Tanne)
FJR 23 (served with 2nd Division from
  November 1944)
FJR 24 (CO Oberstleutnant Hübner)
Pioneer Battalion VIII
Replacement Battalion
Divisional supply units

9th Fallschirmjäger Division
Raised south of Stettin
  (CO Generalleutnant Wilke)
FJR 25 (CO Major Schact)
FJR 26 (CO Major Brede)
FJR 27 (CO Major Abratis)
Fallschirm Artillery Regiment 9
Fallschirm PzJg Battalion IX
Fallschirm Pioneer Battalion IX
Fallschirm AA Battalion IX
Fallschirm Signals Battalion No 9

10th Fallschirmjaeger Division
Raised February 1945 in eastern Austria
  (CO Oberst von Hoffmann)
FJR 28 (CO Major Schmucker)
FJR 29 (CO Major Genz)
FJR 30 (CO Oberstleutnant Wolff)
Fallschirm Artillery Regiment 10
Fallschirm Pioneer Battalion X
Fallschirm PzJg Battalion X

11th Fallschirmjäger Division
This division was set up and used
  piecemeal in March 1945
  (CO Oberst Gericke). Intended
  regiments—FJR 37, 38 and 39

EQUIPMENT & MARKINGS

Above: Paras inside a Ju 52.

Opposite: After landing a fully-equipped Fallschirmjager disengages his harness. Although this man is wearing a Luftwaffe jump suit he is also wearing an Army eagle on his right breast.

Previous page: Paratrooper in second model smock with FG42 assault rifle. The re-enactment colour photographs in this chapter are by Daniel Peterson and reproduced by kind permission of the photographer.

The specialised fighting function of the airborne troops required combat clothing and equipment – and in some cases weapons – adapted to the role, and there were modes of use, also, not previously encountered in conventional ground fighting.

UNIFORMS

Temperate Areas

In Europe standard Luftwaffe service dress and head-dress was worn for parades, walking out, leave and general duties, with the usual Luftwaffe practice of substituting the simplified *Fliegerbluse* in place of the tunic for work wear, combat, or even walking out, at regimental discretion. The appropriate arm-of-service colour (*Waffenfarbe*) was incorporated in head-dress piping, rank badges, and shoulder straps and for paratroops this was golden yellow except for specialist troops such as signallers, engineers, medical attendants, etc., who wore the colour of their branch.

For combat, however, paratroops wore very distinctive specialised clothing, the most revolutionary item, for the time, being the jump smock. The original pattern was of the step-in type. This smock was made in a field-grey (green-grey) drill material and was the pattern originally developed for the Army parachute battalion. It continued in wear after the battalion was transferred to the Luftwaffe. The Army pattern national eagle badge was worn on the right breast and veterans of the Army parachute battalion proudly wore this well into their time of service as Luftwaffe personnel. Despite the original intention that the smock would be discarded for ground combat, it was found to be a good utilitarian garment in its own right and those issued with it mostly retained it in combat. It was secured by two vertical full-length exposed zips arranged so that the front panel came out completely, allowing quick removal on landing, for the original thinking was that this smock would be worn for jumping only, covering personal equipment, and would be discarded once on the ground. The smock had a band that fastened at the neck and tight press-studded cuffs. Zips in the side of the smock gave access through to the trouser pockets.

The Luftwaffe's original smock design was also in grey-green drill, though some were also made in blue-grey, particularly in the early years. This smock also had 'step in' legs at thigh height, but it had a conventional buttoned fly front (soon

replaced by a zip) and a conventional fall collar. It also had side slits to give access to trouser pockets, and the Luftwaffe version of the national eagle emblem was worn on the right breast. To make it more suited to combat wear it was soon modified to give two diagonally-zipped breast pockets and two at thigh level, though there were a number of variations in pocket size and positioning in the 1940 period while the optimum arrangement was developed. Some smocks at this time had only two pockets.

As with the Army pattern smock, the Luftwaffe smock was worn over personal equipment when jumping, and then had to be removed or the personal equipment transferred to the outside once the man was on the ground.

The parachute combat trousers were gathered in at the ankles and had conventional side and (two) hip pockets, plus a fob pocket at the front. However, they also had long slits on each outer seam at knee height, secured by press studs. These gave access to allow removal of the knee pads, worn under the trousers when jumping. Knee pads worn outside the trousers were additional to these. An interior pocket inside the right hand slit held the special paratrooper's knife (primarily designed for emergency release of the parachute lines on the ground), and this had a blade which slid in and out of the handle.

Below: Parachute sergeant with full equipment—MP38 machine-pistol, six magazines pouches, binoculars, water bottle with cup. His rank badge is on his left arm (see page 80).

Jump boots were of black leather, heavily reinforced and rubber-soled. The tops came well above the ankle and covered the gathered-in trouser bottoms. Early boots had side lacing, but later the pattern was changed to conventional front lacing. When emphasis changed to ground fighting after 1941, many men wore conventional service leather ankle boots, in black or brown depending on source, sometimes with canvas or cloth anklets. When jumping the paratroops wore long black leather gauntlets with elasticated tops.

By early 1941 (and first worn in action in Crete), a new 'second pattern' jump smock was being issued. It differed from the earlier pattern in eliminating the 'step in' legs. Instead the skirt was fitted with press studs so that it could be secured tightly round the thighs when jumping, then loosened to form a conventional jacket shape in action. Some of these new smocks were produced in plain olive green, but most were in 'splinter' camouflage pattern. A cloth helmet cover in the same camouflage pattern was also issued, as were some in plain olive green. This 'second pattern' smock was broadly copied in style for British paratroops.

The abbreviated helmet was unique to parachute units, and distinctive as a recognition feature for troops on the ground. The design was intended to eliminate the chances of catching on aircraft fittings and doorways, etc., or on branches or ground objects as the paratrooper landed. The original version developed for the first Army paratroopers was based on the standard Model 1935 German military helmet, reduced in depth all round by taking about 2cm off the rim. The liner was beefed up and the single chin strap was replaced by strong Y-straps. Distinctive was a small horizontal slot on each side just above the rim. The Luftwaffe pattern helmet, which became universal, was similar to the Army design, but without the small side slots and with a slightly more prominent rim. When new, helmets carried a shield decal in national colours (black/white/red) on the right side and

Left: Early Fallschirmjäger attire. TRH Pictures

Below left and right: The second model parachutist's jump smock in Luftwaffe *Splittermuster*. It is seen here with matching helmet cover and bandolier for the K98 Mauser rifle. The bandolier holds 20 five-round clips of ammunition.

the Army pattern eagle decal (original Army parachute units only) or a Luftwaffe pattern national eagle on the left side. Later in the war these decals were commonly omitted, or painted over, or smeared over with mud to reduce their prominence. From 1941 cloth helmet covers were issued, as previously noted, but also used on helmets were elasticated bands, string netting, or even wire netting, to hold foliage as camouflage.

Many items of Army issue, such as smocks, boots, or even helmets of ordinary service pattern could be seen in wear later in the war, and pictorial evidence suggests that even in the early months of the war some men were issued with conventional service helmets while paratroop helmets were in short supply. On the Eastern Front in cold weather, parachute units wore conventional Army style winter combat clothing, notably the reversible (white/olive green) padded smock and trousers.

Tropical Clothing

When the war started the Luftwaffe had no specific tropical clothing, and the first Luftwaffe air squadron personnel who went to North Africa in early 1941 wore Army issue tropical uniforms with Luftwaffe badges and insignia. Specific Luftwaffe items were soon developed, however, notably a tropical tunic which was similar in pattern and style to the ordinary service tunic except that it was slightly looser in cut and was made of biscuit colour cotton drill with brown metal buttons. A specific tropical issue tunic, even fuller in cut, was designed for paratroops, obviously intended to replace the smock. It had the breast pockets replaced by bandolier holders kept in place by brown metal press studs. These were to be troop-tested by the *Ramcke* Brigade in 1942, prior to general issue, but when parachute landings were discontinued there was no further production, though the test tunics remained in use by some *Ramcke* Brigade members. In practice paratroops in tropical dress kept their standard smocks for wear as required.

Matching tropical trousers had a built-in belt, with straps to gather in the bottoms of the legs, tight to the ankles or boots, giving a full cut baggy effect. A deep patch pocket with flap was on the left thigh front, plus the usual trouser side pockets. The matching shorts were in similar style but without the patch pocket. All these garments were made in beige or biscuit colour cotton drill which soon faded or washed out to a light stone shade. While canvas/leather high boots and short brown leather boots were issued for tropical wear, most paratroops preferred to wear their issue jump boots.

The tropical shirt had two pleated breast pockets and a cloth Luftwaffe eagle breast badge. Brown metal buttons were fitted. It came in long or short sleeve versions, was quite loosely cut, and was made of tan cotton drill which, like the other garments, usually faded to a lighter shade. This variation in fading between different items of clothing often gave a 'patchy' appearance to groups of men in tropical clothing.

Issued to paratroops sent to North Africa was the Luftwaffe tropical helmet, made in pith with a tan/beige cloth covering and red inside lining in the crown and green lining under the rim. It had a brown leather chin strap and was similar to the Army pattern except for a narrower more angled brim and a Luftwaffe metal eagle badge on the left side. A shield in the national colours was carried on the right side. Most distinctive of all was the Luftwaffe tropical cap, a soft full crowned, wide peaked cap in beige drill with a button-on cloth neck cover which could be added as required. It also had a chin strap that could be worn down or up. It was issued from May 1942. Also worn was the tropical version of the Army pattern soft

Below: Paras on Crete. Note camouflage smocks and pistols.

peaked *Feldmütze* forage cap with the Luftwaffe eagle emblem, either in cloth or metal, added, and this was mainly taken up before the Luftwaffe tropical cap was on issue. Finally, in 1941, was issued a tropical version of the fore-and-aft *Fliegermütze* forage cap, again in beige drill.

It should be noted that in cold weather in areas where tropical dress was ordered, the standard European issue Luftwaffe blue overcoat was worn, as were other items of European issue clothing, such as head wear and the smock, when the situation justified it.

BADGES AND INSIGNIA

Aside from the standard badges and distinctions of rank worn with Luftwaffe service dress, there were special rank badges for camouflage clothing, introduced for wear on the smock in 1940, though initially only slowly issued. The rank badges duplicated the pattern of stylised wings and bars already in use on Luftwaffe flying suits. The symbols were in white on a grey-green patch worn on each upper arm of the smock. Generals had the symbols in gold instead of white. These badges gave a very logical and distinctive method or recognising rank and command in combat without being too prominent to enemy eyes. Prior to full issue of these special cloth rank badges, officers and men either carried no visible rank badges on their smocks, or transferred the standard rank badges from their service dress.

Also worn, and intended for service dress, were commemorative cuff titles, worn on the left cuff. Sometimes they were seen on smock cuffs also, though this appears to have been an unofficial application. Most famous was the *Kreta* title in yellow and white which was issued to all who took part in the invasion of Crete. Less common was *Afrika* for men, such as those of *Ramcke* Brigade, who served in Cyrenaica, Libya, or Tunis. Some regiments or divisions also had cuff titles, notably *Fallschirm-Jäger 1* issued in 1939, and some subsequent variations and manifestations of the regiments and divisions named for Reichsmarschall Göring.

To qualify as a parachutist a trainee had to complete six jumps successfully. He was then awarded the parachutist badge which was worn on the left breast. The Army badge featured a diving eagle on a laurel wreath with a Nazi eagle and swastika let into the top. The Luftwaffe badge had the diving eagle clasping a swastika in its talons superimposed over a simpler laurel wreath. Former Army parachutists proudly wore the Army badge instead of the Luftwaffe version for years after their transfer to the Luftwaffe.

As the parachute force expanded in the war years, several of the divisions adopted formation signs similar to the Army type. These were as follows:

1. Fallschirmjäger-Division   A green devil astride a red trident, superimposed on a white square. The post-war (1956 onwards) 1st Parachute Division had a white parachute symbol, superimposed on a blue square, and this was also worn as a badge on the upper left sleeve of the uniform.

2. Fallschirmjäger-Division   This was formed in 1942, initially as a brigade known as *Ramcke* Brigade after its commander, and in this form it saw service in North Africa in 1942, before moving to Italy and being reorganised as a division. In both manifestations the formation sign was a kite outline with a large R inside

Above: The workhorse of the Luftwaffe was the Junkers Ju 52, from whose familiar corrugated shell the Fallschirmjäger exited in diving position.

Below: Unlike Allied forces, German paras dropped without equipment. Here is a early war view of a para ready to drop as exemplified by German boxing champion Max Schmeling.

Above left and right: Grenade bags for the Steilhandgranate Models 1939 and 1943. As these are manufactured in the Luftwaffe *Splittermuster* it is highly likely that they were a specialised equipment item for paratroopers, and possibly for Luftwaffe Field Division troops. Barely discernible is the black webbing strap connecting the top inner corners of the bags behind the neck; a second strap across the small of the back connects the bottom corners. The distinctive Luftwaffe splinter camouflage pattern is printed on one side of the cloth only.

Left: Further view of the second model 'bone sack', this time with the bandolier for the paratroopers' FG42 assault rifle. Each pocket carries one 20-round box magazine, totalling 160 rounds.

Opposite, from top to bottom: Emblems were introduced later in the war for some para units. These are:

1	1. FJD
2	2. FJD (or Brigade Ramcke)
3	4. FJD
4	22nd Luftlande Division
5	Postwar 1. FJD para badge (from 1956)

it signifying its commander, General Ramcke. A subsidiary initial (K, vH, H, B) indicated the different regimental commanders according to sub-unit. The sign was usually in black on a white rectangle. The initials indicated the following battalion commanders: K – Kroh or Kargerer, vH – von der Heydte, H – Hübner, B – Burckhardt. The subsidiary initial was not always carried.

4. Fallschirmjäger-Division   This formation had a stylised 'comet' of a white outline star with a blue/red/blue 'flaring' tail, on a white square. Sometimes the star/tail symbol was used in a simplified solid colour (white, red, blue, etc.) without the background.

22. (Luftlande) Panzergrenadier-Division   In the early part of the war up to the Crete operation this was the designated Army air-landing division which worked with 7. Flieger-Division. Its sign was a shield with red/white vertical stripes and a horizontal bar in red/white checks, derived from the state flag of Bremen.

These formation signs could be seen placed variously on front, back, or sides of divisional vehicles though pictorial evidence suggests they were not nearly so frequently applied as formation signs on Army or Waffen-SS vehicles. Where appropriate, Army style tac signs to indicate type of unit could also be seen displayed when divisions fought as ground troops, but again they do not seem to have been so often applied as on Army vehicles. Vehicles also carried a military number plate either painted directly or affixed on front and rear with the index letters WL – Wehrmacht Luftwaffe – prefixing the number. Lettering was black on white.

WEAPONS AND TRANSPORT

While parachute troops were equipped with the standard range of small arms and support weapons used by ground troops, when used in airborne operations there were limitations in artillery and anti-tank weapons they could use since all equipment had to be light enough to be transported by air, and preferably capable of being dropped by parachute as well. The principal equipments used were as follows:

Anti-tank Weapons
Panzerbüsche 39   This was the most recent version of the rifle calibre (7.92mm) anti-tank rifle which had long been used by the Army but was obsolescent when the war started. Its best performance was penetrating 30mm of armour at 100 metre range (1.2in/110yd), so it was inadequate except against light armoured vehicles at close range. Nonetheless it was used in action in the 1940–41 period. It had the advantage of being man-portable.

Panzerbüsche 42   This replaced the Panzerbüsche 39 in 1942 and was a lightened version of the similar 2.8cm taper-bore weapon produced for the Army. It had a tubular steel carriage with small tyred wheels. While the calibre was the same as the Army equivalent the barrel and muzzle velocity were much improved to give a 400 metre range and best penetration of 55mm of armour (2.2in/440yd). This was at the expense of barrel wear, with a barrel life of only 500 rounds. The gun could traverse 25 degrees either side on the carriage, and the weapon could be broken into five parts for parachuting.

PaK 36   This was the standard 3.7cm light anti-tank gun widely used by ground troops, but the largest gun that could be carried inside a Ju 52, weighing in at 450kg (990lb). It could not be broken down and initially could only be delivered

Above: Cuff title and Fallschirmjäger breast badge.

as part of an air-landing operation. However, experiments showed that it could be carried between the undercarriage legs of a Ju 52 and delivered below five parachutes. In this form it was used in later operations. On the ground it could only be hauled by hand, but it was then discovered that it could be pulled by the BMW or Zündapp 750cc motor-cycle combinations also used by the parachute troops, and this became the mode of transport, but the gun team had to be restricted to four men to allow this.

Support Artillery

Gebirgskanone 15   Initially the lightest artillery piece available for the support role was the obsolescent Czech Skoda-built 7.5cm Gebirgskanone 15 which had been designed for mountain troop use. It weighed 630kg (1,390lb) and broke down into seven parts and could be carried and air-landed inside a Ju 52. It still had to be hauled on the ground and it was decided to use small Haflinger horses for this which could also be carried inside the Ju 52. The guns and horse teams were deployed in the air landing in Holland on 10 May 1940, but this proved to be a fiasco as the horses stampeded under fire as they landed. The scheme was abandoned and not used again. Subsequently a few of the later 7.5cm **Gebirgsgeschütze 36** were used, but they were heavier at 750kg (1,650lb) and broke into eight components that had to be carried.

kurzer Granatwerfer 42 Initially the paratroops used the standard 8.1cm German infantry mortars, but in 1940 a special short mortar (the 'Stummelwerfer') was developed specially for airborne use. With a barrel length of 747mm (29.5in), and breaking into three loads each around 18kg (40lb) in weight, it was compact and very portable. It could also be fired at a distance using a lanyard attached to the firing bolt. In service in 1941 it was popular and effective and was also later taken up by the Army and Waffen-SS.

Recoilless Weapons

The air-portable artillery problem was to some extent ameliorated by the production of recoilless guns, which the firms of Krupp and Rheinmetall had both been developing in the late 1930s. Even before the war started they had been asked for lightweight designs for airborne use. By 1940 the first of these, the

Krupp 7.5cm LG 1, was in limited service and was first used in action during the invasion of Crete. (LG = leichte Geschütze = light gun). To keep the weight down it had a simple tubular carriage and spoked bicycle-type wheels. This proved a weak point, with some carriages literally collapsing in action. Rheinmetall took over the design and produced a beefed up version, the 7.5cm LG 40 with a much stronger carriage and smaller metal disc tyred wheels. These could be removed and the carriage could then be emplaced in tripod form. Some 450 were produced and the LG 40 was used in Crete. The LG 40 could be dropped by parachute in four component parts, but containers were preferred in order to ensure all the parts arrived together. An experienced crew could assemble the gun in about two minutes. Some LG 1s were dropped in component parts in wicker baskets. LG 40 range was 6,500 metres (7,100yd), rate of fire 6 rounds per minute.

To give even more punch both Krupp and Rheinmetall produced 10.5cm weapons in 1941–42, the 10.5cm LG 40 (confusingly with the same designation as Krupp's 7.5cm) and the 10.5cm LG 42 (Rheinmetall). Both could be towed by the muzzle, had blast shields, and larger metal tyred wheels, and could be emplaced by removing the wheels. Range was 8,000 metres (8,750yd). These weapons saw relatively limited service, however, because parachute operations were abandoned after Crete. The same fate was suffered by a later development, the 10.5cm LG 43 of 1943, an improved design that was made lighter and more portable for airborne use. When paratroop formations were used in the ground fighting role in the later part of the war they used the same artillery equipment as the Army, such as the PaK 40, PaK 75, etc.

Anti-aircraft Weapons

Initially the parachute flak battalions had the Fla-MG 15 which could be mounted on the motor-cycle combinations, and the widely used 2cm Flak 30 which in its airborne form had the shield removed. This could be towed on its two-wheel carriage by the motor-cycle combination, and could also be broken into six components for manhandling. This weapon had to be carried into an air-landing inside a Ju 52 but some are said to have be dropped by parachute cluster from under a Ju 52. To overcome this problem the 2cm Gebirgsflak 38 was designed with weight in action reduced from the Flak 30's 463kg (1,020lb) to 276kg (608lb) and overall weight only 315kg (694lb). This was an excellent compact design for use both by mountain and airborne troops and it could be para-dropped with its two-wheel carriage from beneath a Ju 52. However, it only saw limited service with the airborne forces since the need for it was gone by the time it was ready.

Above: The standard airborne light mortar (8cm kurzer Granatenwerfer 42)—specially developed for airborne forces.

Vehicles

Vehicles specifically used in airborne operations were the BMW R12 motorcycle, solo or with sidecars, the BMW R75, and the Zündapp KS750, both with sidecars with driven axles. These could tow the airborne artillery pieces as noted above and carry minimal gun crews. They also towed ammunition trailers. All could be carried inside a Ju 52 but early experiments established that they could also be dropped by parachute cluster. Unique was the NSU Kettenkrad half-track motor-cycle which was designed for airborne use and first employed on Crete. This was an extremely useful towing and load-carrying vehicle which could be carried under a Ju 52 or inside the larger gliders.

Below: Parachute riflemen taking arms including MG34 LMG and MP38 machine pistols from an arms container. The metal end of the container has been crumpled on the impact of landing. Note colour-coded container markings.

Containers

Small arms and ammunition in airborne operations were dropped separately in the containers previously mentioned. This was unsatisfactory because parachutists could be engaged by waiting defenders (as in Crete) before they could recover their personal arms from the container. Because of this limitation there were several recorded cases where men ignored the official procedure and carried their small arms with them when they dropped, usually an MP38 or MP40 sub-machine gun, or a rifle, sometimes padded or wrapped in canvas attached to the parachute harness, so that they could go into action immediately on landing. A special item developed was the canvas bandolier carrying up to 200 rounds that could be slung round the neck beneath the smock when jumping. Containers also carried food, medical stores, and radio or pioneer equipment, etc. The later versions had small wheels and a tow handle fitted, these being put in place after the containers were

Left: Detail of right rear panel of a midwar jump smock in *Sumpfmuster*, showing the buttoned fastening of the flare pistol holster, tightening snap, and holes for the metal belt support hooks. The well-used snap has lost its green-grey baked enamel finish, leaving the brass exposed.

Below left and right: The parachutist's jump smock in Luftwaffe *Sumpfmuster*, a special pattern which seems to have been created by modifying the printing rollers originally used to print the air force splinter pattern. It is manufactured from a double-faced twill cotton/rayon blend offering excellent wind resistance. Note the charcteristic jump smock pocket details; and the skirt fastened into separate 'legs' by press studs.

Above right: Tunisia, 1943, with sand-coloured helmet and Luftwaffe tropical trousers. This midwar production jump smock is still made of predominantly cotton blend with rayon and weave identical to that employed in the *Zeltbahn*.

Below right: DFS 230 gliders.

recovered so that they could be used as battlefield barrows. Colour coding and smoke markers were used to help the troops locate their particular containers once on the ground, but the system was wasteful and vulnerable, for it needed four containers for every 12 men as a rule of thumb which took up a lot of payload space. And to compensate for containers going astray it was necessary to drop up to twice the quantity of small arms and ammunition than would be needed by an equivalent ground force.

Gliders

As already noted the DFS 230 was the standard assault glider. This was towed by the Ju 52. A Ju 52 could tow up to three gliders of this type at a time, but in actual airborne assaults only one was towed. The special unit formed to tow the glider assault regiment was known as the Luftlandegeschwader. At the time of the Crete invasion this required 192 Ju 52s to take the entire assault regiment into action. Ten men were carried in one glider, and one platoon needed three gliders. A battalion of 480 men therefore required 48 gliders and 48 tugs and a Luftlandesgruppe of 48 aircraft was allocated to each battalion. Subsequent to the Crete campaign there were no more actual airborne assaults, but the DFS 230 glider and the larger Gotha 242 were used by the airborne forces to transport their men and equipment between various operational fronts such as Tunis and Sicily or Italy and France. However, these were not specifically allocated to airborne forces, and the gliders were also used for general supply and personnel carrier work. Later the giant Messerschmitt 323 was used in the same role.

Above: Paras after the fall of Eben Emael.

Below: Badges worn on Fliegerbluse or camouflage smocks—blue-grey background, generals with gold insignia, otherwise white.

Right: Army or Luftwaffe para in fighting order. Drawings from US official recognition charts.

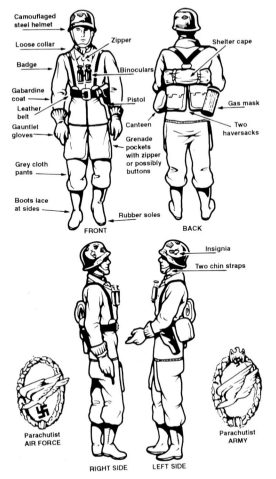

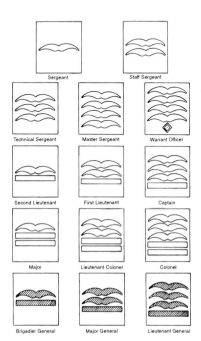

Left: Officers attending an anti-tank course. The 3.7cm PaK36 was the largest anti-tank gun to be air-dropped by the Germans.

Below left: Early war view of para ready to jump, with static line over his shoulder.

Below: The Gigant glider was adapted later in the war to become a heavy transport.

PEOPLE

Above: General Student, the Luftwaffe commander for the invasion of Crete.

GENERALFELDMARSCHAL ALBERT KESSELRING

Born 20 November 1885, Kesselring joined the German Army in 1904. By the end of World War I he was an experienced staff officer. When the Luftwaffe was formed in 1935 he transferred from the Army and was made Chief of Staff of the Luftwaffe after the death of the original post holder. While he was never directly involved at divisional or corps level with 7. Flieger or the airborne forces generally, he did exercise overall control in his various senior command posts. As Chief of Staff he sanctioned the original expansion of the airborne force and the development of its equipment in the late 1930s. As commander of Luftflotte II in 1940, 7. Flieger came under his overall control, just as it (and its expanded successors) did in 1941–45 when he was C-in-C South covering the whole Mediterranean area including North Africa, Italy and the Aegean. He was imprisoned for war crimes (a reprisal killing of Italian civilians) 1947–52, and died in July 1960.

GENERALOBERST DER FLIEGER KURT STUDENT

Born on 12 May 1890, Student finished cadre school training in 1910 and served in the infantry until 1914. He transferred to the fledgling air arm and by 1916 was a squadron commander, giving distinguished service until 1918. In the peacetime Reichswehr he served as Secretary for Technical Development in the Ministry for Aviation (1919–28) before returning to the infantry, first as company commander, then as a battalion commander. When the new Reichs Air Ministry was formed under the Nazi regime in 1933 he became commander of the new aviation test centres, then, as Generalmajor, Inspector General for Luftwaffe Training Schools, which included the parachute school at Stendal. When the airborne forces were expanded in 1938 he was appointed as first commander of 7. Flieger-Division. He retained command of all German airborne forces until 1945 as divisional, corps and army commander as they expanded throughout the war. He died in 1978.

GENERAL DER FALLSCHIRMTRUPPE BERNHARD RAMCKE

Ramcke was the most highly decorated German paratrooper of World War II, and was only the 20th Wehrmacht member to be awarded the Knights Cross with Oak Leaves, Swords, and Diamonds. This came in September 1944 after his doughty defence of 'Fortress Brest'. He had been awarded the DSC as a young NCO in World

War I. He first came to prominence with the airborne forces in 1941. He was by then a colonel on Student's staff, initially liaison officer with the air landing division, but he was called upon at Crete to jump in to replace the injured commander of the air landing assault regiment, After hard fighting in Crete he went to Italy to lead a training mission setting up Italian airborne forces. From there he was nominated to lead the German airborne forces in the projected invasion of Malta in 1942, but when this was cancelled he took his brigade to North Africa to reinforce Rommel's hard pressed *Afrika Korps*. After inspiring leadership there he left Tunis and returned to Europe where he led 2. FJD, most notably and finally as the defender of Brest in 1944.

Above: General Student making a point to a para in early 1941. Behind Student is von Roon (Staff of XI. Fliegerkorps). Note second mark of parachute RZ20.

GENERAL DER FALLSCHIRMTRUPPE EUGEN MEINDL

Meindl commanded the air landing assault regiment on Crete but was badly wounded soon after landing. When II. Fallschirmkorps was formed in 1944, Meindl became corps commander in the rank of General der Fallschirmtruppe.

GENERALLEUTNANT PETERSEN

Petersen was an Army officer who transferred to the Luftwaffe to command 7. Flieger-Division after the death of Walter Süssmann. In this position he led the division in operations on the Russian Front until October 1941 when succeeded by Generalmajor R. Heidrich.

GENERALMAJOR HEINZ TRETTNER

Trettner was Student's original chief of staff, a post he held for some years. He was one of Germany's most experienced airborne forces officers. When 4. FJD was formed he became its commander. Post-war he was the third Inspector General of the Bundeswehr.

GENERALLEUTNANT RICHARD HEIDRICH

Nicknamed 'Arno', Heidrich was older than most generals, tough but fatherly. He took over 7. Flieger from General Petersen and led it through the remaining Russian fighting, then on to Italy where he commanded the division (soon renamed 1.FJD) in their famous defence of Cassino. He died late in 1947.

Below: General der Fallschirmtruppe Ramcke as commander of Fortress Brest 19 September 1944 after his award of the Knight's Cross with Oakleaves, Swords and Diamonds.

FALLSCHIRMJÄGER RITTERKREUZTRÄGER

Eichenlaub mit Schwertern und Brillanten zum Ritterkreuz des Eisernen Kreuzes (in date order)

Ramcke, Bernhard-Hermann	19 Sept 44

Eichenlaub mit Schwertern zum Ritterrkeuz des Eisernen Kreuzes

Heidrich, Richard	25 Mar 44
Heilmann, Ludwig	15 May 44
Kroh, Johannes	12 Sept 44
Ramcke, Bernhard-Hermann	19 Sept 44
Schulz, Karl-Lothar	18 Nov 44
Walther, Erich	1 Feb 45
Meindl, Eugen	8 May 45

Eichenlaub zum Ritterkreuz des Eisernen Kreuzes

Ramcke, Bernhard-Hermann	13 Nov 42
Conrath, Paul	21 Aug 43
Student, Kurt	27 Sept 43
Schmalz, Wilhelm	23 Dec 43
Heidrich, Richard	5 Feb 44
Walther, Erich	2 Mar 44
Heilmann, Ludwig	2 Mar 44

Kroh, Johannes	6 Apr 44
Schulz, Karl-Lothar	20 Apr 44
Egger, Reinhard	24 June 44
Fitz, Josef	24 June 44
Meindl, Eugen	31 Aug 44
Pietzonka, Erich	16 Sept 44
Gericke, Walter	7 Sept 44
Trettner, Heinrich	17 Sept 44
Freiherr v d Heyde, Friedrich-August	30 Sept 44
Meyer, Heinz	18 Nov 44
Schirmer, Gerhard	18 Nov 44
Witzig, Rudolf	25 Nov 44
Rennecke, Rudolf	25 Nov 44
Gröschke, Kurt	9 Jan 45
Rossmann, Kari	1 Feb 45
von Baer, Bern	28 Feb 45
Becker, Kari-Heinz	12 Mar 45
Ostermeier, Hans	15 April 45
Veth, Kurt Major	30 April 45
Gortz, Helmut	30 April 45
Plocher, Hermann	8 May 45
Grassmel, Franz	8 May 45

Ritterkreuz des Eisernen Kreuzes (in alphabetic order)

24 Oct 44	Abratis, Herbert	1. FJD
20 July 43	Adolff, Paul	1. FJD
12 May 40	Altmann, Gustav	1. FJD
4 Dec 42	Arent, Peter	1. FJD
13 May 40	Arpke, Helmut	1. FJD

9 July 41	Barmetler, Josef	7. Flieger-Div
21 Mar 45	Bausch, Friedrich	5. FJD
9 July 41	Becker, Karl-Heinz	1. FJD
5 Sept 44	Beine, Erich	4. FJD
30 Sept 44	Bellinger, Hans-Joachim	FPzD 'HG'
27 Nov 44	Berg, Hartmut von	3. FJD
7 Feb 45	Berger, Karl	5. FJD
15 Mar 45	Berneike, Rudolf	5. FJD
9 May 45	Behre, Friedrich	FPzD 'HG'
28 Mar 45	Bertram, ?	FPzD 'HG'
9 June 44	Beyer, Herbert	1. FJD
18 Oct 44	Birnbaum, Fritz	FPzD 'HG'
29 Oct 44	Blauensteiner, Ernst	II. FsKorps
24 May 40	Blücher, Wolfgang, Graf von	1. FJD
30 Nov 44	Boehlein, Rudolf	1. FJD
26 Mar 44	Böhmler, Rudolf	1. FJD
24 May 40	Bräuer, Bruno	1. FJD
14 Jan 45	Briegel, Hans	FPzD 'HG'
27 April 45	Büttner, Manfred	9. FJD
4 Sept 41	Conrath, Paul	FlaRegt 'HG'
7 Feb 45	Le Courte, Georg,	2. FJD
12 May 40	Delica, Egon	1. FJD
28 Apr 45	Deutsch, Heinz	FstGBrig 12
14 Jan 45	Donth, Rudolf	1. FJD
9 July 41	Egger, Remhard	1. FJD
29 Feb 44	Engelhardt, Johann	2. FJD
8 Feb 45	Erdmann, Wolfgang	7. FJD
17 Sept 44	Ewald, Werner	2. FJD
9 June 44	Foltin, Ferdinand	1. FJD
20 Oct 44	Francois, Edmund	FPzD 'HG'
5 Sept 44	Fries, Herbert	1. FJD
18 Nov 44	Frömming, Ernst	1 FJD
14 June 41	Fulda, Wilhelm	1. FJD
6 Oct 44	Gast, Robert	2. FJD
14 June 41	Genz, Alfred	7. FJD
19 Sept 43	Gerlach, Heinrich	XI. Fliegerkorps
14 June 41	Gericke, Walter	7. FJD
29 Oct 44	Germer, Ernst	1. FJD
13 Sept 44	Gerstner, Siegfried	2. FJD
28 Apr 45	Gersteuer, Gunther	FstGBrig 12
24 May 40	Görtz, Helimuth	1. FJD
6 Oct 41	Graf, Rudolf	FlaRegt 'HG'
8 Apr 44	Grassmel, Franz	1. FJD
9 June 44	Gröschke, Kurt	1. FJD
29 Oct 44	Grünewald, Georg	FstGBrig 12
30 Nov 44	Grunhold, Werner	FPzD 'HG'
9 July 41	Hagl, Andreas	1. FJD
9 June 44	Hahn, Constantin	FPzD 'HG'
5 Sept 44	Hamer, Heino	2. FJD
11 Feb 45	Hansen, Hans-Christian	FPzGD 2 'HG'
23 Feb 45	Hartelt, Wolfgang -	FPzD 'HG'
5 Sept 44	Hauber, Friedrich	4. FJD
14 June 41	Heidrich, Richard	1. FJD
14 June 41	Heilmann, Ludwig	1. FJD
6 Oct 44	Hellmann, Erich	1. FJD
28 Apr 45	Hengstler, Richard	FstGBrig 12
9 July 41	Herrmann, Harry	1. FJD
24 June 44	Heydenbreck, Georg-Henning von	FPzD 'HG'
9 July 41	Freiherr v d Heyde, Friedrich-August	1. FJD
13 Sept 44	Herzbach, Max	2. FJD
18 May 43	Hoefeld, Robert	4./FJR 5
1 Mar 45	Hönscheid, Hans	Kriegsberichter
9 May 45	Hübner, Eduard	1. Fs-Armee
23 Nov 41	Itzen, Dirk	FlaRegt 'HG'
13 Sept 44	Jacob, Rupert	2. FJD
15 May 40	Jäger, Rolf	1. FJD
9 June 44	Jamrowski, Siegfried	1. FJD
9 May 45	Jungwirth, Hans	1. Fs-Armee
29 Oct 44	Kalow, Siegfried	FPzD 'HG'
7 Feb45	Kampmann, ?	FPzGD 2 'HG'
21 Aug 41	Kempke, Wilhelm	7. FJD
24 May 40	Kerfin, Horst	1. FJD
2 Feb 45	Kerutt, Hellmut	7. FJD
18 May 43	Kiefer Eduard	FPzD 'HG'
12 May 40	Kiess, Walter	1. FJD
2 Aug 43	Kluge, Walter	FPzD 'HG'
5 Apr 44	Knaf, Walter	FPzD 'HG'
24 Oct 44	Koch, Karl	5. FJD
10 May 40	Koch, Walter	1. FJD
9 June 44	Koch, Willi	1. FJD
8 Feb 45	Koenig, Franz-Heinz	FPzGD 2 'HG'
7 Feb 45	Koepsel, Herbert	FPzGD 2 'HG'
28 Feb 45	Krappmann, Heinrich	FsPzKorps 'HG'
9 June 44	Kratzert, Rudolf	1. FJD
30 Nov 44	Kraus, Rupert	FPzD 'HG'
9 June 44	Krink, Heinz	1. FJD
21 Aug 41	Kroh, Hans	1. FJD
20 Jan 45	Kroymanns, Wilhelm	4. FJD
29 Feb 44	Kühne, Martin	2. FJD
30 Nov 44	Kuhlwilm, Wilhelm	FPzGD 2 'HG'
5 Sept 44	Kulp, Karl	FPzGD 2 'HG'
18 Nov 44	Kurz, Rudolf	4. FJD
18 Nov 44	Langemeyer, Karl	FSanitäts
10 Oct 44	Lehmann, Hans-Georg	FPzD 'HG'
17 Apr 45	Leitenberger, Helmut	FPzD 'HG'
8 Aug 44	Lepkowski, Erich	2. FJD

Left: Major Gericke led II./FJR6 in an airborne attack on the Italians near Monte Rotondo, 9 September 1943.

Far Left: Leutnant Eckel commanded 14./FJR4 at Cassino 19 March 1944. He personally knocked out three tanks and the rest of his company another 17 of NZ 20th Armoured Division.

2 Feb 45	Liebing, Walter	8. FJD		19 Feb 45	Schirner, Lothar	FsPzKorps 'HG'
26 Mar 45	Lippe, Hans	FPzD 'HG'		11 June 44	Schlemm, Alfred	1. FsKorps
31 Oct 44	Mager, Rolf	2. FJD		6 Oct 44	Schmid, Fritz-Wilhelm	FPzD 'HG'
15 Jan 45	Majer, Hans von	FPzJagdBn		21 May 43	Schmid, Joseph	FPzD 'HG'
31 Oct 44	Marscholek, Hans	5. FJD		24 May 40	Schmidt, Herbert	1. FJD
14 June 41	Meindl, Eugen	7. Flieger-Div		5 Apr 44	Schmidt, Werner	1. FJD
12 May 40	Meissner, Joachim	1. FJD		21 June 43	Schreiber, Kurt	FPzD 'HG'
9 June 44	Menges, Otto	1. FJD		20 June 43	Graf v d Schulenburg, Wolf-Werner	1. FJD
6 Dec 44	Mertins, Gerhard	5. FJD		24 May 40	Schulz, Karl-Lothar	1. FJD
30 Apr 45	Methner, Gerhard	6. FJD		21 Aug 41	Schuster, Erich	7. Flieger-Div
8 Apr 44	Meyer, Heinz	1. FJD		24 May 40	Schwarzmann, Aifred	1. FJD
17 Sept 43	Meyer, Elimar	XI. Fliegerkorps		28 Feb 45	Schweim, Heinz-Herbert	FPzD 'HG'
9 May 45	Meyer-Schewe, Friedrich	FPzErsatzBrig 'HG'		30 Sept 44	Sempert, Gunther	1. FJD
9 Jan 45	Milch, Werner	Granatwerfer-LehrBn		24 Oct 44	Sniers, Hubert	5. FJD
18 May 43	Mitschke, Gerd	1. FJD		28 Apr 45	Stecken, Albert	8. FJD
24 June 44	Necker, Hanns-Horst von	FPzD 'HG'		30 Nov 44	Steets Konrad	FPzD 'HG'
9 June 44	Neuhoff, Karl	1. FJD		28 Apr 45	Stehle, Werner	FstGBrig 12
21 Aug 41	Neumann, Heinrich	7. Flieger-Div		9 July 41	Stentzler, Edgar	7. Flieger-Div
18 Mar 42	Orth, Heinrich	7. Flieger-Div		30 Sept 44	Stephanie, Kurt	3. FJD
18 Nov 44	Paul, Hugo	7. FJD		16 May 43	Straehler-Pohl, Gunther	FBrig Ramcke
29 Oct 44	Peitsch, Herbert	2. FJD		18 Oct 44	Stronk, Wolfram	FPzD 'HG'
5 Sept 44	Pietzonka, Erich	2. FJD		30 Nov 44	Stuchlik, Werner	FPzD 'HG'
30 Nov 44	Plapper, Albert	FPzD 'HG'		12 May 40	Student, Karl	7. FJD
24 May 40	Prager, Fritz	1. FJD		9 July 41	Sturm, Alfred	1. FJD
30 April 45	Probst, Heinz	FsPzKorps 'HG'		9 July 41	Süssmann, Wilhelm	7. FJD
5 Apr 44	Quednow, Fritz	FPzD 'HG'		5 Apr 44	Tannert, Kari	2 FJD
23 Feb 45	Rademann, Emil	FPzD 'HG'		14 June 41	Teusen, Hans	1. FJD
21 Aug 41	Ramcke, Bernhard-Hermann	7. Flieger-Div		30 Sept44	Thor, Hans	FPzD 'HG'
9 June 44	Rammelt, Siegfried	1. FJD		29 May 40	Tietjen, Cord	1. FJD
10 May 43	Rapraeger, Ernst-Willi	Barenthin		3 Oct 44	Timm, Erich-	4. FJD
28, 43	Rebholz, Robert	FPzD 'HG'		14 June 41	Toschka, Rudolf	7. Flieger-Div
13 Sept 44	Reinighaus, Adolf	2. FJD		9 July 41	Trebes, Horst-	7. Flieger-Div
31 Oct 44	Renisch, Paul-Ernst	1. FJD		24 May 40	Trettner, Heinz	7. FJD
9 June 44	Rennecke, Rudolf	1. FJD		6 Dec 44	Tschierschwitz, Gerhard	FPzD 'HG'
6 Dec 44	Renz, Joachim	FPzD 'HG'		30 April 45	Trotz, Herbert	FestGR Breslau
24 Mar 45	Richter, Heinz	5. FJD		29 Oct 44	Uhlig, Alexander	2. FJD
9 May 45	Riedel, Gerd	2. FJD		30 Sept 44	Veth, Kurt	1. FJD
15 May 40	Ringler, Helmut	1. FJD		24 Jan 42	Wagner, Helmut	1. FJD
9 July 41	Roon, Arnold von	1. FJD		30 Nov 44	Wallhauser, Heinz	FPzD 'HG'
12 Nov 41	Rossmann, Karl	FlaRegt 'HG'		24 May 40	Walther, Erich	1. FJD
28 Feb 45	Sander, Walter	5. FJD		24 Oct 44	Wangerin, Friedrich-Wilhelm	III./FJR 3
18 Oct 44	Sandrock, Hans	FPzD 'HG'		21 Aug 41	Welskop, Heinrich	1. FJD
22 Feb 42	Sassen, Bruno	1. FJD		9 June 44	Werner, Walter	1. FJD
12 May 40	Schacht, Gerhard	1. FJD		28 Jan 45	Wimmer, Johann	FPzErsatzRegt 'HG'
12 May 40	Schächter, Martin	1. FJD		18 May 44	Witte, Heinrich	FPzD 'HG'
8 Aug 44	Schäfer, Heinrich	4./FJR 5		5 Feb 44	Wittig, Hans-Karl	1. FJD
21 June 43	Scheid, Johannes	FPzD 'HG'		10 May 40	Witzig, Rudoff	1. FJD
6 Oct 44	Schimpf, Richard	3. FJD		9 June 44	Zahn, Hilmar	1. FJD
5 Sept 44	Schimpke, Horst	1. FJD		28 Apr 45	Zander, Wolfgang	FPzGD 2 'HG'
14 June 41	Schirmer, Gerhard	1. FJD		15 May 40	Zierach, Otto	1. FJD

Above: Generalmajor Schmalz commander of the Hermann Göring Fallschirm-Panzer-Division at Anzio.

Above: General Fritz Morzic was the Ju 52 Assault Transport Group commander for the invasion of Holland, May 1940.

Below: Oberst Heilmann commanded FJR 3 at Cassino and was awarded the Knight's Cross with Oakleaves.

Below: Generalleutnant Richard Heidrich was commander of 1. FJD at Cassino.

POSTWAR

Above: Postwar Bundeswehr 1.FJD jumping from a Luftwaffe Noratlas transport.

In 1955, with the sanction of the NATO Allies and the three-power occupiers of West Germany (USA, Britain, France), it was decided to set up the West German Armed Forces (Bundeswehr) comprising Navy, Air Force, and Army (the Bundesheer) as an integrated part of NATO. The planners decided that an airborne brigade, and an associated airborne school and depot, should be part of the new Bundesheer.

In 1956 the first elements of the new formation were recruited from officers, NCOs and men who had been in the wartime 7. Flieger, the idea being that these should form the backbone of the new force in command, instructional, and administrative roles. Units for recruiting purposes were set up at Ellwangen, Kempten, Esslingen, and Böblingen. The first young volunteers were then recruited and all of them, including the wartime veterans, were then moved to Augsburg to carry out comprehensive parachute training with the 11th Airborne Division of the US Army which was based there at that time.

It was decided early on that the brigade should be expanded to division size and from 1 January 1957, it was designated 1. Luftlandedivision (1st Airborne Division). The first divisional commander was Oberst von Baer who had been Airborne Panzer Corps chief of staff in World War II. The new division was based at Becelaere Barracks, Esslingen. During that year jump training was taken over by the airborne division's own training school, starting in April. First deployment of the still under-strength division was in the autumn exercises of 1957 and just before that Generalmajor Kroh became divisional commander. He had been the wartime commander of the 2nd Parachute Division.

By April 1958 the division was up to full strength and was declared combat-ready to NATO standards and took its place in the order of battle of NATO Land Forces Central Europe. In the NATO exercises that year the division operated for the first time with other NATO airborne units. In 1959 the division was expanded to comprise two full brigades, 25. and 26. Fallschimjägerbrigaden, the latter being the newer formation. The same year's exercises saw the biggest drop yet, in battalion strength at Heuberg. In 1960–61 the various units of the division moved to newer barracks, the 26th Brigade to Bergzabern, Lebach, and Zweibrücken, and 25th Brigade to Calw and Nagold. Divisional and support units moved to Bruchsal and Stetten. In 1961 the division took part in exercises in France and also cross-operated in Germany with US airborne units, while German and US personnel were seconded between the 1st Airborne and US airborne divisions for experience. There was a good degree of standardisation with US airborne techniques and the US Army T10 parachute also became the standard German airborne parachute. Some items of equipment were common, too.

In 1962 Generalmajor Gericke became divisional commander. He was a veteran of Crete (where he won the Knight's Cross) and he had also served in Italy (where he was awarded Oak Leaves to the cross). Oberst Hermann, wartime commander of the 9th Parachute Division, became commander of the airborne and air transport training school. In 1964 divisional HQ was set up at Eichelberg Barracks in Bruchsal. Divisional and support troops included military police, engineer, anti-tank, air defence (flak), signal, medical, maintenance, transport and supply companies. All personnel were trained as parachutists.

Instead of the old Ju 52, the standard airborne transport aircraft of the 1950s was the French-built Noratlas which was supplied to the Luftwaffe. This was of the twin-boom, centre fuselage pod configuration much favoured for tactical transport aircraft in the 1950s. In the late 1960s the Noratlas was replaced by the C-160 Transall, a Franco-German design similar to the Lockheed Hercules. In the 1960s the use of helicopters in the 'vertical envelopment' role was introduced and an Army Aviation Corps wing was attached to the division equipped with American-built H-34, CH-53, and UH-1 Huey helicopters.

The post-war German parachutist was awarded a cloth 'jump badge' on qualifying which was in simplified style but on the lines of the wartime 'jump badge'. This is worn on the right breast pocket. The formation sign of the division was a white parachute on a blue background, worn on the left sleeve on the uniform but also carried on some vehicles and equipment. The historic 7. Flieger name was not perpetuated even though the original key personnel were all World War II parachute veterans, and the post-war German parachute forces were, and remain, an Army (Bundesheer) commitment. While the tradition of fighting efficiency has been retained, the post-war doctrine is, of course, not linked in any way to the Third Reich era.

Below: Airlanding troops of 1. FJD during exercises in 1970.

ASSESSMENT

Above: Composite propaganda photograph purporting to show the landing on Crete in 1941. While it conveys a good impression of a German parachute landing, it is obviously a montage. By Crete the parachutes weren't white, but drab.

The German airborne troops were truly pioneers, for though they were not the first to exploit the idea of using aircraft to bring military men into action from the air – that honour went to the Russians – they were the first to develop the idea to its logical conclusion after Russian efforts were stalled by Stalin's military purges of 1937–39. All the methods of landing sticks of men from the air, complete with equipment, the use of gliders, follow up air-landing components, and even the means of bringing in heavier equipment by air, were all first tackled and developed by the Germans. That they got it right, or largely right given the technology of the time, may be judged by the fact that when the British and Americans formed their own airborne forces in the early years of the war they used the Luftwaffe airborne forces and organisation largely as a pattern to copy, and the copying extended even to the smocks which are still the familiar garb of all military paratroops.

While the German paratroops were arguably the keenest and most professional of all German military forces, second to none in bravery, enthusiasm, fighting qualities, elan and team spirit, they suffered tactically by being the pioneer users of this form of warfare.

Their greatest limitation was the mode of parachute delivery, based on the early Italian Salvatore method, whereby the canopy shrouds were brought to an attachment point in the harness behind the parachutist's back. Therefore he could not reach the shrouds and achieve any kind of directional control. This meant that drops had to be made in calm weather. Even in these conditions it was only too easy for a drop to go wrong, with men being scattered over a wide area or blown well off the intended drop zone.

The parachute design also meant that small arms and ammunition, as well as heavier support weapons, had to be dropped in separate containers (*Waffenhalter*), which added another factor of vulnerability. First, the containers had to be located by the units they were intended for once on the ground, and could just as easily be scattered like the men, if not lost altogether in trees, rivers, etc. Second, any sort of organised ground resistance, as at Crete and Dombås (Norway), could stop or delay the men from reaching their containers and so render them largely impotent as a fighting unit. To some extent this was partly overcome by hardened veterans who jumped with their small arms, against regulations, but the problem was never solved throughout the whole period of German airborne operations, and there was hardly any drop where some problem, large or small, did not arise with scattered men and lost containers.

British and American airborne forces learnt from observing this German experience and adopted parachutes with shoulder harnesses which allowed a degree of directional control by the parachutist, plus a weapons/kit pack which dropped with the parachutist, a huge advance over the German method. By contrast the British and American use of gliders was somewhat crude and basic as a way of getting air-landing troops into area, not always safely. They hardly ever used gliders with the great precision perfected by the Germans, with a skill and daring never equalled or attempted since.

Like Rommel's *Afrika Korps*, the German airborne forces were relatively free from Nazi political interference or indoctrination, possibly because, like the *Afrika Korps*, they were something of a 'sideshow' in the eyes of both the Wehrmacht high command and the Nazi hierarchy. Political 'commissars' and functionaries were absent except that Göring was a benign patron and supporter in his capacity as Luftwaffe chief, so was happy to bask in any honours and successes the airborne forces achieved.

Though the German airborne forces existed for only seven years up to the end of World War II it took only the first year of war for the most important lesson to be learned – that in general airborne drops have only limited potential to hold an objective. It is vitally important to relieve them with heavier forces as soon as possible if setbacks are not to result. Even though the Germans learnt this in their earliest operations, in Norway and the Low Countries in 1940, they tended to overlook it very expediently in later operations, notably at Crete, which nearly ended in large scale disaster and changed the attitude of Hitler and the high command completely when it came to the use of airborne troops. Needless to say the British and Americans had to learn these same lessons the hard way, as Arnhem memorably demonstrated. Looked at half a century on, it seems that the earliest German notion of using small groups of airborne troops as shock troops to take specific objectives by surprise – as at Eben Emael – was always the best way to use them. Most operations based on this principle worked, and those with more ambitious objectives like securing large airfields or areas of ground most often failed. Nothing seems to have changed in this respect over the years.

The bravery, dedication, courage and cameraderie of the German airborne forces became the stuff of legend and it is interesting to note that, even in the final year of the war when most units were made up of new and hastily trained recruits or men transferred from ordinary Luftwaffe units, they quickly lived up to the airborne tradition of team work, initiative, and resolve, taking their cue from the early veterans who still served as the backbone of most divisions. Disparate as the later divisions were, Student, their commander, could contemplate with pride that his original 7. Flieger-Division of 1939 had grown to ten divisions, three corps and an airborne army by 1945, and without exception all these formations fought well and proudly to the end, maintaining the zeal and determination that had characterised the German airborne forces from the time of the first volunteers for the service.

Writing in 1961, Kurt Student, then long retired, wrote: 'The first use of a new weapon is always a risk. For the parachute troops this was indeed the case, for there was no previous example to go by. Their first employment in war was truly a "leap in the dark" in every sense of these words. The employment of parachute troops offered then, as it still does today, undreamed of opportunities for far-sighted military leadership. I gave this weighty and serious complex of questions, with the advantages and disadvantages, my special attention, and took the problem damned seriously. It was clear to me that, in airborne operations, there was a thin line separating defeat from victory, as Crete, and even more Arnhem, made quite apparent. Time for organisation and training was much too short – only 14 months when we started. When I undertook my mission the first lightning flashes of the coming war were already on the horizon.'

Above: Recovering equipment from a container— easily lost during the drop or difficult to recover, this would be a major limitation to all German parachute operations.

REFERENCE

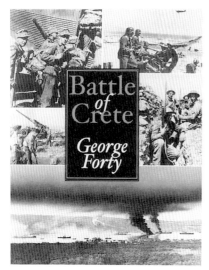

BIBLIOGRAPHY

Battle of Crete George Forty, Ian Allan Publishing, 2001.
A recent account of the battle with numerous illustrations and personal stories. It is particularly good on the German invasion, by air and sea, and the Royal Navy operations that destroyed the latter.

The German Paratroops (UK title)/*Fallschirmjäger* (German title), Rudolf Bohmler and Werner Haupt, Almark Publishing (UK)/Verlag Hans-Henning Podzun (Germany), 1971.
A very comprehensive history of the wartime and post-war period organisation and operations of the German parachute troops in both the German and English languages. The authors were wartime members of 7. Flieger and write with unique knowledge. The book also contains a fine collection of pictures, many of them rare and not seen elsewhere, taken from regimental or personal sources in many cases. There is also a very comprehensive listing of all unit commanding officers, staff officers, award winners, and orders of battle from which some of the details are included in this present book.

Storming Eagles, James Lucas, Arms & Armour 1988.
Another comprehensive history with much extra information on equipment, orders of battle, and some campaign maps. Noted military author James Lucas had combat experience against German paratroops in North Africa and Italy and writes much from personal experience and wartime knowledge. This is a very good single volume book on the subject.

Invasion of England 1940, Peter Schenk, Conway Maritime Press, 1990, (originally published in German as *Landung in England*, Oberbaum Verlag, 1987).
This very detailed and comprehensive book describes every aspect of the planned Operation Sea Lion in 1940, including good coverage of the airborne aspects and planning.

The Lost Battle, Crete 1941, Callum Macdonald, Macmillan 1993.
A highly detailed and thoroughly researched book on the battle of Crete with major coverage of the 7. Flieger part in capturing the island. It also includes much on the political background to the campaign and some history of the birth and training of 7. Flieger and its commitments before Crete. There is good coverage, too, of key personalities.

Weapons and Equipment of the German Fallschirmtruppe, 1935–45, Alex Buchner, Schiffer Publishing 1996.
Useful pictorial coverage with supporting text on all the small arms, heavy weapons, and associated equipment used by the German airborne troops in battle.

Fallschirmjäger in Action, Uwe Feist and Norman Harms, Squadron Signal, 1973.
An excellent collection of photographs of German airborne operations, together with drawings of uniform details, badges and insignia, plus centre-spread artwork of uniform variations. All illustrations have good informative captions.

Uniforms and Insignia of the Luftwaffe, Volume 1, Brian L. Davis, Arms & Armour, 1991.
This very comprehensive reference work, profusely illustrated and detailed, covers all Luftwaffe uniforms and badges, but includes all the paratroop uniform items as well, and is the authoritative book as far as precise details and specifications of uniform clothing are concerned.

Crete was my Waterloo, Neville Chesterton, Janus, 1995.
While this book covers the whole war period it includes chapters giving the author's experience of fighting – and being captured – in the Crete campaign, a good impression from a private soldier.

German Airborne Troops 1939–45, Bruce Quarrie, Osprey, 1983.
This useful book gives a necessarily brief account of the wartime history of the German airborne troops but has good colour plates showing all the uniform variations over the course of the war, plus good details of weapons, uniforms, and equipment, and a good selection of pictures.

Ultra and Mediterranean Strategy 1941-45, Bennett, Ralph, Hamish Hamilton 1989
This book has a particularly good account of the way Ultra intercepts were used and interpreted by the British and how they affected the defence of Crete during the German airborne invasion.

Signal No 12, 1944
This contains a good account, with maps and photographs, of the action on Crete.

INTERNET SITES

http://www.feldgrau.com/
This is probably the most comprehensive site currently on the Web dealing with the German Army before and during World War II. Well-written and researched, and an intriguing in-depth interview with a *Grossdeutschland* veteran, too.

http://www.tankclub.agava.ru/sign/sign.shtml
Russian-language site with excellent illustrations of the tactical signs of the German Armyhttp://www.generals.dk
This is an private project trying to provide biographical data on the army generals of World War II, including many German generals.

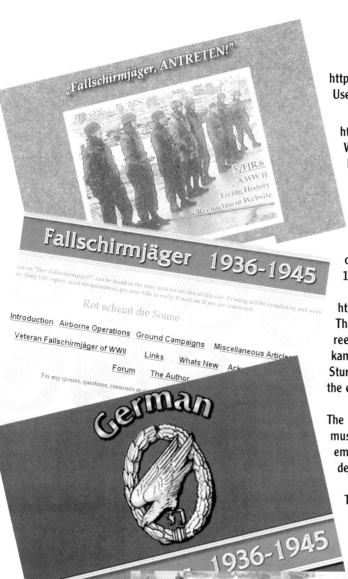

http://www.eliteforcesofthethirdreich.com/
Useful information on Fallschirmjäger and associated units

http://www.geocities.com/~pkeller/fj_index.htm
Website of *Fallschirmjäger Regiment 6* — a US living history group that honors the military service and sacrifices of all World War II veterans, specifically the German paratroopers of World War II.

http://www.eagle19.freeserve.co.uk/index.html
Website of Greg Way aimed at the enthusiast, to give an outlook on nine years of the Fallschirmjäger from 1936–45.

http://www.greendevils.com/
The website of the *Fallschirm Pionier Bataillon 1* reenactment group, part of Kampfgruppe Martz, a kampfgruppe comprised of our unit and the Luftlande-Sturmregiment. A member of the W2HPG, it attends events on the east coast of the United States.

The fort at Eben Emael is still in existence and is now a museum. The website (http://www.fort-eben-emael.be/English/Frame4/10_may_1940.htm) includes detailed coverage of the battle.

The battle of Crete is well-covered on the Web, including an excellent section on the New Zealand History net (http://www.nzhistory.net.nz/Gallery/crete/index.htm) giving details of the New Zealand side of the battle.

British-forces.com has a substantial entry on the battle (http://british-forces.com/world_war2/Campaigns /Crete.html). There are museums about the battle of Crete and the occupation of the island by the Germans — particularly the Municipal Museum of the Battle of Crete and National Resistance in Heraklion on the Doukos Bofor and Meramelou road (telephone 3081246554) is on http://www.culture.gr/4/42/421/42103n/e42103nl.html (or http://www.heraklion-city.gr/english/mus-mah-en.htm); it also has links to the Cretan Naval Museum.

Information on Fallschirmjäger in Africa can be sourced at: http://www.ww2battles.com/afrikakorps/dak/fallschirm jager.htm. This site covers everything to do with the Afrika Korps including details on the Ramcke Fallschirm Brigade. A biography of Ramcke himself (in French) can be found on http://www.1939-45.org/bios/ramcke.htm

The battles at Monte Cassino have a number of sites including http://www.accessweb.com/users/rbereznicki/over.html-ssi. This covers the battle, as well as having many interesting links; it is part of the Wargamer's ring.

SS-Sturmbannführer Otto Skorzeny is well descibed in a biography at http://www.forces70.freeserve.co.uk/Waffen %20SS%Text+ Images/kschol.../skorzeny.ht. A link from this site studies the rescue of Mussolini from the Gran Sasso.

There are a number of wargaming sites, some online some giving wargame information, that cover German Fallschirmjäger, including:
http://home.earthlink.net/~jabo3rdfj/3rdFallschirmjager/ Home/HQ.html
This is an online wargaming site, the Generalkomando der 3rd. Fallschirmjager Division.
http://motiondigital.com/pccs/fallton. htm
Profile of the Fallschirmjäger with weapon value information

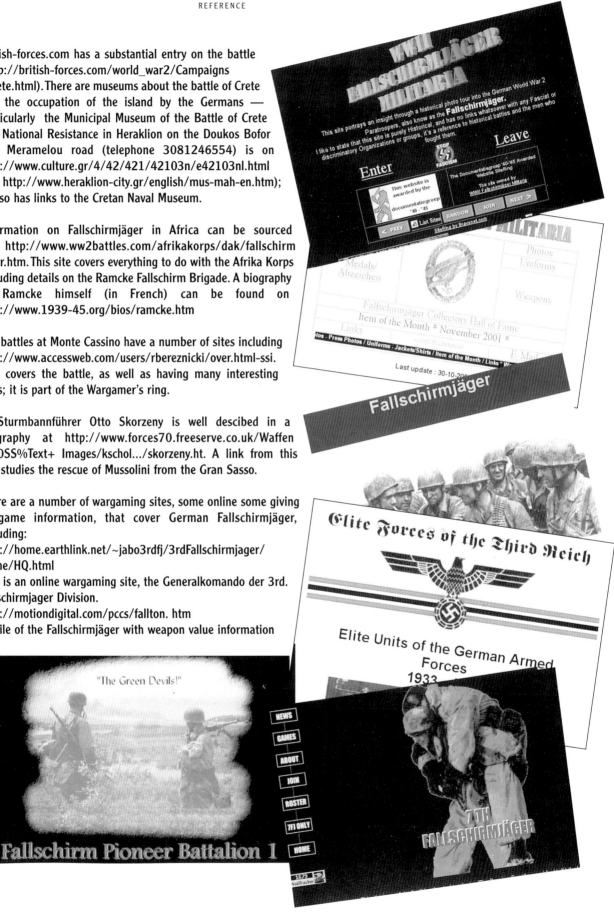

Men of 508th PIR await orders,
6 January 1945. *(via Real War Photos)*

82nd AIRBORNE
'All American'
Mike Verier

ORIGINS & HISTORY

First activated at Camp Gordon, Georgia, on 25 August 1917, scarcely four months after the USA had entered World War I, the 82nd Division was part of the National Army (the term used in WWI to describe drafted soldiers). It drew its original complement of conscripts from states such as Alabama, Georgia and Tennessee. First commanded by Major General Eben Swift, the division's 28,000 men (authorised strength was 991 officers and 27,114 other ranks) soon came to include soldiers from every state of the Union (not to mention that some 20% of inductees proved to be of foreign birth). Once this was realised the name 'All American' was chosen and the red, white and blue 'double A' insignia adopted.

The US was committed to a goal of 'one million men in France by May 1918' and such massive expansion inevitably led to equipment shortages in the short term, In the early stages at least the division was forced to train with wooden rifles. British and French officers with experience in trench warfare were seconded to provide first-hand guidance and training which greatly aided the process. Shortages of grenades and machine guns led to something of an emphasis on the bayonet—which may account for the aggressive reputation the unit subsequently acquired in France.

FRANCE

By early 1918 the division was deemed combat ready, and in April that year embarked for France under the command of Major General William P. Burnham, the second National Army unit so to do. Deployment in 1918 was by sea, and the men of the 82nd were doubtless somewhat relieved to land briefly in England after the long Atlantic crossing. The brevity of their passage onward to Le Havre did not prevent a regiment of the division (the 325th Infantry) from becoming the first American unit to be reviewed by King George V as it marched past Buckingham Palace. In later years reviews were to become something of a speciality when the division was not in combat, but for now there was a war to be got on with.

Combat
On arrival in France the division prepared itself for action, moving up to the line by rail on 16 June from its initial training area near the Somme. As this first deployment was in a French sector the troops were issued with French weapons, including Chauchat and Hotchkiss machine guns, in order to make resupply easier. On 25 June 1918 the All American Division saw combat for the first time, near the city of Toul in the Lagny sector of northeastern France, its assignment being to relieve the 26th Division.

Above: Observation post on the Western Front. (82nd Airborne Museum)

Men of the division had in fact been in the front line prior to this. Officers and NCOs had gained some combat experience with the British on the Somme sector whilst the bulk of the division was working up. The unfortunate distinction of being the 82nd's first casualty had fallen to Captain Jewitt Williams of the 326th Infantry Regiment, who was killed on 9 June.

The first full battalions into the front line trenches were the 2nd/325th, 1st/326th, 3rd/327th, and 2nd/328th. As the 82nd's artillery units were still training, artillery support was provided by the French. By mid-July the division's own machine-gun units had joined the infantry, and on 4 August the first night raid was mounted. Companies K and M of the 326th Infantry, supported by the 320th Machine Gun Battalion, attacked German positions at Flirey, penetrating some 600 yards. By the time the division was moved out of the sector on 10 August it had already suffered 374 casualties.

Respite was brief, the 82nd relieving the 2nd Division in the Marbache sector on 15 August. Finally, its own artillery joined up in the shape of the 157th Artillery Brigade. Supposedly a quiet sector, Marbache was in fact far from restful, artillery bombardment and strafing from the air alternating with aggressive German patrolling.

The first major American offensive of the war, the St Mihiel offensive, was to see the 82nd assigned the village of Norroy as an objective on 12 September. The capture of this was reported as 'relatively easy', although the division suffered 950 casualties during the offensive. One of the 78 killed was the 82nd's first Medal of Honor winner, Lt Colonel Emory Pike. The division was in action until 17 September when it was once again stationed in the Marbache sector, moving on the 20th to prepare for its part in the Meuse-Argonne offensive. The St Mihiel offensive ended on 21 September.

The Meuse-Argonne Offensive

The division was moved to the Clermont area west of Verdun on 24 September to act as reserve for the US First Army. The offensive began on the 26th and on the 29th the 327th Infantry Regiment was committed, at 90 minutes' notice, to bolster the line near Apremont. The regiment force-marched to its positions and held them against strong German attacks until relieved two days later by the 1st Division.

The rest of the division joined the 327th near Varennes on 4 October, and two days later the 82nd moved back into the front line, relieving the 28th Division. Also on the 4th Major General George P. Duncan took command of the All Americans, relieving William P. Burnham (by then a brigadier general).

The division's 164th Brigade was back on the offensive on 7 October, wresting Hills 180 and 223 from the Germans. It was during this action that Alvin York, a former conscientious objector from Tennessee, was to win the divisions' second Medal of Honor and become possibly the most famous American soldier of the war.

Further regiments of the 82nd attacked northwards on 10 October, forcing the Germans from the eastern half of the Argonne Forest. The ground they gained was held for three weeks until the 77th and 80th Divisions relieved the division and continued the offensive.

The 82nd had earned an impressive reputation during the Meuse-Argonne offensive. It had cost the division dear, however, with over 6,000 casualties, including 902 killed. This perhaps was the earliest example for the 82nd of a

Below: 325th Infantry parade in front of Buckingham Palace, London in 1918 reviewed by King George V and the dowager Princess Alexandra. (82nd Airborne Museum)

Left: Ammo dump in France. (82nd Airborne Museum)

problem common to all good military formations, 'the better you are, the more work they give you'.

Some two weeks later came the eleventh hour, of the eleventh day, of the eleventh month, the Armistice.

The road home

The division spent the next three months near Pravthay where it continued to train whilst awaiting orders for home. At last on 2 March 1919 the 82nd began the move to Bordeaux and home. On arrival in New York the division was de-mobilised, de-activation being completed formally on 27 May 1919, the All American Division was to remain a slumbering giant for the next 23 years.

During America's brief involvement in the Great War the men of the 82nd had spent 105 days in the front lines and suffered 1,035 killed in action. A further 378 troopers would succumb to wounds received in combat before the final accounting. In addition to the two Medal of Honor winners, three soldiers of the 82nd won Distinguished Service Medals, and 75 the Distinguished Service Cross. Sergeant York also received the French Croix de Guerre with palm leaves and the Legion d'Honneur, the Italian Croce de Guerra, and the Montenegrin War Medal.

By June 1919 most of the soldiers had been discharged and were on their way back to civilian life. At that point the 82nd Division had passed into history. The flame, however, still flickered and from 1921 until World War II the 82nd Infantry Division, unaware of its destiny, was part of the organised reserves. Until 1942 a reserve HQ was at Columbia, South Carolina.

READY FOR WAR

Whilst the 82nd was slumbering, events in the rest of the world were moving inexorably towards another global conflict. In Germany the emergent military machine was of necessity starting from scratch. This meant that many new doctrines and ideas were embraced. The Germans were not alone in fielding airborne forces; both the Russians and the Italians had developed parachute infantry (the former specialising in what the 82nd now do best, the airfield take-down) but it was the Germans who refined the airborne concept and fully integrated it into their force structure. What the Russians regarded an aerial club hammer, the Germans developed into a rapier.

The Germans saw air power *per se* as an adjunct to the army, almost as long range artillery in fact, but they also recognised the inherent mobility that transport by air could impart. More to the point, they were determined not to get bogged down in the static warfare of WWI. The term Blitzkrieg (lightning war) was coined to describe the new strategy, a word the world was to come to know only too well. The idea was simple: instead of costly frontal assaults on heavily fortified positions, attrition warfare, they would simply go around them. In the case of line fortifications specialist shock troops would go over them, attack from the rear and open breaches for the heavy units to pour through. All this was made possible by the aeroplane.

The concept of airborne assault was not unique or original to Germany for as far back as 1784 Benjamin Franklin had correctly encapsulated the potential of airborne forces, though this potential was naturally unrealisable at the time as the means to transport them were not available. More realistically, in the closing months of World War I Billy Mitchell (who later also correctly prophesied the demise of battleships to air power) planned airborne assaults on Metz. These were more than mere ideas on the back of cigarette packets; the planning was detailed, thorough, and well advanced. The staff officer assigned to this task in 1918 by Mitchell was Lt Colonel Lewis Brereton, who 26 years later would command the First Allied Airborne Army during Operation Market-Garden. With the signing of the Armistice, however, American interest in developing new weapons and tactics ceased, was this not the war to end wars?

The development of General Kurt Student's *Fallschirmjäger* (literally 'hunters from the sky') is beyond the scope of this narrative. Their growth pre-war, and success in the early years was, however, watched keenly by military men of other nations who ultimately copied or adapted most of the German tactics and equipment.* Not least amongst these was one Major William C. Lee, a former infantry officer sent to Germany by Chief of Infantry Major General George Lynch as an observer.

The replication of German equipment was quite thorough (why waste good development?) the jump smock and cut-down helmet being copied almost exactly by the British as were the containers for heavy weapons and ammunition. The similarity between the two forces was such that it later led to some difficulty in telling the two apart once covered in the dust of war. The US airborne forces for their part tried to adapt standard issue items where they could, albeit using the German model as their guide. One item they did take on board, however, (and eventually make their own) was the jump boot.

THE CONCEPT DEVELOPS

Interest in the use of airborne troops was lukewarm in America during the 1930s. There were studies of course, and the usual inter-service rivalry about who should 'own' the soldiers. Claimants included the Engineers, because demolition would be a major role, the Infantry (who eventually won) because once on the ground they would fight as infantry, and the Air Corps who felt that the proposed 'air infantry' unit should be subordinate to it (like the Marines were and still are to the Navy) because it provided the aircraft. Unfortunately, as there were never enough aircraft available, the whole idea was shelved.

Lee meanwhile, returned to the US full of enthusiasm for the development of airborne forces. Serving on Lynch's staff in Washington, DC, he was well placed to lobby those that mattered. His enthusiasm paid off when, in 1940, with most of Europe already overwhelmed by Blitzkrieg tactics, President Roosevelt personally directed that priority be given to the development of airborne (glider and parachute) forces. This was the moment of conception for the Airborne, and the gestation period that followed was to be short.

In February 1940 development of a suitable parachute began at Wright Field, Ohio. The Infantry Board directed that this be accomplished as soon as possible, and that a volunteer unit be formed to test it. The resultant T4 static line 'chute was ready by 25 June when Major Lee was authorised to seek volunteers from the 29th Infantry Regiment (a demonstration unit for the Infantry School). The following month 'Hap' Arnold of the Air Corps also initiated full-scale development of suitable gliders, four companies vying for contracts to develop a suitable aircraft. In May the Fallschirmjäger demonstrated what paratroopers and gliders could do in Holland and at Fort Eben Emael in Belgium.

Above: The first stages of jump conditioning came from training at Camp Toccoa, Georgia. (via Bruce Robertson)

The test platoon

Authorised on 25 June 1940, the Parachute Test Platoon was formed at Fort Benning in July under the command of Lieutenant William T. Ryder. It consisted of 48 hand-picked men selected from numerous volunteers* (there were actually 39 enlisted slots, but the high possibility of injury was taken into account). Its mission was to develop and test equipment, tactics and training methods that would enable the fielding of parachute troops. The men set to with a will.

During the next eight weeks, with France surrendered and the Battle of Britain raging (and the very real prospect of Britain also falling to the Nazis) the men of the Test Platoon trained hard. The programme included physical fitness training, landing techniques, tactics, and tower jumps (which were carried out at a civilian facility near New York, the troopers spending some ten days at Fort Dix). During at least one of the tower jumps General Lynch came from Washington to jump with the men—a firm precedent. The platoon also tested various weapons, items of clothing and equipment, including modified baseball helmets, which were used initially for all jumps. The culmination of the course was to be five live jumps that would qualify the men as parachutists. On 16 August Lieutenant Ryder, leading from the front (as would become standard practice in the Airborne) duly became the US Army's first paratrooper.

Prophetically this first jump was made (reportedly) from a 'C-33'. This was a military version of a revolutionary aircraft for its time, the Douglas DC-2. Very few of these were delivered to the Air Corps because the basic aircraft rapidly evolved into the more capable—and infinitely more famous—DC-3/C-47 Dakota, an aircraft that was to become as familiar to the paratroopers of WWII as the Huey helicopter became to the Vietnam generation.

The last of the five jumps was carried out before an audience heavy with brass (including the Secretary for War and several generals) and took the form of a mock assault. It is not recorded if the 'howling' troopers that so impressed them with the efficiency and ferocity of their assault could actually be heard bawling 'Geronimo!' as they left the aircraft, another tradition begun with the platoon.

Things now moved into high gear. The Test Platoon formed the cadre of the training school that Benning was to become as the first full battalion (the 501st

Some 200 enlisted men and 17 lieutenants volunteered for the Test Platoon, despite the Army's frank admission that the job would require 'frequent jumps from airplanes, which may result in serious injury or death' and a consequent insistence on unmarried soldiers only.

Below: Jump towers were used for training. (via Bruce Robertson)

Parachute Infantry) was authorised by the War Department. By November 1940 three more battalions had been authorised, as well as the first uniform distinctions. The troopers were permitted to blouse (or tuck) their trousers into their boots and wear the overseas cap with parachute insignia. Shortly after Bill Yarborough (while a lieutenant) was to design the distinctive jump wings. (He later went on to develop the M1941 Airborne Field Uniform and the coveted jump boots. See page 87.)

On 20 May 1941, whilst America was just beginning to form the basis of a parachute arm, the cloudless blue sky over Crete was reverberating to the sound of Junkers Ju52 tri-motors. Gliders and paratroopers filled the sky, another powerful demonstration of air assault was underway. Whilst the Germans were successful in their assault on Crete the price was high, the unsupported paratroopers suffering the loss of nearly half their number in the initial assault. Ironically, therefore, whilst Crete galvanised America's development of an airborne force, it actually marked the end (on Hitler's personal order) of large scale assault operations by the *Fallschirmjäger*.

During the next few months, training and the development of gliders proceeded ever more urgently. The 502nd and 503rd Battalions were activated in July and August respectively and the Waco CG-4A glider was chosen for full-scale production.

Initially some 150 pilots were trained to form the initial glider units. On a peacetime basis this would probably have sufficed—America was still trying to keep out of the 'European War'—but then came 7 December 1941, Pearl Harbor, and America was at war.

On 20 December the pilot requirement was increased to 1,000, by April 1942 it had risen to 4,200, and then later to 6,000. Even by scouring draftees for anyone with experience, asking for volunteers and training at civilian schools the demand could not be met. Qualifications were ultimately reduced to the most rudimentary (presumably on the basis that a good landing is 'one you walk away from' and that one good landing would therefore be enough). In fact this shortage was never really overcome. By the time of the Arnhem operations it was common practice for the senior NCO present in a glider to be 'promoted' to co-pilot during the flight to the landing zone. He would thus spend his hour or so bumping along in the slipstream of the towing Dakota being instructed on the basics of landing the thing should the pilot be incapacitated.

In January 1942 the War Department directed that four regiments be formed as the nucleus of Airborne Command. At that time a parachute regiment consisted of three battalions with a total of 1,958 men. In March the now Colonel Lee received his official orders from General Leslie McNair to activate the Command. Lee knew that the burgeoning operation would soon outgrow the facilities at Fort Benning, and began the move to Fort Bragg, North Carolina, where there was vastly more room.

Above: Helmet at a rakish angle, this early war photograph shows a parade-ground para. The weapon is a folding-stock carbine, specially developed for airborne troops; it was not widely used.

REACTIVATION

At the same time all the whole US Army was expanding and moving to a war footing. As part of this rapid expansion the 82nd Infantry Division was reactivated at Camp Claiborne, Louisiana, under Major General Omar Bradley. It was 23 March 1942 and training commenced immediately.

As the 82nd and other infantry divisions got down to hard training the fledgling airborne force continued to expand. In May the first glider regiment, the 88th Glider Infantry Regiment (GIR), came into being, equipped with CG-4s. Through the

The capability to drop whole guns, vehicles and other heavy loads by parachute did not come until the advent of the C-119 after the war. Such equipment either came by glider or was dropped with the troops in disassembled form. In combat dropping a gun in parts proved to be a problem. Not only had the gun to be moved by 'grunt power'—six or eight troopers being needed to tow the thing around—but the loss of a wheel or breech block during the drop rendered the weapon useless.

summer experiments continued with a view to providing artillery for the airborne. Initially these centred on the 75mm pack-howitzer, which was designed to be broken down into mule loads and thus thought ideal for air-dropping.*

Bradley meanwhile had been bringing his command to a high degree of proficiency but was then transferred away. On 15 August the War Department designated the 82nd Infantry as America's first airborne division. Half its manpower was to form the second, the 101st 'Screaming Eagles', with Lee in command. Bradley's deputy, Ridgway, assumed command of the 82nd. Intensive training for the 82nd continued at Camp Claiborne until, on 1 October, it moved to Bragg, destined to be its home to this day.

Training, organisation and doctrine

Apart from the obvious need to train soldiers in parachuting, the new division worked to develop tactics that would best suit its intended role—best summarised as 'assault troops'. The classic use of paratroops, as so ably demonstrated in the Low Countries, is a surprise attack behind an enemy's front line, to take and hold key features such as bridges, eliminate defensive structures and sabotage communications, thus opening the way for supporting heavier forces, which can then exploit the breach.

By definition, paratroops are infantry and therefore lightly armed, though this is a relative term as 'lightly' is not quite the word that comes to mind on seeing pictures of troopers festooned with seemingly their own body weight in weapons, equipment and ammunition. The technology of the time did not allow for precise insertion of units and a pragmatic assumption was made that the lightly equipped troopers would be frequently engaged in small-unit actions. This meant that they were going to have to be self-sufficient and capable of operating on their own initiative almost down to individual level. Paratroopers expected to be unsupported in the initial phase of an attack. Depending on how far from the front line they were, this could be for days.

Such a scenario demanded much of the soldiers individually, and was the reason why only above-average candidates were recruited. A paratrooper, by the nature of his job, was going to need to be intelligent, physically fit, motivated, highly trained and absolutely confident in the abilities both of his officers and his fellow troopers.

The 82nd was selected to convert to this new role because it was considered to be all these things. Bradley had melded the All Americans into a fine fighting force that already possessed a strong sense of identity, and high motivation (there exists a set of grainy pictures showing Bradley and Ridgway tackling the assault course at Claiborne with obvious gusto—no leading from a desk for Airborne generals). All that remained was to turn infantrymen into paratroops or glider-borne soldiers.

At Benning the basic course for paratroops lasted four weeks. The first week was about assessing fitness, with gruelling physical tests and lots of running. This phase varied depending on the quality of the troops, and was sometimes skipped if the incoming soldiers were sufficiently fit. Famously, the men of one of the earliest intakes, the 506th (later to be assigned to the 101st) were so fit that they left their instructors standing. After two days of being thus humiliated the sergeants gave in and moved their charges to the next stage.

The second week still featured the press-ups and the running but this time to the packing sheds where the troopers learnt how to pack their 'chutes. With their lives literally depending on it, folding, packing and checking became second nature. This was interspersed with learning how to exit the aircraft and land properly.

This phase used mock-up fuselages, mounted a few feet above a sand pit. Even at this early stage training was designed to ensure that the men would actually jump when the moment came. They were instructed to look straight out at the horizon—

not down—an obvious enough technique, and more subtly they were drilled to place their hands on the outside of the door when preparing for the jump. This meant that they could not easily resist jumping. The instructors knew that, if a man steadied himself with his hands on the inside of the door and then 'froze', nothing, including the weight of the men behind him, could force him out quickly. Usually the second week also included tower jumps in harnesses attached to steel cables, again this was to work on the landing technique. The third week moved the troopers on to 'free' jumps in parachutes dropped from 250ft towers, with at least one of these jumps at night. Benning also possessed a wind machine to train the men in how to collapse the canopy and avoid being dragged after landing.

The culmination of all this training was the fourth week. Five true jumps would earn the men their wings, and by now they were at peak preparedness, psychologically and physically. The enormity of the first jump should not be underestimated. In the 1940s most of the enlisted men had never even been in an aeroplane and so their first jump was also their first flight, something easily forgotten some 60 years on when air travel is commonplace and casual.

Much time was expended the night before the jump. Parachutes were packed, checked and re-packed. The following morning the troopers double-marched to Benning's Lawson Field and were divided into groups of 24 to await their introduction to the C-47. Once airborne the Dakotas climbed to 1,500ft to begin the drop. On the red light the jumpmasters gave the order 'Stand up and hook up' at which each man attached the snap-hook of his static line main parachute to a cable running the length of the cabin roof. Each trooper would check the next man's line and count off by number when all was secure.

Above: Training drop of troops and equipment containers (those with white 'chutes and single-point attachments). (via Chris Ellis)

Come the green light and the training usually took over. Each trooper, moving now automatically to the door, took up the jump position. The instructor would tap him on the leg and out he would go. Fifteen feet out of the door the static line pulled the back of the parachute pack open and the apex of the parachute out into the airflow. As it reached full extension a break-cord finally separated the soldier from the aircraft, the canopy blooming in the 120-knot slipstream of the departing Dakota. His headlong descent now suddenly slowed, the trooper had a few brief seconds to savour the exhilaration of the moment before preparing for landing. He had done it; he was going to be a paratrooper.

Four more jumps, the parade, the silver wings and the transition from 'legs' to paratrooper. At last allowed to blouse their trousers into their jump boots and wear the distinctions of the Airborne soldier, the newly qualified troopers were permitted a few days leave. Farm boys, college kids, garage mechanics, barmen or office workers when they left home, they all returned as paratroopers, they were now members of an élite.

When they returned to Benning it was not to the spartan wooden huts of the 'Frying Pan' training area, but across the river to rather more civilised accommodation. The training however continued relentlessly. Jumps with full kit and weapons, live training in small unit actions, practice assaults, night manoeuvres, and more weapon training. Things were hotting up and the rumour mills began to generate all sorts of stories about where they might be deployed.

82nd AIRBORNE DIVISION WARTIME UNITS

82nd Airborne Division fought under 10 Allied armies and 19 corps. The following subordinate units were permanently assigned to the division:

Div HQ and HQ Coy
82nd Airborne MP Platoon
325th Glider Infantry Regiment
504th Parachute Infantry Regiment
505th Parachute Infantry Regiment
HQ and HQ Battery Divisional Artillery
319th Glider Field Artillery Battalion

320th Glider Field Artillery Battalion
376th Parachute Field Artillery Battalion
456th Parachute Field Artillery Battalion
80th Airborne Anti-Aircraft Battalion
307th Airborne Engineer Battalion
407th Airborne Quartermaster Company
307th Airborne Medical Company
821st Airborne Signals Company
782nd Airborne Ordnance Maint Company
82nd Airborne Reconnaissance Platoon
82nd Parachute Maintenance Company

These units were attached to the 82nd for long periods of time and were considered vital parts of the division during the combat periods noted:

508th PIR	Normandy, Holland, Ardennes, Rhineland.
2nd Bn, 401st GIR	Normandy, Holland, Ardennes, Rhineland.
507th PIR	Normandy.
666th QM Truck Coy	Holland, Ardennes, Central Europe.

Attached units

The following units were attached to the division during the campaigns and at the dates indicated:

North Africa

Complete records of attachments in North Africa are not available but included the following:
2nd Bn, 509th Pl Engr Company (Cam) (sic)
334th QM Company (Depot)

Sicily

Complete records of attachments in Sicily. are not available but included the following:
39th Regimental Combat Team
26th Field Artillery Battalion
34th Field Artillery Battalion
62nd Field Artillery Battalion
77th Field Artillery Battalion
20th Engineer Battalion (C) (sic)
83rd Chemical Battalion (4.2-inch Mortar)

Italy

Complete records of attachments in Italy are not currently available but included the following:
3rd Ranger Battalion (to 504th Parachute RCT)
Gurkha Battalion (BR) (to 504th Parachute RCT) (sic)

England

Unit	From	To
Quartermaster Truck Coy	20/1/44	27/8/44
HQ and HQ Co, 2nd Airborne Brigade	20/1/44	27/8/44
507th Parachute Infantry Regt	20/1/44	27/8/44
508th Parachute Infantry Regt	20/1/44	30/3/45

Normandy

Unit	From	To
Troop B, 4th Cav Recon Sqn	1/6/44	23/6/44
87th Armored Field Artillery Bn	1/6/44	8/6/44
	1/6/44	8/7/44
Coy C, 746th Tank Bn	1/6/44	11/6/44
Coy A, 746th Tank Bn	13/6/44	21/6/44
Coy A, 712th Tank Bn	1/7/44	8/7/44
188th Field Artillery Bn	12/6/44	8/7/44
172nd Field Artillery Bn	16/6/44	19/6/44
Coy C, 899th TD Bn	1/6/44	19/6/44
Coy A, 607th TD Bn	19/6/44	4/7/44
801st Tank Destroyer Bn	30/6/44	1/7/44
803rd Tank Destroyer Bn	1/7/44	8/7/44
Coy B, 87th Chemical Mortar Bn	15/6/44	21/6/44
Coy D, 86th Chemical Mortar Bn	1/7/44	4/7/44
3809th QM Truck Coy		
3810th QM Truck Coy		
1st Platoon 603rd QM GR Coy		
1st Pl, 464th Amb Coy, 31st Med Group		
493rd Collecting Coy, 179th Med Bn		
374th Collecting Coy 50th Med Bn		
429th Litter Bearing Platoon		
591st Collecting Coy		

Holland

Unit	From	To
Unit A, 50th Field Hospital	17/9/44	
666th Quartermaster Truck Coy	19/9/44	
1st Coldstream Guards (BR)	19/9/44	22/9/44
5th Coldstream Guards (BR)	19/9/44	22/9/44
2nd Irish Guards (BR)	19/9/44	22/9/44
Sherwood Rangers Yeomanry (BR)	19/9/44	10/10/44
Royals Recce Bn (BR) (sic)	19/9/44	9/10/44
Polish Parachute Brigade	25/9/44	30/9/44
231st Brigade (BR)	30/9/44	1/10/44
3rd Guards Brigade (BR)	30/9/44	1/10/44
5th Coldstream Guards (BR)	30/9/44	10/10/44
79th Field Artillery Regt (BR) (sic)	30/9/44	2/10/44
304th Anti-tank Battery (BR) (sic)	30/9/44	3/10/44
506th Parachute Infantry Regt	1/10/44	3/10/44
502nd Parachute Infantry Regt	3/10/44	4/10/44

130th Infantry Brigade (BR)	5/10/44	6/10/44		74th Cml General Coy	4/4/45	21/4/45
2nd Grenadier Guards (BR)	6/10/44	7/10/44		74th Field Artillery Bn	18/4/45	25/4/45
13th/18th Hussars (BR)	10/10/44	10/11/44		12th Tank Destroyer Group (HQ only)	18/4/45	25/4/45
				661st Field Artillery Bn	18/4/45	25/4/45
Ardennes				942d Field Artillery Bn	18/4/45	25/4/45
Unit A, 50th Field Hospital				3rd Coy, 22nd Belgian Fusilier Bn	21/4/45	25/4/45
666th Quartermaster Truck Coy				294th Field Artillery Observation Bn	25/4/45	25/4/45
Coy C, 563d AAA Bn	18/12/44	25/12/44		1130th Engineer C Bn (sic)	25/4/45	26/4/45
Combat Command B, 9th Armored Division	23/12/44	24/12/44		280th Field Artillery Bn	27/4/45	17/5/45
Coy B, 86th Chemical Bn	25/12/44	11/1/45		580th AAA AW Bn	26/4/45	2/5/45
254th Field Artillery Bn	20/12/44	18/2/45			23/5/45	5/5/45
551st Parachute Infantry Bn	25/12/44	12/1/45		13th Infantry	28/4/45	1/5/45
703rd Tank Destroyer Bn	20/12/44	1/1/45		43rd Field Artillery Bn	28/4/45	1/5/45
591st Field Artillery Bn	20/12/44	11/1/45		604th Tank Destroyer Bn	28/4/45	15/5/45
740th Tank Bn	29/12/44	11/1/45		A Squadron, 4th Royals (BR) (sic)	29/4/45	2/5/45
	27/1/45	5/2/45		740th Tank Bn	29/4/45	1/5/45
628th Tank Destroyer Bn	1/1/45	11/1/45		644th Tank Destroyer Bn	29/4/45	1/5/45
517th Parachute Infantry	1/1/45	11/1/45		Coy A, 89th Chemical Bn	29/4/45	9/5/45
	1/2/45	4/2/45		121st Infantry Regt	30/4/45	1/5/45
634th Anti-Aircraft Artillery Bn	5/2/45	18/2/45		56th Field Artillery Bn	30/4/45	1/5/45
887th Airborne Engineer Coy	25/12/44	12/1/45		Coy C, 89th Chemical Bn	30/4/45	1/5/45
Coy A, 87th Chemical Bn	25/1/45	5/2/45		CC 'B', 7th Armored Division	1/5/45	4/5/45
643rd Tank Destroyer Bn	25/1/45	31/1/45		205th Field Artillery Group	3/5/45	17/5/45
400th Armored Field Artillery Bn	25/1/45	18/2/45		207th Field Artillery Bn	3/5/45	17/5/45
32nd Cavalry Reconnaissance Squadron	28/1/45	5/2/45		768th Field Artillery Bn	3/5/45	17/5/45
629th Tank Destroyer Bn	31/1/45	18/2/45				
				Military Intelligence Teams (attached in ETO USA}		
Central Europe				82nd Counter Intelligence Corps Det		
341st Infantry Regt	4/4/45	4/4/45		Interrogator Prisoner of War Team No 40		
417th Field Artillery Group	4/4/45	25/4/45		Interrogator Prisoner of War Team No 43		
746th Field Artillery Bn	4/4/45	25/4/45		Interrogator Prisoner of War Team No 45		
672nd Field Artillery Bn	4/4/45	14/4/45		Interrogator Prisoner of War Team No 47		
541st Field Artillery Bn	4/4/45	25/4/45		Military Intelligence Interpreter Team No 412		
805th Field Artillery Bn	4/4/45	6/4/45		Order of Battle Team No 16		
546th Field Artillery Bn	11/4/45	16/4/45		Photo Interpretation Team No 3		
790th Field Artillery Bn	10/4/45	14/4/45		Photo Interpretation Team No 11		

Above: Wartime units that served as part of or attached to 82nd Airborne Division. Taken from a immediate postwar summary published by the US Army with some missing dates, and some strange unit identifications highlighted (sic) by the editor.

Left: American and British troops rest on the east side of the Elbe after crossing on 30 April 1945. The US troops are of Company I, 505th PIR. (via Real War Photos)

IN ACTION

NORTH AFRICA

After eight months of intensive training at Bragg the 82nd was anxious to get on with the war. The troopers were at a high state of readiness and the war situation was beginning to turn in Africa at least. American paras in the shape of the 509th had been in action during Operation Torch, but the first full-scale use of the Airborne was yet to be undertaken.

In April 1943 orders finally came for deployment overseas to a yet unspecified destination. On the 20th the division began moving by train to Camp Edwards, Massachusetts. This was completed in an air of secrecy, which required the troopers to remove all Airborne insignia and their beloved jump-boots, that they might pass for 'legs' during the transit. Eventually boarding troopships at New York on the 27th the division sailed for North Africa on the 29th.

Conditions on the troopships were less than luxurious but the troopers did their best to cope and keep fit on the long voyage east. Finally, on 10 May the convoy docked at Casablanca. Whilst the ships were unloaded a few days were spent at Camp Don B Passage, before moving out north-eastwards to bivouac camps at Oujda (for the paratroops) and Marnia (for the glider forces).

Here they were joined by the men of the 509th who, with three combat jumps to their credit, naturally felt somewhat superior to the 'green' 82nd. The veterans soon found the newly arrived troopers keen to learn from their experience, however, and the next few weeks of intensive training proceeded apace.

In view of the intense daytime heat, which limited the performance of both men and machines, much of this training was carried out at night. The experience proved invaluable, with the men learning how to group and carry out assaults under a variety of circumstances. The gliders, too, were rehearsed, with much time being devoted to the speedy removal and bringing into action of the heavy equipment they carried.

There was little scope for diversion during this period, although the division attracted its fair share of high-ranking visitors, anxious to see how the new force was shaping up. Visiting 'brass' included their erstwhile commander Omar Bradley, and George Patton who immediately recognised kindred spirits in the tough troopers.

With little outlet for off-duty enthusiasm the troopers turned their energies to occasionally bizarre enterprises. It was for instance considered by some that they needed an animal mascot to replace Max the dog, left behind in the States. This took the form of an unfortunate beast—variously reported as a mule or a jackass—which they tried to train to jump with them. Getting it into a parachute and out of the aircraft was apparently accomplished without problems. Sadly it failed to appreciate the finer points of landing, breaking a leg on its first jump, its consequent demise seemingly a poor reward for considerable equine bravery.

On 24 May Colonel Gavin, one of the regimental commanders, was called to Ridgway's HQ to be briefed on the forthcoming assault on Sicily, Operation Husky, slated for 9 July. Characteristically, Gavin shortly arranged to recce the drop zones (DZs) in person. Gavin, two battalion commanders and two pilots from the 52nd Troop Carrier Wing, took a pair of the unarmed, but very fast British Mosquito aircraft over Sicily. This risky undertaking was fortunately accomplished without loss, and Gavin returned confident that the operation was feasible.

As an aside, the loss, or worse the capture, of such a senior officer would have seriously compromised the operation. Much effort had been expended on disinformation (including the 'Man Who Never Was' operation which allowed the Germans to 'find' a body carrying 'secret' documents indicating an invasion somewhere else). This need to keep the target secret had unfortunate consequences. The troopers were not informed of the presence on Sicily of a Panzer division, lest the fact that they knew that gave away the objective. They were thus insufficiently prepared for the Tiger tanks of the *Hermann Göring* Division they encountered. On 16 June, after six weeks of intensive training, the division moved to Kairouan in Tunisia. The invasion of Europe was about to begin.

OPERATION HUSKY

Above: One of a series (see colour section) of photographs taken in North Africa before Operation Husky. This shows well the 1943 equipment. (82nd Airborne Museum)

The Allies, having finally turned the tide of war in North Africa, saw Sicily as a literal stepping-stone into what Churchill described, with typical floridity, as 'the soft underbelly of the Axis'. As earlier related, the Pyrrhic German victory on Crete had spurred the development of airborne forces on both sides of the Atlantic. Roosevelt and Churchill had both taken a personal interest in the development of parachute forces as they could see the potential they offered. It had been decided that resources would be pooled for airborne operations and Sicily was therefore to be the first major test of the whole concept.

As it turned out Sicily was to be an almost unique engagement, British, American and German paratroopers were to meet in combat and many individual acts of heroism were carried out on both sides. As would be expected fighting was tough with little quarter given. The All Americans may have lacked the combat experience of the British and Germans, but their aggressive training ultimately proved more than equal to the task, and probably decisive.

Sicily was also to provide a salutary lesson in how not to organise a combined-arms assault, and was very nearly an unmitigated disaster. The plan was essentially sound; the execution, however, was another matter.

The problems began with a fairly fundamental dispute between the British and American commanders over who should get what share of the limited number of aircraft assets available. Eventually the British got the bulk of the gliders—and even then had to leave a battalion behind in order to lift all their heavy equipment. The 82nd Regimental Combat Team (RCT) on the other hand would be parachute only.

Whilst the brass were thrashing out the details the troopers were training hard. Although they had not been told of their objective (and would not be until almost the last moment) a training area had been laid out in the desert to simulate the sixteen or so pill boxes surrounding the Gela drop area. These were assaulted with live ammunition until the men were thoroughly rehearsed. As ever the rumour factory was at full production with suggested targets running through most of southern Europe, and at least one that they were to jump on Berlin in order to capture Hitler!

The plan essentially was for the airborne forces to assault key bridges and defensive positions immediately ahead of amphibious landings on the south and east coasts. This, it was hoped, would allow an early breakout from the beachheads and a rapid drive to secure the island.

The British were to go in first in order to secure three key bridges on the east coast road. Shortly behind them the Americans would jump into an area around Gela on the south coast. The British Eighth, and American Seventh Armies respectively would simultaneously follow with sea-borne landings in the same sectors. The first phase airborne landings would go in on the night of D-1/D and be codenamed Husky One (American) and Fustian (British). Support would also be provided in the form of naval gunfire, a provision which very nearly proved to be the undoing of the whole enterprise.

As H-Hour approached the troops bivouacked around Kairouan began assembling at the ten satellite airfields it served. First off were the British at 19.00hrs. They had a motley fleet of 128 Waco CG-4 gliders (provided by the Americans and therefore new to the British pilots) and eight Horsas. Towing aircraft included 109 Dakotas, 21 Albemarles and eight Halifaxes.

A little over an hour later the American lift, some 3,400 soldiers of the 505th and 504th, plus some support elements, also took off. A total of 266 Dakotas formed into flights of nine and headed out over the Mediterranean. Each man had with him a slip of paper with a message from Gavin. 'Slim Jim' did not go in for the grandiloquence of some of his contemporaries, but the inspiration was clear and effective.

> 'Soldiers of the 505th Combat Team.
>
> 'Tonight you embark on a combat mission for which our people and the free people of the world have been waiting for two years.
>
> 'You will spearhead the landing of an American Force on the island of SICILY. Every preparation has been made to eliminate the element of chance. You have been given the means to do the job and you are backed by the largest assemblage of air power in the world's history.
>
> 'The eyes of the world are upon you. The hopes and prayers of every American go with you.
>
> **James M. Gavin'**

Right: The 82nd trained at Oujda and left for Sicily from Kairouan, the aircraft being routed via Malta. During the invasion of Italy, the division saw action at Salerno, and in January 1944 at Anzio. Leaving the theatre in April 1943, the 509th would return in August 1944 to participate in the invasion of southern France.

Both lifts were routed via Malta at low level to avoid detection until the last moment. Only as they crossed the coast of Sicily would they gain height to approach the drop zones. Unfortunately visibility was poor, and winds were exceptionally high. Worse, as they flew directly over the naval elements near the beaches the nervous, inexperienced (and unbriefed) gunners below fired upon the lumbering transports of the British lift, believing them to be German bombers. Already dispersed and in some confusion, nearly half the gliders came down in the sea. The paratroops fared little better being dropped far and wide, only one group actually making its allocated DZ. Because of the high winds drop injuries were high, too.

In their turn the Americans also found themselves over Sicily with only the broadest notion as to exactly which part. As was to become typical, Gavin was the first man to jump. not far behind him was 'Red' Ryder, who had commanded the Test Platoon and was now a lieutenant colonel. Also jumping with the 82nd that night was war correspondent Jack Thompson of the *Chicago Tribune*. If anything the 82nd was even more widely dispersed than the British, being spread over some 60km in small groups.

At this point, with the plan in tatters, it might be thought that disaster was inevitable. Although the troopers did not know it yet, fate had actually placed the paras well. For the time being, however, the 82nd's initiative and training in small unit actions took over, and the results were remarkable.

Because of the scattered drop, the German and Italian defenders were faced with ambush and assault by groups of the tough Americans seemingly coming out of the night from all directions. The troopers cut communications, destroyed bunkers and vehicles and generally created havoc in the enemy rear. In some sectors they linked up with the British after an understandable exchange of fire in at least one spot.

Numerous small actions were fought that night. Landing almost amongst the enemy at Ponte Dirillo, G Company, 505th set about clearing the Germans from their trenches and pillboxes, quickly seizing a bridge that would assist the US 45th Infantry Division in its breakout for the beach. Elsewhere 14 paratroops took on a group of pillboxes which they knocked out, capturing some 250 Italians.

Jack Thompson described another such engagement:

'One group of the 1st Battalion, including Lt Colonel Arthur Gorham, landed four miles south of Niscemi, about 2½ miles from the scheduled DZ. They were just east of a very sturdy, thick-walled farmhouse which had been converted into a military fort held by 60 men with 4 heavy machine guns and 6 lights. It was well wired in with trench defences. Colonel Gorham ordered an assault on the house, and it was organised and led by Captain Edwin Sayre and 22 men.

'Their first attack was launched at 2 o'clock in the morning. They were held up then, but attacked again just before dawn, with rifles, grenades, one 60mm mortar and a bazooka. They forced the Italians back out of the trenches and into the house and attacked the house with grenades. Sayre led the assault, carrying one hand grenade in his teeth and another in his left hand, with his carbine in his right hand. It was after they had taken the farmhouse that he discovered that the man who was covering him was armed only with a trench knife and not a tommy gun as he had thought. A rifle grenade fired at about ten feet blew open the door, but the door swung shut again. Sayre walked up, threw open the door, and pitched a hand grenade inside.

'They found a total of 15 dead and took 45 prisoners, some of whom were Germans. Four paratroops were wounded, one of whom later died. The house soon came under fire from an 88, and Col Gorham withdrew his men back to another hill.'

All of this gained time for the beachheads to be consolidated as such action reduced or prevented adequate response from the defending forces. Matters were not all one-sided, however. Unbeknown to most of the troopers, the *Hermann Göring* Panzer Division was on the island, and armed in part at least with the formidable Tiger tank. This division had the potential to throw the invaders back into the sea. The lightly armed paras on the other hand, had only the woefully inadequate bazooka with which to respond. Only marginally effective against medium tanks, its rounds often failed to halt the German behemoth.

Biazza Ridge
Here fate played its hand. Gavin had been separated from most of his command, but by D+1 had managed to link up with around 250 men, mostly from

Above: Gavin jumped with his men and led from the front. Here he is 'chuting up for the D-Day jump, note his preferred weapon, a rifle. (82nd Airborne Museum)

the 3rd Battalion, 505th. Instinctively he headed for high ground overlooking the 45th Infantry's defences in order to drive the Germans off such a commanding position. It was as the Americans pursued the fleeing defenders that they encountered the first Tiger tanks.

The counter-attack was repulsed with some difficulty. A single pack howitzer from the 456th Parachute Field Artillery (PFA) used direct fire, forcing the Germans back at least temporarily. The paras had by chance been dropped between the beach and the Panzers. Keeping the two apart was to prove vital. With the aid of artillery support and naval gunfire Biazza Ridge was held, but at a high cost in casualties amongst the All Americans.

Other elements of the *Hermann Göring* Division encountered the tenacious Americans dug-in with two captured Italian anti-tank guns along the Niscemi–Biscari Highway. Here the 3rd Battalion, 504th drove off a German column heading for the beaches. One or two Tigers actually traded fire with off-shore destroyers, but thanks to the courageous efforts of the paras there was to be no armoured attack on the beaches of any consequence.

The plethora of actions underway all over southern Sicily actually led the defenders to believe that they were under attack by 'five or more' airborne divisions. In fact, fewer than 200 paras had seized and held all the objectives assigned to the whole combat team. The massive disruption caused by the rest, however, had ensured that the response by Axis forces to the sea-borne assault was blunted.

Disaster strikes

The plan called for a second wave to jump on Farello airfield on D+1. Despite the lessons of the first drop, and against Ridgway's misgivings, it went ahead as planned, there being no time to re-plan such a complex undertaking. It was to prove the biggest disaster of the 82nd's war.

The drop was to consist of the rest of the 504th, the 376th Parachute Artillery, and the balance of the 307th Parachute Engineer Battalion. Commanding the 2nd Battalion, 504th was Bill Yarborough.

The first C-47s over the DZ dropped their charges without incident, but as the second wave came in, all hell broke loose. It was never established exactly who had fired the first shot, but an AA gunner who fired at the lumbering Dakotas, believing them to be enemy bombers, panicked those around him into opening up. Almost instantly a fire-storm of machine-gun and cannon fire enveloped the hapless transports.

Some 23 out of 144 C-47s were destroyed, and dozens of others were terribly shot-up. Worse, the AA batteries continued to fire on the paras that did jump, and on aircraft that had managed to ditch in the sea. More than 300 aircrew and paras were killed and hundreds more badly injured. Less than 25% of the lift made it onto the DZ.

This incident almost led to the demise of Airborne units in the post mortem that followed the Sicily operations. As with the German experience in Crete, there were those who felt that the cost could not be justified. Certainly the Marine Corps, which had been considering forming parachute units, quietly shelved its plans in the light of such a predictable disaster—the cause of which was routing friendly transports over surface elements who were inevitably under attack from enemy aircraft.

By this time the Germans had already realised that Sicily was going to fall. This did not mean they were going to give up without a battle and a fighting withdrawal was planned that would make the Allies pay for every yard gained.

For the rest of the Sicilian campaign the 82nd served as infantry with Patton's Seventh Army. In view of the casualties suffered in the initial jumps (and the need to conserve the highly trained paratroops for future use) they were not assigned the hardest missions. This in no way reduced their aggressiveness or resolve and the 82nd continued to lead by example, capturing at one point the vital port of Trapani and some 5,000 prisoners.

By 22 July the Americans were in Palermo, and Sicily effectively fell to the Allies on 14 August. On the 16th, just hours ahead of the British, Patton's men entered Messina. The battle for Sicily was over.

INTO ITALY

With Sicily secure, the Allies were anxious to press on across the Straits of Messina and into Italy proper. They rightly surmised that the Italians were minded to surrender or even change sides following the removal of Mussolini from power.

Hitler, having reached the same estimation of Italian steadfastness, had vastly strengthened his forces on the peninsula, and at one point had Student's *Fallschirmjäger* amongst troops poised to take part in the 'arrest' of the entire Italian government and the Crown Prince. In the light of this somewhat fluid situation Allied planning went through several iterations. At least six plans for airborne assault were considered and discarded.

The Taylor Mission
A plan that very nearly happened saw the 82nd actually 'chuted up' for a drop on Rome, where, with the assistance of Italian forces, they were to seize the city from the Germans. Fortunately for the troopers this dangerous plan was cancelled at the last moment following a remarkable personal meeting between the 82nd's Divisional Artillery Commander Brigadier General Maxwell D. Taylor and Marshal Badoglio, the head of the new Italian government, actually in occupied Rome.

This mission was the stuff of adventure movies, placing a member of the 82nd at a pivotal point in history. It also proves that whilst fighting skills may be fundamental to the success of airborne soldiers, their innate quick thinking and ability to adapt in changing situations is equally important. It also possibly demonstrates that the best officers and soldiers are attracted to élite units, which in turn is why they perform better than 'average' formations.

The Italians were indeed anxious to capitulate, but feared massive German reprisals against Rome the moment the surrender was announced. The plan therefore called for a drop to prevent this, timed to coincide with the sea-borne landing at Salerno. The Italians were to provide security and support which would be essential to the success of the mission. Their actual ability to do this was

Below: General Mark Clark speaks to members of the 325th Glider Infantry near Salerno. The 82nd had been able to stabilise the beachhead at Salerno, and Clark later specifically requested elements of the 82nd remain in Italy after the bulk of the Division returned to the UK. (U.S. Army)

Above: General Mark Clark flanked by British Generals Alexander (left) and McCreery on the beach at Salerno. (US Army via George Forty)

severely doubted and it was decided that a face-to-face meeting was necessary. General Taylor spoke Italian and accompanied by Colonel Tuder Gardiner, left Palermo on 7 September for the clandestine meeting.

Just off Ustica island they transferred to an Italian corvette for the short voyage to the port of Gaeta. The execution of the drop now depended on a radio message from Taylor. On arrival the two Americans 'roughed themselves up' and, masquerading as prisoners, were bundled into a car by their Italian escort. A dangerous trip through hostile territory and German roadblocks eventually brought them to Rome.

Much to Taylor's frustration the ageing Badoglio had to be roused from his bed for the immediate conference that was needed. It soon became apparent that the Italians were in no position to guarantee the support that the 82nd would require. Taylor's first task was to cancel the drop. Coded radio messages were urgently sent and finally at 16.30hrs—as the first troopers were boarding their aircraft—the drop for that evening was cancelled. Had Taylor been captured or killed and not sent the abort message, the 82nd would have dropped into a disaster that night.

Taylor meanwhile found himself the *de facto* Allied negotiator for the Italian armistice. He insisted that Badoglio write a message to Eisenhower confirming that the Italians could not support Operation Giant II (as the Rome drop was code-named) and that he (Taylor) was to return to Sicily to convey the views of the Italian government. The signed, longhand, message now in his hand, Taylor radioed its content and awaited orders.

Having sat through an American air raid, Taylor eventually received orders to return. Together with Deputy Chief of the Italian Defence Staff, General Rossi, the two American soldiers once again embarked on a hair-raising trip past the occupying Germans (at one point a column of infantry passed within yards of the small truck they were trying to be inconspicuous in). Safely reaching an Italian airfield they were flown to Algeria in an Italian SM 79 (with the attendant risk of being shot down by their own forces).

As planned Eisenhower announced the surrender as the first soldiers were hitting the Salerno beaches on the 9th. An hour later Badoglio, despite his fears about German reprisals, confirmed it in a radio broadcast to the Italian people.

Salerno

The Allied invasion of Italy began with landings at Salerno (Operation Avalanche) on the east coast, and simultaneously at Taranto (Operations Gibbon and Slapstick). German resistance at Salerno proved stiff, and the attackers were soon bogged down on the beachheads. Matters reaching a critical point on the afternoon of the 13th when Ridgway, at the time en route by air to a command conference, received a radio message from Lieutenant General Mark Clark, commander of Fifth Army, urgently requesting a drop to stem a threatened Axis breakthrough of Allied lines.

In a remarkable demonstration of their ability to respond the 504th RCT was stepping out over the drop zone to execute an almost text-book landing exactly eight hours later, the soldiers having been briefed in the aircraft as the engines were started. Together with the 325th GIR the troopers quickly established a perimeter in the area of Paestum. The paratroopers had taken on three German divisions.

The following day the position was consolidated when 1,900 more men of the 504th were dropped. Gavin's 505th RCT also dropped on the beachhead on the 14th, whilst the 2nd Battalion, 509th (attached to the 82nd) dropped in the Avellino sector and set about disrupting defences, communications and supplies in the enemy rear.

This latter drop, into mountainous terrain, again suffered from dispersion, with the 640 men dropped spread over nearly 100 square miles. Only 510 eventually made it back to Allied lines, but for nearly three weeks their activities tied down a totally disproportionate number of German troops (more in fact than the number available to the whole Allied command) who were thus unavailable to the action around Salerno.

Whilst the drops were going in, the 325th Glider Infantry, together with 3rd Battalion, 504th were sailing for Salerno from Licata. On arrival on the night of the 15th the 325th moved to begin operations in the Sorrento peninsula, whilst the 504th's men rejoined their regiment at Albanella. The following morning the 504th marched some four miles to occupy the town, and by noon Colonel Tucker was briefing his battalion commanders to seize and hold high ground overlooking Altavilla, key positions that would protect the security of the beachheads.

This was to be no small undertaking. Not only was a greatly superior force ranged against the Americans, but the valley floor they were going to have to cross had for some years been a German artillery range. This meant that hostile fire was very accurate and could concentrate on almost any spot with precision. Most of the American casualties over the next three days were directly attributable to artillery fire.

By the 17th the 504th had nevertheless taken all its objectives. The regiment was, however, now cut off from Allied lines and that night it was suggested by General Dawley, commander of the VI Corps, that the 504th withdraw and try to form a line closer to the beaches. Tucker's famous 'Retreat, Hell!' response resulted in the reinforcements he wanted being sent and the ground was held, enabling the Fifth Army to move northwards towards Salerno and Naples.

The advance continues
Meanwhile F Company, 325th took to boats to occupy the island of Ischia in the Bay of Naples. The remaining elements of the 82nd also arrived by sea at the tiny village of Maiori, which clung to the sheer rock of the mountains above. The aim was to drive the Germans from the heights, and, together with Colonel Darby's Rangers, the 325th RCT and 3rd Battalion, 504th started climbing, successfully clearing the enemy as they went. Mt San Argela and the Chiunzi pass were taken,

Below: Anzio X-Ray beach soon after the landings. (US Army via George Forty)

enabling a link up with H Company, 504th, which was holding out alongside the 319th Battalion Glider Field Artillery and the Rangers. The remainder of the 504th took up positions on the Chiunzi pass on 25 September, and by the following day was overlooking the Naples plain. The pass quickly became known as '88 pass' for the concentration of enemy fire directed on it.

By the 29th the 505th, now attached to the British 23rd Armoured Brigade, was moving towards Naples. The next day elements of the 505th became the first reconnaissance troops in the city. The 504th, with the British XX Corps, meanwhile skirted the base of Mt Vesuvius to bypass the city. When, on 1 October, Naples duly became the first major European city to fall to the Allies, the 82nd was in the vanguard of the victorious troops that marched in.

For most of the 82nd there followed a period of policing duties in Naples. Whilst sporadic German attacks continued, and they had to deal with sabotage attempts and booby traps, the troopers had time for some relaxation finding the bars (and other rather less salubrious establishments) much to their liking after the deserts of North Africa.

The 505th on the other hand, continued north towards the Volturno River with the British, spending the 3rd to the 9th clearing pockets of resistance. Characteristically the 505th was amongst the first across on the 13th.

On 29 October the 504th began an epic drive through the mountains. With the Fifth Army on its left and the Eighth Army on its right the leaders were eventually 22 miles ahead. Crossing the Volturno the paratroops entered Isernia, a major road and rail junction, and cleared Calli, Macchio, Fornelli, Cerro and Rochetta. During the entire period all actions were small unit engagements. There was no defined front line and both sides roamed the area. The men of the 82nd, however, were masters at this type of work, besting the Germans on virtually every occasion. The terrain was extremely difficult and roads were all but non-existent. Everything had to be carried by mule or by man-power. Evacuating casualties meant hours toiling down mountain tracks with stretchers.

Despite all problems it was eventually just 15 troopers who crossed a minefield to take Hill 1017, Fifth Army's primary objective.

In November the bulk of the division was due to move to Ireland to begin training for the forthcoming invasion of France. At the specific request of Mark Clark, however, the 504th along with the 376th Field Artillery Battalion and elements of the 307th Airborne Engineers remained in Italy with his Fifth Army. The rest of the 82nd sailed on the 18th. Between 10 and 27 December the 504th was in combat in the Venafro sector, participating in the seizure of Mt Summairo.

ANZIO

On 21/22 January Fifth Army's assault on Anzio (Operation Shingle) commenced, the 504th landing near Nettuno. The landing at first proceeded like a training exercise, but as the leading LCTs were unloading, the Luftwaffe arrived. Despite ferocious AA fire from the ships the attacking aircraft wrought terrible destruction on the beachhead. Under repeated attack the men and equipment mostly got ashore, but considerable losses were sustained. After some two days the regiment was ordered to the right flank of the beachhead, taking up positions along the Mussolini canal.

Over the next few days the Allies attempted to break out, the 504th capturing several bridges after bruising firefights with a heavily armed enemy. Attacks on the

25th by all three battalions pushed towards Borgo Piave, an important road junction. Whilst the attacks were successful initially, the Germans countered with an armoured force which eventually pushed the 504th back to the canal.

This situation continued for several days, until the 504th was relieved by the 179th Infantry. After a short respite in reserve the 3rd Battalion, now attached to the 1st Armored Division, was committed with the British 1st Division in the Carroceto sector.

There the battalion suffered many casualties to unprecedented enemy artillery fire, and when German infantry finally attacked it was only the tough troopers' iron-will and steadiness under fire that enabled them to repel repeated assaults. Accounts of the often hand-to-hand fighting are harrowing and it is clear that lesser troops would have buckled.

The fighting between 8 and 12 February was savage. At one stage H Company was able to recapture a senior British officer from the Germans, and with the assistance of I Company fight its way back to the Allied lines. Such actions earned the 3rd Battalion one of the first Presidential Unit Citations awarded in the European theatre.

The battle for Anzio quickly became a static defensive, matter of attrition—not what airborne troops are trained for, and a waste of their skills. It was with considerable relief therefore that the men of the 504th finally received orders for England on 25 March. They left Anzio for Naples in LSTs, still under fire, and finally arrived in England on 10 April. The 82nd's war in Italy had finished. The troopers had more than proved themselves in combat but suffered terrible casualties in the process. Ahead of them was an even bigger task.

Below: The landings at Anzio were heavily contested. The 82nd came in by sea, the 504th PIR landing under attack from the Luftwaffe. (US Army via George Forty)

THE INVASION OF NORMANDY

In November 1943, as the bulk of the 82nd prepared to leave the Mediterranean, General Gavin had already gone to London to help plan the airborne part of the forthcoming invasion of France. The soldiers, after months in warm climes, were shortly to find themselves in Northern Ireland in winter. There might not be anyone shooting at them there, but the change from southern to northern European weather was certainly going to test their hardiness. The 82nd had suffered terrible casualties and was going to need some time to get back to full strength. It had also proved beyond doubt the value of the Airborne and that meant the call would not be long in coming.

The division was not to stay in Ireland for long. Early in the New Year a more permanent facility was set up near Leicester. To make up strength the 507th and 508th PIRs were now assigned to the division. Additionally volunteers were sought amongst suitably qualified replacement troops arriving from the US—in most cases only too happy to leave the miserable tented camps in the dank Welsh countryside they were 'holding' in. A jump school was established near Leicester to qualify those not previously parachute trained, and training at all levels was stepped up.

The nine months spent in England were generally happy ones for the troopers. They found that they had much in common with their British counterparts and, of course, there was a social life. The locals were for the most part welcoming and friendly, the girls pretty and the beer, if unfamiliar to American tastes, was good. Again from the modern perspective, it should be remembered that many of the troopers had known nothing of the world outside a farm in Nebraska or Tennessee a few months before.

Another important step came in England. The glidermen, long denied parity with the paratroops they so ably supported, finally received their pay increase and their own wings. No one truly begrudged it—jumping was always regarded as far safer than going by glider.

As the intensive training continued, so did the build-up of men and material for the invasion. Over 2,000 Waco gliders were shipped to the UK and assembled. In order that the 101st should benefit from the combat experience of the 82nd Gavin was put in charge of standardising tactics and procedures throughout the Airborne.

The British Isles became a vast hive of military activity as every arm of service from dozens of nations prepared for the biggest invasion in history. The Reich was pounded by the RAF at night and by the US Army Air Force during the day. Every possible logistic need was considered, huge floating harbours and fuel pipelines were devised; new equipment was developed and tested and assaults from the sea and air rehearsed. Occasionally the exercises were all too real. Terrible slaughter was wrought off the Dorset coast one night when German E-Boats got in amongst landing craft full of troops. (Kept secret at the time lest it effected morale, the disaster at Slapton Sands has only recently been fully reported.)

There were problems at the top, too. For all the public unity amongst the Allies there were disagreements and conflicting agendas, both political and military. Later on this was to cost the Airborne dear. For the time being a consensus was eventually reached, and planning for Operation Overlord went into the final stages. Gavin rejoined the division on 6 February.

D-Day plans

There were a number of possibilities considered, including the extremes of an airborne assault on Paris (which would be held until a link up with the sea-borne invasion force) and dropping the troops directly on the coastal defences at the

Above right: Waco CG-4 (Hadrians to the British) gliders in invasion stripes landing in Normandy, June 1944. the stripes were put on the wings in great secrecy a few days before the invasion. (82nd Airborne Museum)

Below right: Build-up to D-Day: assembling CG-4 gliders out of packing cases somewhere in England, 1944. (82nd Airborne Museum)

Above: Gavin briefing officers for a jump. The photo was taken in England prior to D-Day—the carefully posed group appear to be in a British Nissen hut, prefabricated building built largely from corrugated iron sheets. These were universal on UK bases and many survive to this day (82nd Airborne Museum)

beaches. More sanguine heads prevailed and eventually it was decided that the first Allied soldiers on French soil were indeed to be paratroops dropping ahead of the sea-borne landing. They would, however, drop inland to serve as a blocking force preventing reinforcements reaching the invasion beaches, and simultaneously seizing vital roads and bridges that would enable a breakout from the beachhead in due course. As ever they would also create as much confusion and havoc as possible in the enemy rear.

The US airborne troops were to arrive in Normandy in three different ways. Some 18,000 men from the 82nd and 101st would drop by parachute. Close behind them would be the gliders, and finally a small contingent (principally artillery) would come in across Utah Beach.

The final plan—its last revision made only a few days before the invasion—called for the 82nd to drop on both sides of the Merderet River in order to secure Neuville-au-Plain, Ste-Mère-Église, Chef-du-Pont, Etienville, Amfreville and their surrounding areas. They were also to destroy bridges across the Douve River denying German reinforcements that route to the beaches.

To provide some measure of mutual support should things go badly on the beaches, the 101st's DZs were close to those of the 82nd. Some re-assignment of objectives saw the 82nd draw Ste-Mère-Église originally slated for the 101st. This irony was reversed a few months later when the 101st got the toughest assignment at Bastogne by equal happenstance.

The gliders were to undertake the first operational night landing ever attempted, hopefully with the aid of beacons set up by pathfinders dropped ahead of them. There were not going to be enough gliders or pilots so some of the glider infantry and artillery were going to have to be part of the amphibious landing and link up with the rest of the division as soon as possible.

Originally D-Day was to be 5 June, but bad weather forced a postponement. Troopers by this time were already at the airfields and ports. The 456th PFA for instance had boarded ship at Rothgate dock in Cardiff on 3 June, its vehicles and guns having been loaded over the previous few days. Airfields all over southern England were lined with aircraft bearing the hastily applied black and white 'invasion stripes' mandated for the day. (Aircraft recognition was poor throughout armies in 1944, and the Allies wanted no repeat of the Sicily debacle.)

At 17.15hrs on the 5th the 456th was amongst a growing armada that set sail for France, at about the same time as the paratroopers were checking their equipment and weapons. They expected to be on their own for a while before the 'legs' got off the beaches and were consequently heavily armed in addition to their bulky T5 parachutes and reserves. Troopers carried as much ammunition, grenades and fighting knives as could physically be managed. Most men hefted nearly 100 pounds of equipment—making the mandatory yellow 'Mae West' life preserver a somewhat doubtful assistance in the event of a water landing. Surprisingly few accidents were reported in the circumstances, although the 505th suffered three killed and ten wounded when a grenade exploded as its men were boarding their aircraft.

At around 23.00hrs the first pathfinders took off, and a little over an hour later over 1,000 C-47s were following them. The greatest invasion in history was under way. Some 378 of these aircraft carried the 82nd's three regiments with 52 gliders accompanying them with anti-tank guns and other heavy equipment.

The assault force was to fly what today would be called a 'lo-hi-lo' profile. Crossing the English Channel at 500 feet or less to avoid radar, they would climb

Below: Soldiers of the 508th PIR checking their T-5 parachutes on an airfield in England prior to D-Day. Note the variety of fighting knives and pistols, as well as the cargo pockets bulging with extra ammunition or supplies. None of the soldiers has yet donned his reserve 'chute, so the harness detail can be seen. (US Army)

to 1,500 feet while crossing the coast in an attempt to escape German small-arms fire and light flak, before dropping once again to 500 feet as they approached the drop zones.

D-Day
The first pathfinders were on French soil at 01.21hrs on 6 June. Unfortunately many were off course and consequently did not turn on their beacons. First aircraft over the DZs were carrying the 101st who managed a reasonably accurate drop. Unfortunately for the following 82nd this meant that the defences were now thoroughly alerted. Heavy flak forced many aircraft off course and Gavin's men were widely scattered. The gliders, too, had eventful flights. Broken tows and other problems forced some back. One CG-4 had the hinged nose section unlatch in flight, and since this contained the pilots, a fairly hairy few minutes were had whilst frantic attempts were made to secure it. With considerable difficulty this section made it back to base.

Meanwhile the paratroopers were discovering that aerial reconnaissance had failed to reveal marshy ground—at best this slowed them down, and at worst literally swallowed some of their heavy equipment. Some troopers came down in rivers. Only the 505th was dropped near its planned drop zone. Men of the 3rd/505th under Lt Colonel Krause headed for their objective, Ste-Mère-Église. To their horror they found the bodies of troopers who had fallen directly on the town in the drop and had been killed by the Germans before they could assemble their weapons and defend themselves.

Before dawn—less than four hours after the drop—Ste-Mère-Église became the first town in France to be liberated, at 04.30hrs Krause's men raised the same Stars and Stripes that had flown over Naples when it too was liberated. (Today the same, somewhat battered, flag is proudly displayed in the 82nd Division's museum at Fort Bragg.) The men had precious little time to savour the moment, for at 09.30hrs the Germans counter-attacked, supported by tanks. With some time yet to pass before they could be reinforced from Utah Beach, the troopers of the 82nd were going to have to tough it out.

The 2nd/505th was diverted from its advance on Neuville-au-Plain to reinforce its colleagues. The CO, Lt Colonel Vandervoort, detached a reinforced rifle platoon, together with one of the few 57mm anti-tank guns to survive the landings, with orders to block German attempts to reach the town. This decision proved vital in the coming hours. For four hours the 48 men under Lieutenant Turner Turnbull held off a far superior German force, but suffered some 20% casualties. Together with the defence of Ste-Mère-Église itself the 82nd's heroic stand that morning blunted the German counter-attack on the beaches. Later that evening glidermen from the 325th reinforced the hard-pressed paras.

The 1st/505th meanwhile was attempting to take the bridge over the Merderet River at La Fière. Three assaults, however, had failed with heavy casualties. Gavin, dropped some three miles away, had managed to gather some 500 troopers and sent half of them to assist at La Fière, whilst the rest were ordered to take the Chef-du-Pont bridge, which also crossed the Merderet River. Both bridges were served by narrow causeways across the surrounding boggy ground and were vital if the Utah infantry were to get off the beaches. The problem with this strategy was that bridges work both ways, so keeping them open also meant that the enemy had access to the beaches if they were not held.

The village was taken, as was the eastern end of the bridge, hours later. However, the attackers had not managed to gain the other side, and were considering

Above: They look too young to go to war—82nd glidermen in a CG-4 over England in 1944. On the night of 5/6 June these men would land on the Cotentin Peninsula. (82nd Airborne Museum)

blowing the bridge instead. Ridgway meanwhile ordered Gavin to take and hold the La Fière causeway and bridge 'at all costs' and efforts were re-doubled. Eventually a company from the 507th (who had suffered bad scattering, some troopers landing 20 miles away) forced its way across the bridge, clearing the Germans from the other side. Inexplicably they then kept going, leaving a vacuum quickly exploited by the Germans who held the western side for a further two days. Despite this, and again with the aid of one of the few 57mm guns available, the 82nd made sure that the Germans could not advance either, knocking out a tank actually on the bridge and interdicting the eastern causeway.

Like the 507th, the 508th had been badly scattered, getting only seven sticks into the regimental DZ. Many of its members found themselves fighting alongside the Screaming Eagles of the 101st (proving the wisdom of standardising tactics) whilst the rest, as in Sicily, fought numerous small actions wherever they could stir up the most chaos. Once again this caused great confusion amongst the Germans who assumed that they were under attack by a far greater force, and were unable to pinpoint the best counter-attack. One group ambushed a staff car and killed General Wilhelm Falley, commander of the German 91st Infantry Division, a major blow to the German command structure.

Elsewhere, the CO of the 2nd/508th, Lt Colonel Thomas J.B. Shanley, rounded up enough troopers to try for his original objective, a bridge over the Douve River. Meeting more resistance than his small force could overcome he withdrew to 'Hill 30' which they then held for two days against numerous counter-attacks. Since this position interdicted the German advance on Chef-du-Pont and thus Ste-Mère-Église it became key to the 82nd Division's entire area. Again the ability of Airborne soldiers to adapt to a changing tactical situation quickly and decisively had proved its value.

Above: Dated 4 June 1944, this photograph of a group of 'Glider Riders' (probably the 325th) have been hanging around for some time waiting for the order to go (the drop was eventually postponed for 24 hours). Note the chap 'aiming' his bazooka at someone off camera. The two troopers to his left are carrying containers of ammunition for the bazooka. The Horsa they are about to board speaks of hasty reassignment— it displays very roughly applied invasion stripes and someone has marked out, but not had time to finish painting, a US 'star 'n' bar' cockade over the British roundel. The blue part of the insignia has been applied, probably sprayed with a stencil, but only a couple of brush strokes of white. (82nd Airborne Museum)

Left: 509th drop into Southern France, August 1944. (via Bruce Robertson)

Opposite page, Above: Horsa gliders loading for D-Day in England. Once the decision to go was made the troops were confined to barracks and the aircraft painted with the distinctive black and white 'invasion stripes' shown here. Two of the three troopers in the foreground wear (rather loosely) the yellow Mae West life jacket issued for over water flights. The men under the glider wing on the left of the picture are checking the attachment point for the towing yoke. All the gliders visible in the original print have the yoke fitted and are ready to go. (82nd Airborne Museum)

Opposite page, Below: Hamilcar glider in Normandy seen with a DD (swimmable) Sherman.

Right: The airborne landings and the German reaction. The landings on both flanks of the invasion beaches succeeded in drawing away from the beaches German reserves that would otherwise have been used on the 6th. Initially, 21st Panzer was directed at the British on the eastern side of the Orne, while the American units were counter-attacked by 91st and 352nd Divisions. (Map info from Kershaw: *D-Day: Piercing the Atlantic Wall*)

Below: The 82nd and 101st landings were considerably widespread—some 25 miles long by 15 deep. On the morning of the 6th, the 82nd could muster only 33% of its strength, the 101st only 38%. However, this did have the advantage of giving German counter-attackers the problem of where to focus their attacks. (Map info from Kershaw: *D-Day: Piercing the Atlantic Wall*)

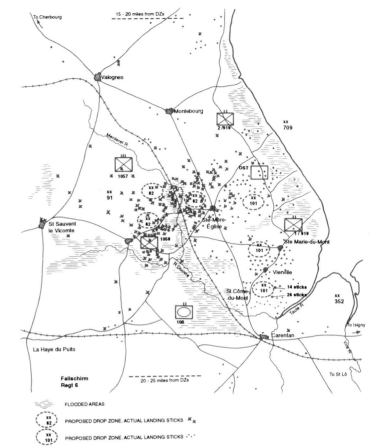

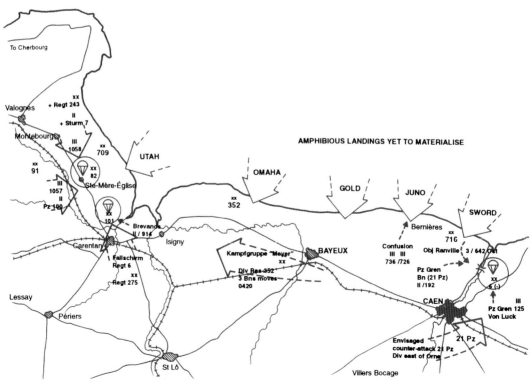

The situation changed so quickly because of the imprecise nature of airborne arrival. The paratroopers suffered scattering for a number of reasons: navigational errors were common; anti-aircraft fire could force the aircraft to take evasive action; wind speeds and directions might differ from those estimated. Furthermore in the time it took a stick of troops to exit the C-47's single door the aircraft would travel nearly a mile. Finally wartime T5 and T7 parachutes were designed simply to get the wearer to the ground. They were not the sophisticated 'flyable' canopies that can be deployed today (albeit that they were vastly better than their German WWII equivalents which were not steerable at all).

During the chaotic first few hours of the invasion some troopers literally fell into the hands of the Germans and were captured. One such was 3rd/508th's Battalion Surgeon, Captain Briand N. Boaudin. Released by his comrades a few days later near Orglandes he commandeered, amongst other souvenirs, a rather fine German medical kit which survives at Fort Bragg to this day.

The 'glider riders' faced many of the same problems, including of course, the fact that once free of their tug aircraft they were committed to land in short order no matter what. In Normandy the first night glider landings ever were undertaken, multiplying the dangers. During the two phases (the bulk of the glider force was scheduled for the evening of D-Day) some 11% casualties were suffered just in landing, and only one in four gliders landed undamaged.

Where LZs were blocked, mined or flooded the pilots had to find the nearest open space and try to get in, hedgerows and other obstacles, natural or man-made, notwithstanding. In the confined spaces available many landings were little more than controlled crashes. A final hazard was the load itself. Several aircraft were found with their crews crushed by loads that had torn loose in the landing. Generally, however, the smaller American CG-4s, with their welded tube construction, proved more survivable in Normandy than the bigger, heavier British Horsas. Their wooden construction splintered in a bad landing, giving rise to even more potential for injury amongst the unfortunate occupants.

Above: Liberated Ste-Mère-Église, 6 June 1944. (via Real War Photos)

Below: This picture has often been miscaptioned. It actually shows two 82nd infantrymen, Capt Briand N. Boaudin (left) and Lt Paul E. Lehman. They were captured on D-Day but liberated a few days later. In the process the pair have acquired a number of souvenirs (the French Wine was also liberated from the Germans). Boaudin, a medical officer, holds the German medical valise, with its distinctive cowhide cover, now in the Divisional Museum. (US Army)

Above: Paratroopers move cautiously through a French village in Normandy in June 1944. (US Army via Chris Ellis)

Left: Unidentified Paratroopers move through Carentan in the Cherbourg peninsula. Heavy fighting had secured the town but resulted in considerable damage as can be seen. (US Army via Chris Ellis)

Right and Inset: Lt Kelso C. Horne on the road to St. Sauveur, Normandy in late June 1944. Festooned with bandoliers of extra .30 ammunition for his M1 Garand rifle, Horne also has a grenade clipped to his webbing and a .45 automatic in a leather holster. Although not terribly accurate the .45 was a powerful weapon at close quarters and was reputed to be able to stop a truck. One of the sequence of photos taken at this time later became famous on the cover of *Life* magazine. (US Army via Chris Ellis)

AUGUST 14, 1944 10 CENTS

Presidential Unit Citation for HQ and HQ Company, 82nd Airborne cited in War Department General Orders 69 of 22 August 1944

Division HQ and HQ Company, 82nd Airborne Division, is cited for outstanding performance of duty in action against the enemy between 6 and 9 June 1944 during the invasion of France. The Forward Echelon of Division HQ and HQ Company landed by parachute and glider on D-day . . . on the Cotentin Peninsula in the area surrounding Ste-Mère-Église, France. The enemy opposed drops and landings with intense antiaircraft fire and immediately surrounded the secured area with mobile antiairborne landing groups which attacked with machine guns, mortars, and artillery. Shortly after 0200, a division command post was established west of Ste-Mère-Église. HQ personnel were augmented by predawn glider elements landing about 0410, and by further gliderborne increments during the day. HQ personnel from many gliders, which had landed in areas not secured by parachute troops, fought their way to the Division Command Post, into which they infiltrated during the first 48 hours. The Division Staff and HQ Company remained in close proximity to the forward lines at all times. During the first 37 hours, enemy action was often not more than a few hundred yards from the command post. The officers and men of Division HQ and HQ Company labored without rest or relaxation day and night during the first 3 days of the invasion, at times under direct attack by artillery and small-arms, immediately adjacent to active fighting and frequently subjected to bombing attacks directed against it nearby artillery batters. Duties were performed unhesitatingly with utter disregard for personal safety and with superior efficiency and tireless devotion to duty. The courage and perseverance shown by members of the Division HQ and HQ Company, 82nd Airborne Division, are worthy of emulation and reflect the highest traditions of the Army of the United States.

The second landings should have been easier with the advantage of daylight. Unfortunately not only were the planned LZs still contested, but Ridgway's radios had dropped in the river and he thus had no way of warning the incoming gliders that new sites had been hastily marked out.

Again fate played a hand. Still unaware of the situation on the ground the gliders actually arrived an hour early at around 20.00hrs. In this case the almost inevitable navigational errors led to many gliders being off course and actually missing the worst fire from an enemy massed around their intended LZ. The following morning, when the last of the 325th's glidermen arrived, they too suffered from the difficult terrain, losing nearly 200 killed or injured during the landings.

Joining up with elements of the 4th Infantry Division, tanks and their own infantry driving up from the beach, the 325th fought its way towards Ridgway's positions. There the La Fière Bridge was still in German hands and one battalion was sent to help the hard-pressed paratroopers fighting for its control.

By the 8th the 82nd was in control of most of its area of operation, but still the bridge held out. During the day, however, Ridgway learned of a submerged crossing over the Merderet which would enable him to flank the Germans and at 23.00hrs the 1st/325th began the assault.

The fighting was fierce. During this action one platoon became cut off and was threatened with annihilation. As the Germans moved in for what they assumed would be an easy kill Pfc Charles N. de Glopper, already wounded, left cover blazing away with his Browning Automatic Rifle (BAR). He was eventually cut down by return fire but his sacrifice allowed the rest of his platoon to escape. He was posthumously awarded the division's first Medal of Honor in WWII.

It was to take a further assault led by the 3rd/325th, supported with tanks and artillery, before the bridge was finally cleared the following morning. Gavin immediately led a drive to relieve Shanley's men, still holding out on Hill 30. Even at this late stage where operations in the airhead were regarded as 'mopping up' another German counter-attack against La Fière had to be fought off before the area could truly be considered secure.

As the beachheads were consolidated the 82nd found its men being used as assault troops. Driving across the Douve on 14 June they cleared the enemy from some 100 square miles of territory in less than 48 hours. By the 16th they were in control of St Sauveur-le-Vicomte, allowing the 9th Division to pass through their lines and reach the coast on the following day in preparation for the drive on Cherbourg.

During the ensuing days the division turned south and took dozens of objectives against tenacious German resistance to consolidate the bridgehead. Often they were days ahead of the 'legs' divisions designated for the objectives who were moving much more slowly.

After 33 days of constant combat the 82nd was withdrawn from the front line having suffered almost 50% casualties. It had undoubtedly been pivotal in preventing the Germans pushing the allies back into the sea. The Airborne had once again demonstrated its value, but at terrible cost. Captain Charles W. Mason wrote a succinct summary:

'33 days of action without relief, without replacements. Every mission accomplished. No ground gained ever relinquished.'

A better tribute to those who died would be hard to find.

NIJMEGEN

During 33 days of fighting in Normandy the division had suffered the highest casualties of any of its campaigns, 46%. This sacrifice, however, certainly prevented far greater slaughter on the beaches. The 82nd's aggression and skill at arms was self-evident. During that time it took on five German divisions, virtually eliminating two of them as effective forces. In this process it destroyed 62 tanks and 44 assorted artillery pieces, plus other materiel too numerous to list. With a record like this it was always going to be at the sharp end—indeed high casualties were expected and allowed for in the macabre calculations of war.

Returning to its bases in England the 82nd set about re-building. Replacements had to be trained, lessons learnt put into practice, equipment replaced and weary troopers given some respite. Whilst the 82nd was recovering the war went on. The division's old friends the 509th had become part of the 1st Airborne Task Force which launched Operation Dragoon, the assault on the French Mediterranean coast, on 15 August. During this operation 90% of the gliders involved were wrecked beyond recovery—but the objectives were taken in less than half the time planned, another vindication of the Airborne.

There was slow progress in the Normandy battles into July but the breakout into northern France then got going with remarkable speed, Paris was liberated on 25 August, and the Allies were rolling back German forces so fast that they were in danger of outrunning supplies. Amidst all this success, however, there were cracks in the alliance that threatened the whole process.

At the highest level the Free French leader General de Gaulle was barely speaking to Roosevelt and on less than friendly terms with Churchill. At the next level down things were little better amongst the military commanders. Many were already thinking about their post-war careers and acting accordingly. Supreme Commander Eisenhower found himself embroiled in conflicting proposals from rival commanders. On the one hand there was the autocratic Montgomery who, despite his success in the Western Desert, had a reputation for slow and ponderous manoeuvre. On the other were the redoubtable Omar Bradley (original commander of the re-activated 82nd Infantry Division) and his subordinate George Patton for whom the word 'aggressive' might have been invented. With political considerations and personal vanity also factors it is little wonder that relations between the senior commanders came close to open hostility at times. This distracted Eisenhower and led to a compromise that was to see the Allies defeated for the only time in the European campaign.

The Airborne divisions meanwhile focussed on the 10,000 replacements they were going to have to train, and a major re-organisation. Activated on 2 August the First Allied Airborne Army was to be the biggest ever formed, combining American, British and Polish assets, and commanded by Lieutenant General Lewis Brereton with British General 'Boy' Browning as deputy.

Brereton, who had planned the proposed parachute assaults during WWI, was an Air Force officer and staunch advocate of the effectiveness of air power. This apparently excellent qualification masked a lack of understanding of what happened once air power had delivered the soldiers to the battlefield. His deputy was an extremely able Guards officer who had been responsible for the formation and training of British glider and parachute forces. Not immune to idiosyncrasies he had also designed his own rather unique uniform. (Browning's other contribution to Airborne uniform, however, was the red beret. It has subsequently been adopted by airborne forces the world over, not least amongst them the US Airborne who wear it with pride to this day.)

Ridgway meanwhile had been promoted to command the US XVIII Airborne Corps, his deputy, Gavin, assuming command of the 82nd on 28 August. As part of the Change of Command ceremonies that month, Generals Eisenhower, Ridgway, Brereton and Gavin reviewed the 82nd. During that review Ike made the comment about 'owing you (the 82nd) a lot' and never a more prophetic word was spoken.

The components of the new force were:

- US XVIII Airborne Corps: US 17th, 82nd, and 101st Airborne Divisions
- I British Airborne Corps: 1st and 6th British Airborne Divisions, 1st Polish Independent Parachute Brigade, 52nd (Lowland) Division (Airportable)
- USAAF IX Troop Carrier Command
- Nos 38 and 46 Groups, RAF

Eisenhower eventually decided to give priority to Montgomery's 21st Army Group as it thrust through Belgium towards Holland, securing the Channel ports and overrunning V-2 sites that were dropping the world's first operational ballistic missiles on London. This priority was, however, to be temporary, for once the great port of Antwerp was in Allied hands, it would switch to Bradley's 12th Army Group for a direct attack across the Rhine.

Slightly to the surprise of all, Montgomery moved fast. Brussels was liberated on 3 September and the city of Antwerp, but not its vital sea approaches, the following day. By the 12th Monty's men were in Holland. During August and early September no less than 18 plans to speed the advance even more had been formulated, many involving the Airborne, only for these to be dropped, overtaken by the unexpectedly rapid advances on the ground. At this point, as British Lieutenant General Sir Brian Horrocks later commented 'We made the mistake of underestimating our enemy— a very dangerous thing to do when fighting the Germans.'

On 5 September Monty was offered the First Allied Airborne Army to speed his advance. His response was an uncharacteristically daring plan. An 'airborne carpet' was to be laid from Eindhoven to Arnhem with the objective of capturing vital bridges and securing a route for the British XXX Corps which would drive rapidly to cross the Rhine at the last one, Arnhem. Speed was of the essence, which made the plan risky. During the planning Browning is reputed to have made the famous comment about the attempt on Arnhem possibly being 'a bridge too far'.

The airborne part of the operation was to be Operation Market, whilst the ground assault became Operation Garden. It was set to begin on 17 September,

Above right: Reconnaissance photograph of the bridges over the Waal. The rail bridge (multi-span at right) was taken first by 3rd Battalion 504th PIR after a river assault; the road bridge (left) fell later on the same day, 20 September 1944. (82nd Airborne Museum)

Below right: Checking equipment and loading up at the start of the operation. The man in the foreground is wearing an M1A1 carbine-carrying case; behind him, one trooper checks another's T5 parachute; at the aircraft, a weapon's bag is passed into the interior (US Army)

leaving little time for fine detail in the planning or the collection of up-to-date intelligence regarding German dispositions (and what intelligence there was, it transpired, was woefully inaccurate). Worse, there was insufficient co-ordination at the highest levels.

Briefly the plan was for the 101st Airborne to secure the first part of the corridor around Eindhoven. The 82nd was to seize the bridge across the Maas at Grave, a number of canal crossings, and the vital Nijmegen bridges across the Waal. One road and one rail, both were substantial enough to take armour and the only crossings for some 20 miles. High ground around Groesbeek was also to be occupied to block any German advance out of the Reichswald Forest. Finally the British were to jump on the last bridge in the chain, Arnhem. Theirs of course was the farthest point from relief.

The whole plan rested on the speed with which the armoured thrust on the ground could link up with the airborne troops and force the corridor. Once launched the plan would be obvious to the enemy and any delay would increase the risk to those holding the farthest parts of the 75 mile 'carpet'. The payoff, however, was a flanking of the Siegfried Line that would place the Allies close to Germany's industrial heartland of the Ruhr. Market-Garden had the potential to shorten the war.

Because there simply were not enough transports to lift this huge force in one go, the drops were to be incremental over three days. The good news, however, was that because the Allies enjoyed near total air superiority the assault would go in during daylight hours. This it was hoped (and subsequently proved) would reduce the scattering so prevalent in night drops. Lessons learnt in Normandy were also taken on board. Paratroopers were not going to be shot up before they hit the ground this time, they were going to jump with loaded weapons so they could come down blazing. The artillery was going to make its first parachute insertion, too, the 376th PFA jumping alongside Gavin's men.

As D-Day neared preparations went into overdrive. Every artillery and flak emplacement along the route was bombed and strafed from high, medium and low levels. B-17s, B-26s, American P-47 Thunderbolts and British Typhoons all added their firepower. Such was the Allied control of the skies that the Luftwaffe had no real counter and the Germans discerned no plan amongst all the other bombing.

As 1,545 transports and 478 gliders began loading with troops and materiel on the morning of the 17th there were the usual nerves for the newly trained and the studied nonchalance of their battle-hardened comrades. Much gallows humour centred on the 504th who were to jump on Grave. Some officers tried to fend it off by talking about 'Gravey' but to little avail amongst the unit wits (actually it is pronounced to rhyme with 'starve')

At 11.09hrs the take-offs began and the vast aerial armada headed in two streams towards Holland. First on the ground were the pathfinders who landed at 12.47hrs. Less than 15 minutes later Gavin, first out as ever, led the 505th down onto DZ 'N' just south of Groesbeek. Jumping with the infantry was the 376th PFA whose men had their ten 75mm pack howitzers assembled within minutes of landing. Moving 1,000 yards to the first gun line, the 376th was able to provide fire support to the 508th by 18.00hrs and was soon supported by the 456th who arrived by glider with jeeps and more artillery the next day.

Also arriving by glider in the 505th's area was General Browning and his HQ. Slightly to the north and east of Groesbeek Colonel Roy Lindquist's 508th jumped on DZ 'T', whilst on the left flank Rueben Tucker's 504th jumped on both sides of the bridge over the Maas River at Grave. This proved the most successful drop of the day as Tuckers' men quickly overran both ends of the bridge. The 52nd Troop

Above right: The journey—this map shows the track and waypoints on the northern and southern routes to Holland. (Based on drawings in the USAAF's Secret report on Operation Market Garden)

Below right: The landings—this map shows the drop zones used on 17 September. 505th PIR dropped on DZ 'O' near Grave. Grave bridge over the Maas was taken swiftly. 505th and 508th PIRs were dropped or landed at LZ 'N' and 'T' respectively, 456th Parachute FA Battalion landing on LZ 'N'. The artillery—75mm pack howitzers—was decisive in the early part of the battle, the only support for the infantry until Allied armour closed on the 19th. (Based on drawings in the USAAF's Secret report on Operation Market Garden)

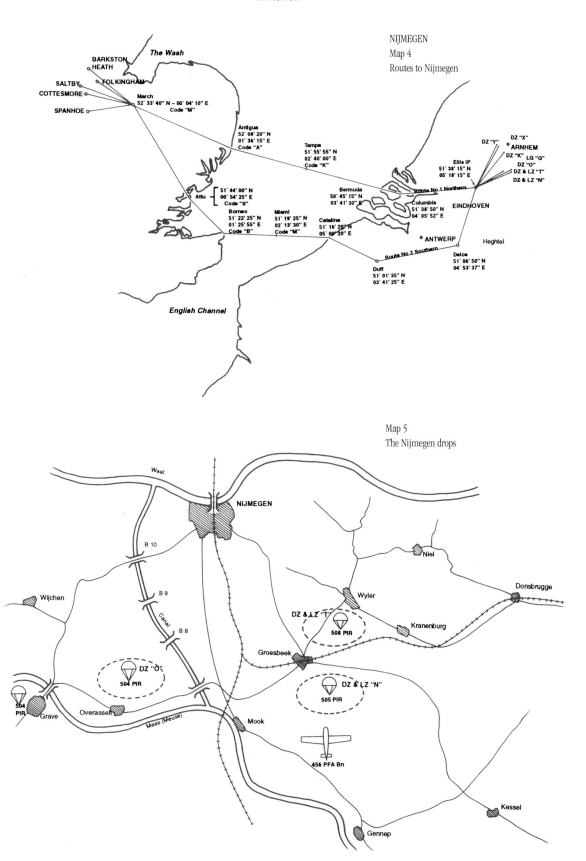

NIJMEGEN
Map 4
Routes to Nijmegen

Map 5
The Nijmegen drops

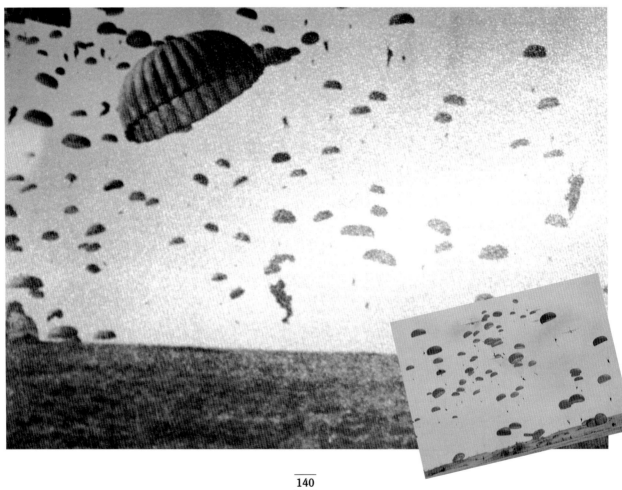

Left: C-47 full of paratroopers awaiting take-off, 17 September 1944. (via Real War Photos)

Right: The Nijmegen drop. This C-47, serial 2100833, is from the 439th Troop Carrier Group (squadron code L4). 'Chalk 3' was a stick of 14 men from Charlie Company, 307th Engineer Battalion, who took part in the Waal crossing. The aircraft also dropped para packs containing mine detectors, radios, BARs, tools, mines and explosives. Taken by the CO of the 439th (the wing of whose C-47 can be seen) the picture is made more interesting as everyone on the aircraft is known. 1-Lt Melvin Ullrick led the stick which consisted of S/Sgt Noel E. Morrison, Sgt William Kero, T/5 Russel S. Anderson, Pfcs Garo Kirkorian, Raymond H. Slocum, Carmen J. Western and Pvts Alexander S. Nemeth, Robert R. Freel, Joseph E. Jobora, Hutchel B. Stansbury, Raymond H. Geroux, James W. Pembleton and Howard Miller. The aircraft was piloted by 1-Lt Henry L. Harris with co-pilot 2-Lt Stephen V. Sajawies. Crew chief was S/Sgt Howard E. Gerard and Radio Operator T/Sgt Howard T. Love. (Col Charles Young).

Below left: DZ 'T' Groesbeek. A poor quality but historically interesting picture taken by one of two American war reporters who jumped with the troops that day. Col Roy Lindquist's 508th PIR are seen landing here. There are well over 100 parachutes visible in this shot indicating how tightly the formations of Dakotas flew. Comparison of this shot with one taken nearly 50 years later (inset) shows that certain things don't change. (US Army/inset Mike Verier)

Below right: Another view of the landings. (US Army)

Above: The drop was one of the biggest of WWII and extremely accurate—but not as accurate as this spring 1945 practice drop. (via Real War Photos)

Carrier Wing's after action report has a map showing where the actual drops were made in relation to the planned DZs. It shows all the drops were extremely accurate and, where the dots for the 504th do not match the DZ, there is a slightly sniffy note pointing out that this was at the unit commander's insistence!

This drop was at the time the biggest ever attempted, and it was not without its problems, the hung loads (including one or two paratroopers caught in the static lines), engine failures and flak damage were almost expected, but there were human costs, too. Serial A-9 of the 316th Troop Carrier Group (42 C-47s, 3 C-53s) dropped 677 men of the 504th and 270 parapacks on DZ 'O'. One aircraft had to land at Feltwell to discharge a paratrooper who had 'gone out of his mind'. Having done so it immediately re-joined the formation and completed the drop. On the return journey the same aircraft ditched in the Channel, all the crew being picked up by the air-sea rescue organisation.

Rather bizarrely, above this armada was a B-17 full of war correspondents and photographers calmly observing the operation for posterity, but not all were content with such a detached view, Serial A-7's manifest included the famous CBS commentator Ed Murrow, and his technician Mr Maselle who had insisted on being in a C-47 with the troops.

Once on the ground, Gavin quickly set about establishing the enemy's dispositions, with his Dutch liaison officer Captain Arie Bestebreurtje, soon in telephone contact with the Dutch resistance from a local house. The British paratroops were to regret their lack of Dutch liaison in the days that followed.

Groesbeek was also a railway junction, and during the night one train passed through the area unchallenged, a fact that apparently did not please Gavin (his testiness more than somewhat due to a painful back injury suffered during the jump). Ever willing to please their commander the troopers set about the next two with bazookas. One was carrying fuel for V-2s, the resultant spectacular explosion nearly taking the troopers with it.

By the end of D-Day, whilst all the landings had been successful, none of the main objectives of Market had been taken, and the armoured thrust had not even begun. The Allies, however, were committed and as D+1 dawned efforts were re-doubled. Three times that day Gavin's soldiers reported the bridge in their hands, but the German defences held and each time the Americans were forced to withdraw.

In the 82nd's sector the defensive perimeter was pretty thin and Gavin was finally forced to withdraw the 3rd/508th from attacking Nijmegen to prevent German counter-attacks from overrunning the glider LZs. With some difficulty they were cleared just in time for the gliders that arrived overhead around 14.00hrs.

Once again most of the gliders made an accurate landing despite heavy flak. This time the lift brought in the 319th and 320th GFA, and the 456th PFA plus the balance of the 307th Airborne Engineers, the 80th Airborne Anti-Aircraft Artillery and some medics. Materiel delivered included 30 howitzers, eight 57mm anti-tank guns and over 90 jeeps. Twenty minutes later a supply drop by 135 B-24 Liberators was also successfully made. Some 25 gliders overshot, some landing up to five miles inside Germany, but remarkably more than half the personnel involved eventually fought or infiltrated their way back to Allied lines.

By the end of the second day Major General Taylor's 101st Airborne and the British XXX Corps commanded by Horrocks had at last broken out from Eindhoven and were on their way to link up with the increasingly hard pressed 82nd. The bridges at Nijmegen were still in German hands, although engineers had managed to disable the demolition charges during the night so that at least they remained intact.

On the 19th (D+2) the Guards Armoured Division, spearheading XXX Corps, finally linked up with Gavin's men at Grave bridge, the leading elements making contact with the 504th at 08.20hrs. With no time lost, the 2nd/505th was placed under the command of the Guards and the tanks and infantry moved towards Nijmegen. Initially they met only light resistance and moved into the town, taking the post office, which was rumoured to contain demolition apparatus for the bridges. Short of their objectives, however, both columns were stopped by heavy enemy fire which knocked out the lead tanks. Flanking attacks by Grenadier Guards on the road bridge, and a combined force of grenadiers and paratroops on the rail bridge failed to make headway and by nightfall a stalemate had been reached. Elsewhere the 508th was still fending off probing attacks by the Germans on its thinly stretched defensive lines.

Gavin and Browning had become increasingly anxious for the British paras at Arnhem, who would not be relieved unless the bridges were carried. Gavin concluded that the only way to break the stalemate was to get troops across the river and flank the defenders. To this end he requested that Horrocks' engineers bring up their boats from the rear, planning that the 504th would cross at 08.00hrs the next morning, under cover of an artillery barrage.

In the event the boats were late, the vehicles making very slow progress on the one congested road open to them. For the moment, however, Gavin's immediate attention was on Mook and Beek, heavily under attack by the 6th *Fallschirmjäger* Division—no second rate formation. Leaving to take personal charge of the situation Gavin supervised the counter-attacks. In Mook the 505th re-took the town street by street, whilst at Beek the 508th, who had been asked to hold the

Netherlands Orange Lanyard

HQ and HQ Company, 82d Airborne Division
Cited in Department of Army General Orders 43 of 19 December 1950:

Considering that the outstanding performance of duty of the 82d Airborne Division, United States Army, during the airborne operations and the ensuing fighting actions in the central part of the Netherlands in the period from 17 September to 4 October has induced HER MAJESTY, THE QUEEN, to decorate its divisional color with the Military Order of William, degree of the knight of the fourth class, considering also, that is desirable for each member of the personnel of the 82nd Airborne Division, United States Army, who took part in the aforesaid operations, to possess a lasting memento of this glorious struggle; decrees: that each member of the personnel of the 82d Airborne Division, United States Army, who took part in the operations in the area of Nijmegen in the period from 17 September to 4 October 1944 is allowed to wear the Orange Lanyard of the Royal Netherlands Army.

Above: The ubiquitous 'Jeep' (a contraction of 'GP' as in 'General Purpose') provided most of the Airborne's mobility. This one is the Divisional G-1 jeep (note the star plate over the 82A/B stencil on the bumper) awaiting its passenger at the 508th's Harness CP. (US Army)

position if possible, went on the attack and that night re-took the town, pursuing the Germans all the way back to the Rhine.

The Waal crossings
When the British canvas boats finally arrived, the troopers set to preparing them. There were 26 assault boats, holding ten men each. It was nearly 15.00hrs before this small force pushed out into the fast current of the Waal led by Captains Thomas M. Burris and Carl W. Koppel.

Preceded by rocket-firing Typhoons, a ferocious artillery barrage had been laid down ahead of the assault, along with smoke to try and give some cover. When reports reached German commanders they initially dismissed the idea of an assault across the river—they simply did not think it could be done. The German troops on the spot, however, some 400–600 soldiers, lost no time in opening up on the boats as the smoke screen was blown away, leaving the frantically paddling Americans exposed in mid-river.

Terrible carnage was wrought as the troopers struggled against the current, so much so that only 13 of the boats returned. Those that did get ashore, however, sought vengeance. The ferocity of their attack quite overwhelmed the Germans, who faltered in the face of screaming troopers coming at them with bayonets and grenades. Seeing the destruction of the boats some troopers on the far shore simply took bandoliers of ammunition and their rifles and swam across (which says much for the physical condition of paratroopers). Tanks acting as artillery pounded the Germans from across the river in an attempt to support the troopers on the far side.

Gradually (some six return trips were necessary) the 1st and 3rd/504th got their men across and drove the Germans eastwards. First the railway and then the road bridge was cleared. The 504th suffered over 100 casualties during this action, but the Germans lost four times as many men.

Whilst the hand to hand fighting for the northern shore was going on the Grenadiers and the 505th hit the southern end of the bridge. By 17.00hrs the Germans were routed and the 82nd had control of the north end of the bridges. The

Right: Men of the 50th Anti-Tank Battalion pause at a roadside shrine in Belgium during December 1944. Left to right: Pvt Chas A. Badeaux, T/5 Theodore B. Sohoski and Pvt John H. Bogdan. (T/5 Emil Edgren, US Army)

first tanks of the Grenadiers, supported by the 2nd/505th were across by 19.00hrs. It took some time to secure the vast road bridge fully, several Germans being winkled out from hiding places under its structure as late as the following morning.

As British and American troops began to stream across the bridge and dig in, the Germans were re-grouping. The counter-attack came the next day (21st) at noon. Supported by tanks it nearly succeeded in dislodging the Allies. During this action Private John Towle used his bazooka to drive off two tanks and destroy a house being used as a strong point before succumbing to enemy fire. His heroic action earned a second Medal of Honor for the division.

Bad weather had meanwhile delayed the arrival of the 325th Glider Infantry and Gavin was reduced to forming an ad hoc battalion from 450 glider pilots who released some paratroopers for action by guarding the divisions' growing number of German prisoners. Fortunately Gavin's foresight in making sure that there was artillery with the first lift meant that the thinly spread paratroopers at least had some support.

Support was sadly lacking in other areas. A terrible lack of co-ordination at the highest levels meant that the Luftwaffe was able to get in amongst the transports and attack both ground and air targets. The Allies, having started from a position of air superiority, failed to maintain it. The consequences of this for the encircled British paras were all too obvious.

Despite the best efforts of the Airborne soldiers it did not prove possible to relieve the British paratroops at Arnhem. The Poles, delayed by weather, were finally committed but the first wave of gliders arrived unescorted and was cut to pieces on the LZ. The full story is beyond the scope of this narrative but of the 10,300 men who jumped on Arnhem only 2,587 made it back to Allied lines. Montgomery's plan had indeed proved too ambitious.

Market-Garden as planned was abandoned by Eisenhower on the 22nd (D+5) but the fighting went on unabated and the men of the 82nd found themselves serving as 'legs' under General Horrocks (who they regarded as a good commander). The battle for Nijmegen was not over as far as the Germans were concerned and they continued to attack the bridges with their newly acquired jets, the Me 262 and Ar 234, as well as swimmers with mines.

The 325th finally arrived on D+6, 3,385 troops being delivered into the 82nd's area, and an airhead was established at an abandoned Luftwaffe field near Grave where supplies could be flown in. This also permitted the repatriation of the badly needed glider pilots. Gavin, meanwhile, finally got his second star and promotion to major general.

The 82nd was to be given no rest for, despite protests from Brereton, Montgomery had persuaded Eisenhower to keep it in the line along with the 101st. The 82nd remained in combat until November suffering more casualties than during Market-Garden itself. Finally it was relieved and sent to the rear for some much-needed rest.

Based near Reims the 'resting' paratroopers kept in fighting trim by scrapping with the 101st at any opportunity and vying for the favours of local girls. Conscious of the possibility of their being summoned for fire-brigade duties, Gavin made sure that full stocks of ammunition and supplies were to hand even though the division was supposed to be in reserve. His prudence was justified.

Above: Pfc Richard Stafford of the light machine gun platoon, HQ Company 1st Battalion 508th PIR at Nijmegen. Picture was taken on the Dammen van Poldesveldtweg. Stafford was the first trooper to walk down the street. The weapon is a water-cooled .30 cal. Browning, the M1917A1. (via 82nd AB Division Museum)

Above: 'Somewhere in Belgium' (it was actually taken around Christmas day, between Bra and Frature). This photo of an 82nd soldier running to a new scouting position, Thompson in hand, was a source of inspiration for General Gavin who kept it in his office. When, in 1958, the soldier was eventually identified as Earl E. Potter, Gavin wrote that it 'epitomised something fundamental; the spirit the individual has that motivates him in the middle of danger to take every risk and do the right thing is far more important to us than all the equipment that we can buy.' (82nd Airborne Museum)

THE BATTLE OF THE BULGE

Whilst the 82nd was re-fitting the Allies pushed on. On 8 November the US Third Army began its drive to breach the German West Wall defensive line, whilst on the 16th the First Army began the Hürtgen Forest campaign. The results of this latter were to become all too apparent to the 82nd in the spring. In the meantime the Germans were already planning a massive counter-offensive in the west. By the time the US First Army began attacking the River Roer Dams on 13 December the Germans were already massing in their forward assembly areas.

Much of the Allied campaign in Europe was characterised by poor intelligence (or, more accurately, a failure to recognise information for what it was). Such was the case with the German assault in the Ardennes in late 1944. Despite considerable reconnaissance information clearly showing troop movements and supply build-ups that presaged an armoured assault, the Allies were caught completely flat-footed in the Ardennes. Quite apart from intelligence failings the Allies were seriously over-stretched. They had failed to predict the heavy losses of the autumn and were short of both men and equipment; worse they felt that the Germans were already beaten and had allowed a certain degree of complacency to set in.

The Germans on the other hand were not about to admit defeat, Hitler's ambitious plan called for an armoured drive that would reach Antwerp, splitting the allied armies in two. The Germans were, moreover, used to the terrain—after all they had used this route of attack in 1870, 1914 and 1940. Combined with parachute assault in the rear, and the confusion that the 'Greif' commandos (using captured equipment and wearing American uniforms) would cause, the offensive had a real chance of success against the small number of 'green' troops holding the more than 80-mile line that would be attacked.

There were many flaws in the plan, which was clearly too ambitious for the resources available. Many of Hitler's senior commanders argued against it in fact, but to no avail. They had also not reckoned with the resilience of the ordinary American soldiers. They may have been green, in under-strength units and ill-prepared, but they held out long enough for the Airborne divisions (the only reserve SHAEF had) to arrive and plug the gaps. The Airborne in its turn stopped the German advance, refusing to surrender in the face of overwhelming odds, until Patton's Third Army and Hodges' First Army finally arrived.

The operation known to the Germans as *Wacht am Rhein* and to history as the Battle of the Bulge was to prove the US Army's biggest battle of WWII, and cost it 80,987 men killed, wounded or missing.

The assault begins

At 05.30hrs on 16 December the German attack fell without warning on the American front. Artillery and mortar barrages preceded infantry assaults backed by armour. To their credit the front line troops, overrun in some places, turned and fought, slowing the Germans who had reckoned on punching through and driving relentlessly west. The defences in the Losheim Gap began to give, but elsewhere the Sixth Panzer Army made little progress against the US 2nd and 99th Divisions. Fifth Panzer Army was also making less headway than planned against the 28th Division.

The situation was extremely tenuous, however, and the American command quickly realised that the thin line of troops in place could not hold for long. That night the Losheim Gap was breached, leaving the 106th Division almost surrounded. The following morning Obersturmbannführer Joachim Peiper's 1st SS

Panzer Division captured Bullingen, and the 18th Volksgrenadier Division captured the Schönberg Bridge completing the encirclement. Later that afternoon Peiper's SS troops massacred 85 unarmed American prisoners in a field near Malmédy.

Still thinking that the German attack was little more than a spoiling operation designed to divert troops from the Roer dams, the Allied High Command, having released the 7th and 10th Armored Divisions from reserve, relaxed. Bradley and Eisenhower spent the evening playing bridge. Finally, late that evening, it sank in that a major incursion was underway and that help was needed fast—at last the alarm bells were ringing. The only reserves available were the re-fitting Airborne divisions, the 82nd and the 101st. Eisenhower released them immediately.

Having received the alert at around midnight, Gavin's foresight in having ammunition and supplies ready was quickly repaid. The 82nd was moving towards the front by 07.00hrs. This was partly achieved by side-stepping the Army's ponderous bureaucracy—the trucks needed were in SHAEF's huge motor pool and the written orders needed for their release were certainly not available in the middle of the night. Undaunted, the paratroopers' senior NCOs simply 'arrested' any rear echelon type who dared to challenge them, taking some 500 trucks and virtually kidnapping 300 drivers. By the time the 101st arrived on a similar mission there were only cattle trucks left.

This somewhat unconventional approach had two consequences, the 82nd arrived at the front line in time to block the Germans—24 hours later and the battle would have been very different in outcome. Secondly their original orders were for Bastogne, but because the division was already on the move they were changed for Werbomont (further north) and the following 101st directed to Bastogne instead. (Gavin had overall command of XVIII Airborne Corps briefly as Ridgway was in England and the 101st CO, Taylor, was in America.)

By the 19th the Germans were pressing on the whole front. The vital crossroads at Bastogne and St Vith were holding but only just, both being all but surrounded. Meanwhile the 82nd fanned out from Werbomont to take up a defensive line along the Salm River, finding itself in a similar position to that they had held in Holland— German forces to their north, south and east. Such was the Airborne spirit, however, that the 82nd generally held German forces in its area as being in far greater trouble than it was. The optimism was not shared by all, for that afternoon some 7–8,000 American troops surrendered on the Schnee Eifel.

Left: An interesting shot from December 1944 simply captioned 'two recon boys in the Bulge.' Their jeep has been turned into a scout car by the installation of improvised armour and a .50 cal machine gun (a formidable weapon, still in use today). The rear wheels have been fitted with snow chains and the vehicle appears to have been painted white in a concession to local operating conditions. Appropriate clothing, however, was by no means universal as can be seen from the crew. (US Army)

Above: An improvised defensive position in the Odrimont sector (Belgium) provides cover for S/Sgt Charles O. Marible (left) and Pfc Louis E. Jenkins of the 325th Glider Regiment. Aside from the .30 cal machine gun, note that rifle and grenades are also close to hand. (T/5 Norbuth, US Army)

Below: Men of the 508th PIR with their jeeps in the Ardennes—a picture that gives some inkling of the terrible conditions the soldiers had to cope with during the winter campaign. (US Army)

Gavin had been ordered by the now returned Ridgway to hold the widest possible area. Consequently the 325th was deployed to Barvaux in the west, and Grandmenil and Mouhan to the south. The 505th initially went to Habiemont, then on the following day further east to Basse-Bodeaux and Trois Ponts. The 504th also moved east over a couple of days, first to Rahier, then on to Cheneaux and Trois Ponts. Finally the 508th was sent to the heights of Their Dumont. As the divisional artillery arrived it was deployed to support the paras and glidermen.

Gavin was in no doubt that his troops would soon encounter German armour. This time, however, the 82nd was better prepared, for not only had the battle-hardened troopers evolved effective tactics for dealing with tanks, they also had some new tricks up their sleeves.

Throughout the war the Americans had suffered from poor anti-tank weapons, the 57mm gun and the infantry bazooka having little effect on newer German tanks, which also out-gunned the standard Allied tank, the Sherman. The wily paratroopers, however, had come across a considerable quantity of German Panzerfaust hand-held anti-tank rockets in Holland. Gavin himself was seriously impressed with this weapon and they were put to good use in the Ardennes. His gunners had also noted the British discarding sabot round for the 57mm (6-pounder) gun with its far greater penetrating power and traded whatever they could for some carefully hoarded rounds they were now to make good use of.

The 504th in fact quickly made use of its Panzerfausts. On the afternoon of the 20th it encountered a battalion of the 2nd SS Panzer Grenadiers and after fierce hand-to-hand combat captured over a dozen flakwagons and a battery of 105mm howitzers (prompting the unit wits to call themselves the '504th Parachute Armored Regiment'). It is perhaps fortunate for the 38 prisoners they took that afternoon that the paratroopers were not aware that they were from the battalion who had perpetrated the Malmédy massacre.

By now, however, St Vith and Bastogne were completely cut off and their survival depended on the 82nd preventing a German crossing of the Salm River. Around dawn on the 21st the 1st SS Panzer Division fell on the positions of Lt Colonel Ben Vandervoort's 2nd/505th. Calmly declining Gavin's offer of reinforcements, Vandervoort's men held off the best the Germans had.

The 82nd's front now extended some 25 miles, and the following morning the 325th on the right flank was assaulted by an armoured force and forced to withdraw some distance, although not before the 82nd's 75mm artillery had inflicted severe losses on the Germans. The German advance was halted by the engineers blowing a bridge, and the timely arrival of the 325th's reserve battalion.

Whilst this was going on General McAuliffe of the 101st was delivering his famous 'Nuts!' response to the German call for the surrender of Bastogne. St Vith on the other hand had to be abandoned. The 508th, which was holding the corridor through which its heroic defenders were retreating, found itself under attack by the 9th SS Panzer Division.

By the following day, with retreating troops passing through its positions, the regiment was under attack by three SS Divisions plus other German units. Despite the US 3rd Armored Division pulling out

(which exposed their right flank) the paratroopers held out through the night of 23/24 December until tanks of the 9th Armored Division were finally assigned to give them some support.

The 82nd had bought the time that the besieged defenders of Bastogne needed. Re-supplied by air, the 101st fought off a massive attack on Christmas Day and held out until the 26th when Patton's 4th Armored Division finally broke through and lifted the siege.

Meanwhile, on Christmas Eve, now under command of Monty's 21st Army Group, the 82nd received orders much to its disgust to withdraw to more compact defensive lines, By Christmas Day it was in place. German probes of the new lines were not long coming and on the 27th a massive attack by the 9th SS Panzers was repulsed with some difficulty by the 504th and 508th. This attack, however, seemed to mark the end of serious German offensive action which simply ran out of steam. The initiative was about to pass to the Allies.

Above: An airborne bulldozer of the 307th Engineer Battalion pushes a German tank destroyer aside on a narrow forest road whilst troopers wait anxiously to get on. (US Army)

Counter-attack

On 3 January the Allies went on the attack. On the first day the 82nd, augmented by the 551st Parachute Battalion and the 517th Parachute Infantry Regiment, and supported by the 740th Tank Battalion, lost no time in assaulting the Germans. The 740th was much respected by the paras—unlike many armoured formations it shared the Airborne's aggressive spirit. Between them they overran the 62nd Volksgrenadier Division and the 9th SS Panzers, taking some 2,500 prisoners. To their incredulity they were then ordered to stop. Monty's other troops lacked the drive of these two élite units and had to catch up—there was much bitching in the ranks.

Below: Major General James Gavin directs troops in Belgium, 28 January 1945. (via 82nd Airborne Museum)

Unleashed again on the 8th the 82nd pushed on through Vielsalm, where divisional artillery caught and decimated a German column of 35 vehicles and 500 troops at a crossroads. Moving on to the Salm River it quickly re-took the territory relinquished a couple of weeks earlier. During this drive 1st Sergeant Leonard Funk of the 508th, in an action that would have been incredible if Hollywood had written it, deservedly won the division's final Medal of Honor of WWII. The 82nd finally received some hard-earned rest when the 75th Infantry Division relieved it on the 9th allowing the paras back some 20 miles to Chevron.

During this brief respite some troopers managed to wangle leave and get into the usual trouble (that side of military life remains little changed). Towards the end of the war a slightly more relaxed attitude allowed some troopers to furlough in more exotic places such as Nice on the French Mediterranean coast, although even in such idyllic surroundings high spirits led to the odd scrape. One group, who had 'borrowed' an MP jeep for a couple of days, was finally rounded up and triumphantly incarcerated by the aggrieved owners of the vehicle whilst higher authority was summoned. Locking paratroopers in a second floor room with open windows was not the smartest move, however. The miscreants were long gone by the time the officer arrived!

Above: Men of the HQ Company, 508th PIR take a
break during the march to assembly areas, La
Avenanters, Belgium, 6 January 1945. A variety of
improvised winter dress employed by the troopers is
evident. The trooper in the foreground appears to be
wearing a British leather jerkin. (US Army)

Into the dragon's teeth

Early on the morning of 27 January the
82nd again began a move back into
combat. Boarding trucks and heading
east it was to spearhead the assault on
the last great German defensive barrier,
the Siegfried Line. This formidable
defence stretched along the German
border from the Waal to the Rhine, belts
of bunkers, trenches, machine-gun
nests, minefields and dragon's teeth
were tiered to provide overlapping fire
support and were over a mile in depth.
Virtually impervious to artillery or
aerial bombardment by the weapons of
the day they presented a formidable
obstacle.

At 04.00hrs on 2 February the All
Americans led the assault on the West
Wall destroying bunkers systematically as they went, often with the Germans' own
weapon, the Panzerfaust. Once through they seized the German towns of Udenbreth
and Neuhof, as well as the Hertserott Heights. To their disgust no real effort was
made to exploit the breach they had made.

There followed a few days rest and re-fit before the troopers were back in
combat, this time in the dreadful conditions of the Hürtgen Forest. As mentioned
earlier the US forces had tried to take this ground the previous autumn in an
operation that Gavin was to criticise heavily post-war. It had turned into a meat
grinder. Seven divisions had lost 33,000 men to no avail.

What awaited the 82nd in the early thaw of 1945 was sickening even to
hardened troopers. As the snow began to melt countless thousands of bodies from
the winter debacle began to emerge. The 82nd found evidence of wounded soldiers
simply abandoned and left to die at an aid station. To a unit that prided itself on
caring for its wounded this was appalling, more so that such an act was perpetrated
by their own side.

Between 8 and 17 February the 82nd pushed through Kommerscheidt and then
into Schmidt before reaching the swollen Roer River (the Germans had succeeded
in blowing the dam). Fortunately for the 82nd the proposed assault crossing was
cancelled, the division having received orders to return to France, with its long
winter war finally over.

ON TO BERLIN

The Ardennes battle had taken a terrible toll on the US forces, and very nearly split
the Allied High Command (which of course had been Hitler's intention). It had,
however, cost the Germans more, 220,000 casualties, including the last really
effective troops they possessed, and nearly 1,500 tanks and armoured vehicles that
their increasingly pressed industries simply could not replace.

As the net closed round Germany from both the east and the west the 82nd was
back at camps around Sissone-Suippes near Épernay in France. Gear and clothing
badly needed replacement, and the troopers needed rest and good food. Otherwise

the war ground relentlessly on. The 9th Armored Division had captured the bridge at Remagen intact and was across the Rhine on 7 March,

Meanwhile the usual potential uses for the Airborne were dreamed up by the generals and the rumour mill in equal measure. One old suggestion was less far-fetched than might be thought, for as far back as November 1944 Brereton had been asked to plan for a potential drop on Berlin. This was to be an operation that was to become an 82nd speciality post-war, the airfield take-down. Accordingly the paratroopers practised. Even on practice jumps some injuries were inevitable, but on one particular occasion, a Dakota that had just discharged its troopers suffered what appeared to be a propeller runaway and dived straight into the stick in front of it, taking five men to their death.

The Berlin jump was never to take place, since possibly for the first time in the war the 82nd was actually being held back to preserve its highly trained troops. The reasons, however, were entirely cynical. Unbeknown to Gavin the division was earmarked for the invasion of Japan, an assault which could well mean the sacrifice of the Airborne to achieve the aim.

Consequently it was the US 17th and the British 6th Airborne Divisions who made the last major drop of the war, Operation Varsity, on 24 March. Sent to to secure a bridgehead near Duisburg on the east bank of the Rhine the paras showed they had learned the lessons of Holland. In a little over two hours 1,696 aircraft and gliders landed 21,680 troopers. Losses were significant but the armour linked up the same day and the objective was secured.

Above: Colonel Charles Billingslea commanded the 325th Glider Regiment during the Battle of the Bulge. (82nd Airborne Museum)

The 82nd finally left the Sissone-Suippes area on 31 March, moving by road and rail to take up positions around the devastated German city of Cologne. There they found themselves guarding some 10,000 Russian slave labourers and PoWs abandoned by the retreating Germans, in addition to occupation duties. Whilst they were not supposed to be in 'combat' the troopers saw no reason for not conducting aggressive night patrols into German-held territory across the Rhine, or exchanging fire with the other side when possible. Off duty the men found it equally difficult to resist the charms of the local girls, despite this being technically 'fraternisation' which was forbidden.

Below: Men of the 508th PIR process German prisoners on 3 January 1945. (US Army)

The patrols across the Rhine became a major incursion on 6 April when a company of the 504th occupied the town of Hitdorf for nearly 24 hours. With the aid of reinforcement by another company they held off counter-attacks by 'seriously pissed'* German infantry and Tiger tanks. By the time the two companies withdrew the Germans had suffered some 200 casualties and drawn so many men from other positions that 13 miles away American forces broke through the resultant thinned lines—another good day for the Airborne.

By mid-April the Allied advance had slowed at the last major obstacle, the Elbe. Slated to cross this were the 82nd, along with 7th Armored and 8th Infantry, together with the British 6th Airborne. Accordingly the troopers once more boarded trucks for the front. During the journey they witnessed much of the devastation and destruction of the once great Reich.

On 23 April Soviet forces reached Berlin.

By the night of 28 April the 505th was at the banks of the Elbe and preparing for the crossing. Germans could be seen digging in on the other side but appeared somewhat half-hearted—few wanted to die for an already lost cause. The following night the collapsible boats were brought up and at 01.00hrs on the 29th the 505th surged across near the hamlet of Blekede, taking the Germans completely by surprise and encountering only sporadic resistance. The 504th followed and by noon the following day, despite a fierce artillery barrage, a pontoon had been

constructed and the 82nd was across in force. That same day Hitler committed suicide in Berlin. 1 May found the troopers of the 82nd driving deeper into German territory with their preferred support, the 740th Tank Battalion.

Throughout the European fighting the paras had regarded tankers with some disdain, indeed they had suffered in the Ardennes when tanks 'cut and ran' instead of supporting them. Consequently when, on 29 December, Lt Colonel George K. Rubel had reported to the 505th that he was there to assist them he received a frankly hostile response. 'Tanks,' he was told, were 'more of a liability than an asset, they can't keep up with our troops.' Somewhat rankled by this, Rubel assured the paras that he would keep up if 'your guys get up off the ground and fight.' Within the hour infantry and tankers had surprised each other and hostility had changed to mutual respect. So it remained in May as the troopers of the 82nd pushed across Germany riding on the 740th's tanks.

Even so they never ceased to amaze the uninitiated. One newly arrived tank commander radioed his CO that he could not see the infantry following him—he was advised to look to the front for the 82nd. A little later on he again radioed that troopers were now passing him on bicycles. Shortly after that a horse and buggy with seven or eight troopers passed him. Later still, to his utter incredulity, he reported some 20 troopers on horseback rounding up Germans. Briefly formed that day the '505th Parachute Cavalry Regiment' continued to spearhead for the tanks.

Reaching Ludwigslust that night, the paras began to encounter increasing numbers of Germans fleeing westwards to avoid capture by the Russians. The culmination of this was a unique event in American military history, the surrender of an entire army to the 82nd. On 3 May Lieutenant General von Tippelskirch surrendered his Twenty-first Army of some 150,000 men, 2,000 vehicles and all their equipment to the paras. For them at least the war was over. On the same day patrols from the 82nd met Russians from VIII Mechanised Corps at Grabow.

Meanwhile other patrols had made a grim discovery just outside the town, the concentration camp at Wobelein. That night the mayor of Ludwigslust, who had been diverting rations intended for the prisoners to his own people, shot his wife and daughter before committing suicide. Although it was a small camp by German standards, the men of the 82nd were deeply shocked by the inhumanity and deprivation they found. Despite their best efforts many of the inmates were too weak to be saved. Shock was soon replaced by anger with the local townspeople and surviving German officers were made to dig graves.

That the German people might confront their complicity in such atrocity 200 bodies were laid out by these graves, dug in the town square, and the entire population forced to view them and pay some respect to those so grievously treated so close to their comfortable homes. Three chaplains from different denominations then held a memorial service at which the locals were left in no doubt of their responsibilities.

Many of the townspeople had simply refused to acknowledge what the Nazis were doing on their very doorstep, worse, many of the prisoners at Wobelein were 'political', including people from most of the occupied countries of Europe who had in some way offended the regime. For some the shame was too much to bear, and there was a rash of suicides following the memorial service.

The Russians

On the 5th contact was made with the main Russian formations. At first there was much back slapping and hand-shaking, a good deal of it for the benefit of those we would now call 'the media'. The 82nd attempted to socialise but quickly found that the Russian capacity for drink was almost limitless. Worse, the Russians were an undisciplined bunch concerned only with rape and pillage of the local population. Within days fraternisation was forbidden and all the appalled troopers could do was try to come between the locals and marauding bands of Russian soldiery whenever they could.

At midnight on 7 May Germany surrendered, and the 8th, VE Day, was celebrated throughout Europe with great euphoria. The men of the 82nd, many of whom were already on leave, began to think of home.

On 1 June the division returned to France where the troops began to wonder about Japan. Any campaign against the fanatical Japanese promised to be long and bloody in the extreme. Reports from Okinawa of heavy fighting and high casualties did nothing to calm their (entirely justified) fears that sooner or later they would once again find themselves at the sharp end. But then on 6 August a lone B-29, the *Enola Gay*, released a single weapon at 31,600 feet over a city called Hiroshima. In a blinding flash 52 seconds later world history changed forever.

OCCUPATION

The men of the 82nd were not to go home just yet. In August and September they were moved to be part of the occupation force in Berlin. Like many élite units their elan meant that they could bull as well as they could fight. During the spectacular VJ Day parade at Templehof Airport a special guard was laid on for General Patton. The proud troopers with their white cravats and spit-shined boots so impressed him that he commented, 'In all my years in the Army, and of all the honor guards I've seen, the 82nd Berlin Honor guard is the best', thus bestowing on the All Americans another sobriquet, 'America's Guard of Honor'.

Berlin was not all parades. There were jumps on the airport, as much for the benefit of the Russians as for continued training, and police duties in the shattered city. Once again the troopers found themselves trying to control the worst excesses of the Russians, who had taken to systematic looting. In particular they were boarding refugee trains at the last station before the American sector and robbing

Above: Company B, 325th Glider Regiment, in Belgium, 28 January 1945. The white snow clothing is a mixture of snow suits and white capes and hoods. (via Real War Photos)

Below: Rotating back to rest areas after a spell in the front line, 22 December 1944. (via Real War Photos)

Above: Crews check out an M24 Chaffee, 19 January 1945. Chafees were introduced into the ETO in December 1944 and was well liked by its crews. Thinly armoured, they were used well into the 1950s nearly 4,500 being produced up to June 1945. Light reconnaissance vehicles were used by 82nd Airborne postwar, the M551 Sheridan—the only airdroppable tank—seeing service until the late 1990s, including the Gulf War. (via Real War Photos)

the occupants of anything of value. Even gold teeth were ripped out and anyone protesting was beaten or killed, with no exception made for age or infirmity either.

The trains would arrive in the American sector with several dead and many injured. This daily occurrence greatly angered the troopers who were powerless to intervene. Eventually their anger reached General Gavin who went personally to witness the situation. Having passed through a particularly harrowing train load of injured and dead refugees his party came upon the perpetrators roughing up an old lady. As the Russians ran off laughing Gavin had to be restrained from shooting them himself.

Orders were thereafter changed. American guards were authorised to challenge and arrest anyone caught in such acts. Should they refuse to submit a warning shot was to be fired. If they still did not stop the guards were authorised to shoot them. Shortly after that three Russians made the mistake of thinking they could outrun an 82nd marksman. It was not long before the attacks ceased.

For the majority of the 82nd the closing months of 1945 were to see them gradually shipped home (the US Army operated a points system, those with the longest service—and therefore the most points—went first). By Christmas most of the division was back in the States.

TRIPLE NICKLE—THE 555TH

There is an often-overlooked part of the 82nd Airborne's history during the 1940s that nevertheless shaped the development of the US Army as it is today.

During WWII US forces were segregated. Through ignorance and prejudice America's black people were only allowed to serve in separate formations, often in second line roles. Even so, where they were allowed to show their mettle, black soldiers fought with bravery and skill every bit the match of their white contemporaries.

Encouraged by President Roosevelt, the McCoy Commission (named after the Secretary for War John T. McCoy) recommended in December 1943 that a test platoon of black paratroopers be formed, and this was activated on the 30th of that month as the *555th Parachute Test Platoon. (The * prefix was used by the Army to designate what was then known as a 'colored' unit.) Inevitably, the men of the 555th called themselves the 'Triple Nickles', with 'Nickles' deliberately misspelt, a unit tradition.

It was not made easy for them—just to get in the platoon the soldiers had to be better than the best. Senior NCOs had to sacrifice their stripes if they wanted in. Training was conducted at Fort Benning, Georgia, a location where prejudice was

endemic and overt. Despite all the obstacles placed in their way 17 of the 20 men gained their wings. It is worth noting that in percentage terms that is a much higher success rate than is ever achieved today.

From the beginning the Nickles carried themselves with great dignity; they knew that they were pioneers, there to prove that it both could and should be done and they were not going to buckle in the face of any provocation. From this cadre grew first a company and then a battalion. In July 1944 the unit moved from Fort Benning to Camp Mackall, North Carolina. On 25 November the unit was re-organised and re-designated as the *555th Parachute Infantry Battalion. The soldiers continued to train hard, anxious to get to Europe and avenge the German insult to athlete Jesse Owen at the 1936 Olympics. This was not to be, however. Despite being combat ready, and despite the massive losses suffered by the Airborne in Normandy, Holland and the Ardennes, the nearest they got to combat was helping to pack parachutes for the Normandy invasion.

When at last secret orders were received in March 1945 sending the Triple Nickles to Camp Pendleton in Oregon it was assumed they were headed for Japan, training in demolitions and EOD (Explosive and Ordnance Disposal) giving some credence to the rumour factory. The mission was to be called Operation Firefly.

Attached to the 9th Service Command, the paratroopers soon found that they had been 'volunteered' as smoke jumpers to augment the few crazy guys who jumped into trees for the US Forestry Service. The reason for this, and the EOD training, was one of the most bizarre attacks of any war, Japanese balloon bombs.

Lacking the ability to attack the US in any substantive way the Japanese came up with a number of bizarre schemes (including a submarine aircraft carrier intended to attack the Panama Canal). The concept of the balloon bombs was simple, hang incendiaries from balloons which would reach high enough altitudes for the prevailing winds to carry them across America. A simple

clockwork release would then drop the weapons which would then start forest or crop fires. Great precision was not necessary—America is a big target—and bombs were scattered from Canada to Mexico, one falling as far away as Boise, Idaho.

The majority of the bombs, however, came down in the north-western forests, On 6 May 1945 a lady called Elsie Mitchell was on a fishing trip with five kids in Oregon, and they became the first victims of the bombs when a device they had found exploded.

This incident, and others where bits of balloon and equipment with Japanese writing on were found, prompted the Forestry Service to ask for help from the Army. Great secrecy was maintained at the time for fear of both the panic that might ensue amongst a population not used to being attacked, and backlash attacks on the Japanese-American population. Not mentioned was the far greater fear that these weapons could be used to dispense chemical or biological agents. It was also vital that the Japanese did not learn of any success and increase their efforts.

Disappointed though they were at not going to war, the 555th set about the task of becoming the world's first Airborne fire-fighters with great professionalism. From Pendleton four officers and 96 troopers were also detached to Chico, California, and the jumps commenced.

Specialised equipment was needed, for jumping into trees is dangerous and something most parachutists try to avoid. Modified baseball helmets with mesh face-guards became de rigeur as did initially a 50ft rope to allow the trooper a descent from the treetops. Over their standard fatigues the men also wore Air Force fleece-lined flying jackets and trousers, the tough leather giving additional protection.

Whilst there were the usual injuries through jumping (including one man who suffered a spinal injury and walked 18 miles to the airstrip for pick up rather than burden his colleagues), the only fatality the unit suffered in 1,236 jumps was a trooper who fell to his death after running out of rope when jumping into giant redwoods. Following this incident a 150ft rope became standard issue.

The 555th also used a modified

Below: The 'Triple Nickles', the 555th Parachute Infantry Battalion. (US Army)

'chute, known as the 'Derry', with one panel missing which allowed more manoeuvrability than the standard model. This of course presaged modern 'chutes which can be steered with some precision.

The tree jumping continued from May to August 1945, following which the Nickles returned to Fort Bragg where they were initially attached to 27th Headquarters and Headquarters Special Troops First Army. In December they were attached to the 13th Airborne. Still retaining its own authority and discipline the 555th was in something of a limbo during this period as men began to receive their discharge papers and go home. Finally in February 1946 the Triple Nickles became a battalion attached for administrative purposes to the 504th. The 504th's colonel at the time was a man who was to rise to great prominence later—William Westmoreland. Gavin, who knew good soldiers when he saw them, made sure that the Triple Nickles were part of the victory parade as full members of the 82nd Airborne. The Army meanwhile was only slowly coming to recognise their worth.

What made the 555th unique amongst 'colored' units in US service was that it was the only formation which was all-black, officers and men (other units had black enlisted men and white officers). The troopers had also had to deal with the ignorance and bigotry of the time throughout their existence. This they accomplished with the professionalism, self-confidence and pride that comes with being Airborne. Whatever ill-informed society thought, these men knew they were the best of the best. So well did they acquit themselves in fact that in 1947 Gavin went personally to Washington to request that they become a permanent part of the 82nd. This far-sighted move was made at some professional risk—there remains a feeling in some quarters that Gavin retired without a fourth star because of his support for the 555th.

On 13 December 1947 the 555th was de-activated, its colours cased, and it became the 3rd Battalion, 505th. History was not done with the Nickles yet. In July 1948 President Truman ordered that the US forces be integrated and in December the 3rd/505th was de-activated and its personnel absorbed into the 82nd as a whole. The process of integration was greatly aided by the officers and men of the unit who gradually took their professionalism out into the wider Army community as they dispersed on different assignments.

More than one member of the 82nd has commented to this author that much of the heartache and racial tension of the fifties and sixties would have been avoided if men of all races had served together in WWII. Bonds and mutual respect forged in the crucible of war are not easily broken—'there are', as one veteran said, 'no racial or religious differences in a fox hole.'

The modern US Army owes a considerable debt to the 555th, a debt most recently acknowledged by no lesser person than Colin Powell, America's most senior black soldier. He credits the 555th with setting the stage that enabled his rise to the very top of his profession.

Many of the original members of the 555th went on to achieve high rank and do great things in the post-war Army. One of the original platoon members, Sergeant Roger S. Walden won a Silver Star in Korea for instance. Today, wherever the veterans go, young paratroopers want to shake their hands—one ex-trooper, Cecil Malone, still jumps, drawing thunderous applause as he executes perfect landings in front of three generations of paratroopers. The Nickles will not be forgotten, or for that matter fade away.

Below: The US flag goes up over a town in East Germany during the final days of the European campaign. During three years of war 82nd had notched up 422 days in combat. Over 3,200 personnel had been killed in action out of a total missing, wounded, injured or killed of over 15,000—more than the strength of a complete late 1944 division, approximately 13,000 men. (82nd Airborne Museum)

PARATROOP RIFLE COMPANY AIRCRAFT LOADING FOR MARKET GARDEN

AIRCRAFT #1—15 men, 2 containers

Company CO
2 x Radio operators
2 x Messengers
2 x ATRL squads (gunner and asst gunner)
2 x Riflemen
Armorer artificer
QM sergeant
Cargo sergeant
1st sergeant

A5 Container # 1
2 x ATRLs in frame
4 x bags ammo (ea 6 rockets)
2 x blankets

A5 Container # 2
1 x Gas alarm
1 x SCR 300 radio
1 x SCR battery
1 x Panel, AP50A, set
1 x EE8A
2 x blankets and 2 x 2 by 4s

Eleven aircraft were needed to carry a paratroop rifle company during Operation Market Garden, loaded as shown here. On D-Day, 17 September 1944, 413 C-47s and C-53s carried 6,312 paratroops to the dropzone.

AIRCRAFT # 2—16 men, 2 containers
1st Squad 1st Platoon

1st Platoon leader
Radio operator
1 x LMG squad (gunner, asst gunner, ammo bearer)
AT grenadier
Aid man
Messenger
1 x Rifle squad (leader, asst leader, 6 x riflemen)

A5 Container # 3
1 x LMG and spare barrel
1 x pair shoulder pads
4 x boxes MG ammo
1 x camo net
2 x ammo bags (ea 5 AT gren)
2 x blankets

A5 Container # 4
7 x boxes MG ammo
20 rounds 60mm ammo
2 x blankets and 2 x 2 by 4s

AIRCRAFT #3—19 men, 3 containers
2nd Squad 1st Platoon

Platoon sergeant
1 x LMG squad (gunner, asst gunner, ammo bearer)
AT grenadier
1 x Rifle squad (leader, asst leader, 6 x riflemen)
1 x Mortar squad (leader, gunner, asst gunner)
3 x Ammo bearers

A5 Container # 5
1 x 60mm mortar
4 x ammo vests (ea 10 rounds)
1 x camo net
2 x 2 by 4s
2 x blankets

A5 Container # 6
1 x LMG and spare barrel
1 x pair shoulder pads
4 x boxes MG ammo
1 x camo net
2 x ammo bags (ea 5 AT gren)

A5 Container # 7
7 x boxes MG ammo
20 rounds 60mm ammo
2 x blankets and 2 x 2 by 4s

AIRCRAFT #4—15 men, 2 containers
3rd Squad 1st Platoon

1st Platoon assistant leader
Messenger
1 x LMG squad (gunner, asst gunner, ammo bearer)
AT grenadier
1 x Rifle squad (leader, asst leader, 6 x riflemen)
Signal corpsman

A5 Container # 8
1 x LMG and spare barrel
1 x pair shoulder pads
4 x boxes MG ammo
1 x camo net
2 x ammo bags (ea 5 AT gren)

A5 Container # 9
7 x boxes MG ammo
20 rounds 60mm ammo
2 x blankets and 2 x 2 by 4s

AIRCRAFT #5—16 men, 2 containers
1st Squad 2nd Platoon

2nd Platoon leader
Radio operator
1 x LMG squad (gunner, asst gunner, ammo bearer)
AT grenadier
Aid man
Messenger
1 x Rifle squad (leader, asst leader, 6 x riflemen)

A5 Container # 10
1 x LMG and spare barrel
1 x pair shoulder pads
4 x boxes MG ammo
1 x camo net
2 x ammo bags (ea 5 AT gren)
2 x blankets

A5 Container # 11
7 x boxes MG ammo
20 rounds 60mm ammo
2 x blankets and 2 x 2 by 4s

AIRCRAFT #6—19 men, 3 containers
2nd Squad 2nd Platoon

Platoon sergeant
1 x LMG squad (gunner, asst gunner, ammo bearer)
AT grenadier
1 x Rifle squad (leader, asst leader, 6 x riflemen)
1 x Mortar squad (leader, gunner, asst gunner)
3 x Ammo bearer

A5 Container # 12
1 x 60mm mortar
4 x ammo vests (ea 10 rounds)
1 x camo net
2 x blankets and 2 x 2 by 4s

A5 Container # 13
1 x LMG and spare barrel
1 x pair shoulder pads
4 x boxes MG ammo
1 x camo net
2 x ammo bags (ea 5 AT gren)

A5 Container # 14
7 x boxes MG ammo
20 rounds 60mm ammo
2 x blankets and 2 x 2 by 4s

AIRCRAFT #7—15 men, 2 containers
3rd Squad 2nd Platoon

2nd Platoon assistant leader
Messenger
1 x LMG squad (gunner, asst gunner, ammo bearer)
AT grenadier
1 x Rifle squad (leader, asst leader, 6 x riflemen)
Signal corpsman

A5 Container # 15
1 x LMG and spare barrel
1 x pair shoulder pads
4 x boxes MG ammo
1 x camo net
2 x ammo bags (ea 5 AT gren)

A5 Container # 16
7 x boxes MG ammo
20 rounds 60mm ammo
2 x blankets and 2 x 2 by 4s

AIRCRAFT #11—15 men, 2 containers

Company executive officer
Radio operator (300 set)
Messenger
2 x ATRL squads (gunner and asst gunner)
4 x Riflemen

A5 Container # 24 and # 25
2 x ATRLs in frame
4 x bags ammo (ea 6 rockets)
2 x blankets

AIRCRAFT #8—16 men, 2 containers
1st Squad 3rd Platoon

3rd Platoon leader
Radio operator
1 x LMG squad (gunner, asst gunner, ammo bearer)
AT grenadier
Aid man
Messenger
1 x Rifle squad (leader, asst leader, 6 x riflemen)

A5 Container # 17
1 x LMG and spare barrel
1 x pair shoulder pads
4 x boxes MG ammo
1 x camo net
2 x ammo bags (ea 5 AT gren)
2 x blankets

A5 Container # 18
7 x boxes MG ammo
20 rounds 60mm ammo
2 x blankets and 2 x 2 by 4s

AIRCRAFT #9—19 men, 3 containers
2nd Squad 3rd Platoon

Platoon sergeant
1 x LMG squad (gunner, asst gunner, ammo bearer)
AT grenadier
1 x Rifle squad (leader, asst leader, 6 x riflemen)
1 x Mortar squad (leader, gunner, asst gunner)
3 x Ammo bearers

A5 Container # 19
1 x 60mm mortar
4 x ammo vests (ea 10 rounds)
1 x camo net
2 x 2 by 4s
2 x blankets

A5 Container # 20
1 x LMG and spare barrel
1 x pair shoulder pads
4 x boxes MG ammo
1 x camo net
2 x ammo bags (ea 5 AT gren)

A5 Container # 21
7 x boxes MG ammo
20 rounds 60mm ammo
2 x blankets and 2 x 2 by 4s

AIRCRAFT #10—15 men, 2 containers
3rd Squad 3rd Platoon

3rd Platoon assistant leader
Messenger
1 x LMG squad (gunner, asst gunner, ammo bearer)
AT grenadier
1 x Rifle squad (leader, asst leader, 6 x riflemen)
Signal corpsman

A5 Container # 22
1 x LMG and spare barrel
1 x pair shoulder pads
4 x boxes MG ammo
1 x camo net
2 x ammo bags (ea 5 AT gren)

A5 Container # 23
7 x boxes MG ammo
20 rounds 60mm ammo
2 x blankets and 2 x 2 by 4s

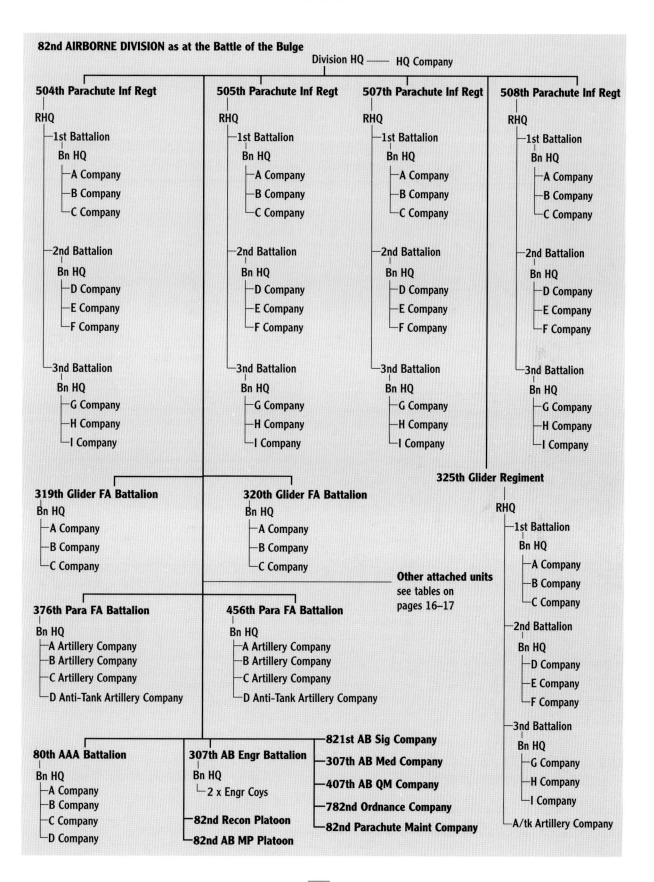

82nd AIRBORNE DIVISION as at the Battle of the Bulge

Division HQ —— HQ Company

504th Parachute Inf Regt

RHQ
- 1st Battalion
  - Bn HQ
    - A Company
    - B Company
    - C Company
- 2nd Battalion
  - Bn HQ
    - D Company
    - E Company
    - F Company
- 3nd Battalion
  - Bn HQ
    - G Company
    - H Company
    - I Company

505th Parachute Inf Regt

RHQ
- 1st Battalion
  - Bn HQ
    - A Company
    - B Company
    - C Company
- 2nd Battalion
  - Bn HQ
    - D Company
    - E Company
    - F Company
- 3nd Battalion
  - Bn HQ
    - G Company
    - H Company
    - I Company

507th Parachute Inf Regt

RHQ
- 1st Battalion
  - Bn HQ
    - A Company
    - B Company
    - C Company
- 2nd Battalion
  - Bn HQ
    - D Company
    - E Company
    - F Company
- 3nd Battalion
  - Bn HQ
    - G Company
    - H Company
    - I Company

508th Parachute Inf Regt

RHQ
- 1st Battalion
  - Bn HQ
    - A Company
    - B Company
    - C Company
- 2nd Battalion
  - Bn HQ
    - D Company
    - E Company
    - F Company
- 3nd Battalion
  - Bn HQ
    - G Company
    - H Company
    - I Company

319th Glider FA Battalion

Bn HQ
- A Company
- B Company
- C Company

320th Glider FA Battalion

Bn HQ
- A Company
- B Company
- C Company

325th Glider Regiment

RHQ
- 1st Battalion
  - Bn HQ
    - A Company
    - B Company
    - C Company
- 2nd Battalion
  - Bn HQ
    - D Company
    - E Company
    - F Company
- 3nd Battalion
  - Bn HQ
    - G Company
    - H Company
    - I Company
- A/tk Artillery Company

376th Para FA Battalion

Bn HQ
- A Artillery Company
- B Artillery Company
- C Artillery Company
- D Anti-Tank Artillery Company

456th Para FA Battalion

Bn HQ
- A Artillery Company
- B Artillery Company
- C Artillery Company
- D Anti-Tank Artillery Company

Other attached units
see tables on
pages 16–17

80th AAA Battalion

Bn HQ
- A Company
- B Company
- C Company
- D Company

307th AB Engr Battalion

Bn HQ
- 2 x Engr Coys

- 82nd Recon Platoon
- 82nd AB MP Platoon

- 821st AB Sig Company
- 307th AB Med Company
- 407th AB QM Company
- 782nd Ordnance Company
- 82nd Parachute Maint Company

EQUIPMENT & MARKINGS

EQUIPMENT

No analysis of the 82nd in World War II would be complete without some discussion of its equipment, particularly the aircraft, gliders and parachutes that gave the Airborne its special capabilities.

Douglas C-47 Dakota

The Dakota, developed from the civil DC-3, was so successful that it quickly became the backbone of Allied air transport operations, British and American. Capable of lifting cargo or troops, and towing gliders it quickly replaced the motley collection of aircraft (usually converted obsolete bombers) used by the British Airborne for dropping paratroops. Post-war demobbed C-47s formed the core of many a nascent airline, and considerable numbers fly to this day.

Capacity: 3 crew + 24 paratroopers
Span: 95ft 6in
Length: 63ft 9in
Weight, empty: 17,700lb
Weight, loaded: 26,000lb
Cruising speed: 160mph
Top speed: 230mph
Ceiling: 24,000ft

Curtiss C-46 Commando

Designed to do the same job as the Dakota, the C-46 had a much greater capacity (in both weight and volume) and featured doors on both sides of the fuselage to allow more efficient dispatch of troops. The aircraft was trialled during the Arnhem operation but suffered high losses with an apparent tendency to burst into flames rather easily. It was not used in the European theatre after that.

Capacity: 3 crew + 40 paratroopers
Span: 108ft
Length: 76ft 4in
Weight, empty: 29,300lb
Weight, loaded: 50,000lb
Cruising speed: 235mph
Top speed: 270mph
Ceiling: 22,000ft

Above right: C-47 showing under-fuselage equipment container stowage. (See page 158 for contents of these.) The unusual combination of British and United States' national markings in this wartime photograph suggest that the aircraft is flying over North Africa in 1943. (Museum of Army Flying)

Below right: Preserved C-47 with invasion stripes outside the Airborne Museum at Fort Bragg. Behind is a C-46—used briefly in Europe, it proved unsuitable and was relegated to the Far East. Another excellent C-47 can be seen at the new museum in Ste-Mère-Église. (Mike Verier)

This sequence of photos (see also pages 166–167) is obviously posed. Its quality, however, is so good that the pictures might have been taken yesterday. They represent a unique colour record of Airborne uniforms and equipment just before the Sicily landings.

Far left and Below: Paratroopers 'chuting up with T5 parachutes. Note the paratrooper boots and cumbersome entrenching tool. The trooper nearest the camera is just attaching his reserve to the harness. (US Army via 82nd Division Museum)

Left: This next soldier is wearing a parachute but interestingly seems to have a standard M1 'infantry' helmet. The Flag patch is worn on the left shoulder—the right was more common—and prominent on the left thigh is the canvas gasmask cover. (US Army via 82nd Division Museum)

Above: Landing a glider was never straightforward—indeed, most of the time it was particularly dangerous. The risks were not restricted to enemy gunfire or uneven landing grounds, some crews were killed by their own loads breaking loose and crushing them. This casualty is a Waco CG-4A. (Museum of Army Flying)

Below: A British Horsa takes-off for Normandy towed by a Halifax. Note the twin tow attachments under the glider's wings. (Museum of Army Flying)

Waco CG-4A

The most numerous of the Allied types, the CG-4 was a workmanlike machine of welded tube and fabric construction. The nose section was hinged upwards to permit unrestricted access to the essentially square-section fuselage capable of accommodating a jeep or artillery piece. In British service it was named Hadrian, a sobriquet not apparently used by the Americans.

Capacity: 2 crew + 13/15 soldiers (or 1 jeep/artillery piece and 6 soldiers)
Span: 83ft 6in
Length: 48ft
Weight, empty: 3,400lb
Weight, loaded: 7,500lb

Airspeed AS 51/AS 58 Horsa

Whilst a competent enough aircraft, the Horsa was constructed entirely of wood and roundly disliked by British and American troopers alike because of the way it would splinter in the barely controlled crash that a combat landing so often became. It was capable of accepting a jeep or similar. Two variants were built, the slightly larger Mark II having a hinged nose making access to the load more straightforward—the Mk I's tail had to be removed after landing. It was built (often in sub-assemblies by furniture factories) in large numbers and saw service on most Allied operations

Capacity: 2 crew + 25 soldiers
Span: 110ft
Length: 67ft (Mark I); 67ft 11in (Mark II)
Weight, empty: 8,370lb
Weight, loaded: 15,500lb (Mark I); 15,750lb (Mark II)

Above: View of General Aircraft Ltd's factory showing the prototype Hamilcar and, in front, the production line of the smaller Hotspur. Designed along the same lines as the German DFS 230, it was relegated to a training role by the much bigger Horsa. (Museum of Army Flying)

Left: Waco CG-4 gliders collected together for return to the UK following landings during the Dutch campaign. More survived the daylight landings here, when compared with the vast numbers written off during the Normandy operations. (via Bruce Robertson)

General Aircraft GAL 49 Hamilcar

The largest glider built by the Allies, the Hamilcar was designed to bring heavy loads and vehicles to the battlefield. The cockpit sat above a 'straight through' cabin accessed via a hinged nose. The Hamilcar had the distinction of a tank (the Tetrarch) specially designed to fit in it. A powered version was trialled, but the war ended before it could be put in service.

Capacity: 1 x Tetrach or Locust; or 2 x Bren carrriers; or bulldozer
Span: 110ft
Length: 68ft
Weight, loaded: 32,500lb

Below: Study of a General Aircraft Hamilcar. The last remaining Hamilcar fuselage—discovered performing as a garden shed—is on show at Middle Wallop. (Museum of Army Flying)

Above: Officers at a briefing. Note the variety of shirt colours and the inconsistent placing of the 82nd Division patch. The man with his back to the camera wears American belt equipment (including, presumably, the .45 automatic behind him) but the beret suggests he may be French. (US Army via 82nd Division Museum)

Left: Despite the C-47 in the background (note red outline to National insignia confirming date as 1943), this lieutenant is a gliderman as evidenced by his infantry leggings. He has a field dressing taped to his left leg and carries binoculars in a brown leather case, as well as the ubiquitous right-angle torch. The large pouch at his thigh is for a gas mask and bears the markings of the Chemical Corps under the 'US'. The 82nd Division patch is worn on his left shoulder and the Stars and Stripes patch can just be made out on the other arm. He is to be wearing the M1C airborne helmet. (US Army via 82nd Division Museum)

Right: Fully rigged paratroopers by the door of a C-47. The aft door was for bulky items of freight (in the freighter role the Dakota could carry a jeep) For dropping paratroops, however, this door was not used. Two crewmen are taping over the handle to ensure there is nothing to foul the jumpers' harnesses or static lines. (US Army via 82nd Division Museum)

Part of the Presidential Unit Citation of Company A, 504th PIR for crossing Rhine River at Hitdorf, Germany on 6 April 1945.

Company A . . . is cited for outstanding performance of duty in the armed conflict against the enemy . . . This company crossed the Rhine River at 02:30 hours 6 April 1945, and seized the mile-long town of Hitdorf on the east shore with the mission of providing a base for further patrolling and to cause the German High Command to commit disproportionate forces against them in the belief that it was to be a major river crossing . . . the Germans assembled and directed a considerable portion of two divisions to the mission of containing and annihilating the . . . [US forces]. In mid-afternoon the entire area was subjected to a withering and devastating artillery barrage for two hours, after which counter-attacking forces in overwhelming strength with tank support assaulted the defending troopers from every direction . . . The troopers of Company A doggedly stood their ground, fought at close quarters, and at point blank range and inflicted terrible casualties on the masses of the enemy. Fighting with relentless ferocity throughout the afternoon and night, this gallant company held its ground and carried out its mission until it was finally ordered to withdraw to the west bank of the Rhine on the night of 6-7 April . . . Eighty prisoners were taken and evacuated and conservative estimates indicate that 150 of the enemy were killed and 250 wounded. The conduct of Company A reflects great credit on the Airborne Forces of the United States Army.

Parachutes

The three major airborne forces of WWII used 'chutes that were superficially similar in that they all had 28ft diameter canopies. In their detail operation they were quite different however.

The US Airborne's first attempt was the T4. A workmanlike job, the rig featured a reserve (emergency) 'chute which was carried vertically on the trooper's chest leaving little room for other equipment. Like all the parachutes for assault troops, it relied on a static line to open the main canopy once the soldier dropped clear of the aircraft (the reserve of course was manually operated). The T4 was superseded by the T5 by the time of the first operational jumps. The principal observable difference was the horizontal stowage of the reserve 'chute. (The Americans were the only combatants to use a reserve. With typical British phlegm their decision not to was originally based on the small size of the 'hole in the floor' exit on a Whitley, and later on cost. The Germans jumped from much lower altitude with a rig that in any case made a reserve impracticable.)

Both the American designs suffered from not having a single point quick-release (it was felt that troopers might fall out of the harness too easily). This, however, meant that getting out of the harness on the ground could be a struggle, taking up precious seconds and making the trooper vulnerable. This latter point was addressed by the T7 (first issued in 1944) which did have a quick-release.

A more serious complaint was that all three US parachutes had the canopy opening first, before all the rigging deployed. This resulted in the wearer going from 120mph to almost zero in a few feet as the canopy 'stopped' to deploy whilst the shroud lines paid out and then snapped the falling trooper to a halt. Such was the violence of this arrested motion that in Normandy some troopers found that grenades in their pockets simply burst through the seams and were lost.

The Germans also had a 'canopy first' 'chute, the RZ 20, which was even more demanding of the trooper. Unlike the British and American rigs in which the canopy lines were gathered into four risers, the Germans had a single point suspension which met an inverted V-strop attached to rings either side of the jumper's waist (inexplicably, as their standard aircrew parachutes were entirely conventional). This meant that the *Fallschirmjäger* had no control over direction or rate of descent. Worse, when the canopy snapped open he would jacknife due to being suspended from the waist. This arrangement resulted in a 'face forward' landing attitude. The one tactical advantage of the RZ 20 was its ability to cope with very low altitude drops. In Crete some sticks went out as low as 250 feet.

The British X-Type parachute on the other hand had none of the vices suffered by its contemporaries. Like the American T-Series it had four risers and the incumbent rode down in an almost sitting posture. Like the American rig the ability to 'spill' air from the canopy by pulling on the risers gave a measure of control, enabling the jumper to turn into wind for landing and to a certain extent steer away from obstacles (not that there was much time for such niceties at 500 feet in the dark). The X-Type also featured the classic 'turn and strike' quick-release, which made getting out of the harness a simple operation, saving vital seconds after landing.

Its most important feature, unlike the others, was a 'canopy last' deployment. Essentially the static line pulled the canopy out of the pack in a bag or sheath. The shroud lines then paid out evenly until they pulled the canopy out of its bag. The deceleration for the paratrooper was thus more even as the canopy developed. The downside was that it was therefore slower-opening than the German or American models, and less able to cope with low altitude drops. It was nevertheless acknowledged as the most reliable of all the parachutes used during the conflict.

Above: King George VI inspects British Paras wearing X-Type parachutes. (via Mike Verier)

Left: In full flight under his RZ 20, a Fallschirmjäger had no control over his descent because of the single point harness and bacause the shroud lines were too high above his head to be reached—well illustrated despite the poor quality of this photograph. (via Chris Ellis)

Left: 82nd Airborne re-enactor in full equipment—T5 parachute (the white of the static line that operates it just visible) on his back; reserve 'chute with red ripcord handle on his front; full belt, webbing, canteen, pistol, entrenching tool and knife; life vest; pack hanging between his legs; Griswold bag (on his right side and only visible under his right knee) containing his rifle; compass attached to shoulder strap; black waterproof bag (on left thigh) containing gasmask; Hawkins mine (the brown can on his left ankle); AN/PPN-2 transmitter/receiver beacon (in canvas bag in his left hand); unlined horsehide riding gloves; and, of course, M1C helmet and field dressing. (Tim Hawkins)

Right: Another re-enactment photograph showing a well-laden paratrooper (but not fully laden! In combat every pocket would bulge with grenades, K-rations and field dressings). Apart from the kit outlined above, this man carries a Thompson M1 sub-machine gun, a TL122C right-angle flashlight; and an ammunition pouch for the M3 (on his right hip). Note the white rope skein and the bottom of his pistol and knife holsters. (Tim Hawkins)

PEOPLE

Above: Pike.

Above right: de Glopper.

Below right: Towle.

Below: York

MEDAL OF HONOR WINNERS

Lieutenant Colonel Emory J. Pike
From Columbia City, Iowa, Pike was Division Machine Gun Officer and won his medal for action near Vandieras, France, 15 September 1918. While on a front line reconnaissance mission, heavy artillery shelling disorganised advancing infantry units of the 325th. He re-organised the men, secured the position against attack, and went to the aid of a wounded soldier in an outpost, before being severely wounded by shell fire. He later died from these wounds.

Corporal Alvin C. York
From Fentress County, Tennessee, York was in Company G, 328th Infantry, and won his medal for action near Châtel-Chehery, France, 8 October 1918. Corporal, later Sergeant, York is one of the truly great names in American military history. His story is all the more remarkable that he was originally a conscientious objector who only agreed to volunteer for combat after much soul-searching.

As ever in the fortunes of war, York's platoon just happened to draw the assignment of silencing some machine guns. Frontal assault had failed and the four NCOs and thirteen privates were to attempt to steal up unobserved. York, a Tennessee woodsman, had the point and led the patrol so skillfully that they completely surprised some 75 Germans. York was forced to shoot one who resisted upon which the rest surrendered.

At this point other German machine guns opened up on the Americans killing nine, including the other three NCOs. Whilst the remaining seven soldiers took cover and tried to guard the prisoners, York calmly took his rifle and began picking off the MG crews with precisely aimed shots. The 1917 Enfield rifle only had a five round magazine, and realising this a German lieutenant led five men in a charge on York's position.

They had clearly never encountered someone who had grown up hunting turkeys in the Tennessee hills. York made every round count, and as the last man got close calmly drew his pistol (the famed .45 automatic, not a weapon noted for its accuracy) and dispatched him, too. Eventually, after some 25 Germans had been killed, the cowed survivors surrendered. York and his remaining soldiers rounded them up and marched them back, even acquiring one or two others en route. When they finally reached the battalion lines they had no fewer than 132 Germans including four officers, along with the captured Maxims.

York's exploits were immortalised by Gary Cooper in the Hollywood film *Sergeant York* (xxx).

Private First Class Charles N. de Glopper

From Grand Island, New York, de Glopper was serving in Company C, 325th Glider Infantry Regiment, when he won his medal for an action on 9 June 1944, at La Fière, France, on the Merderet River. Part of a platoon that had penetrated the German lines but found itself in danger of being completely cut off, de Glopper and his comrades were pinned down in a ditch. Seeing that the only way for them to withdraw was to provide covering fire, de Glopper stepped out onto the road with his BAR and began firing on the German positions.

He immediately drew a large volume of rifle and automatic fire but, although severely wounded, continued to return fire. Falling to his knees he still continued to fire burst after burst at the German positions until he was finally killed.

Through his sacrifice his fellow troopers had been able to get to a more secure position and continued the fight, securing the bridgehead. Afterwards many wrecked machine guns and dead Germans were found to attest to the effectiveness of his fire.

Private John R Towle

Of Cleveland, Ohio, Towle served in Company C, 504th Parachute Infantry Regiment. He won his medal in action near Oosterhout, Holland, 21 September 1944, during the Nijmegen action. Armed with a rocket launcher, Towle single-handedly, and without orders moved into an exposed position and broke up a German counter-attack against the recently taken bridge, driving off some 100 infantrymen supported by two tanks and a half track. He then turned his bazooka on a house being used as a strong point and destroyed that before he was mortally wounded by a mortar shell.

First Sergeant Leonard Funk Jr.

Funk came from Braddock Township, Pennsylvania, and was in Company C, 508th Parachute Infantry Regiment when he won his medal, in action at Holzheim, Belgium, 29 January 1945. Funk, a small unassuming man, probably ranks as the 82nd's greatest hero, since he won every major decoration it was possible to win, culminating in the Congressional Medal of Honor at Holzheim.

Funk was one of many troopers scattered in the Normandy drop. Despite a badly sprained ankle he eventually rounded up a group of 18 men and set out to regain friendly lines some 20 miles distant across hostile territory swarming with German troops. After three men at the point had been lost Sergeant Funk himself took the lead rather than jeopardise any more of his men. He

Above: Funk about to undertake a jump complete with dog 'Shorty'—the original note on the back of the photo (in his own handwriting) attributes the location as 'somewhere in France' and the date as April 1945.

Below: 20 January 1945. During a lull in the fighting men of the 82nd receive the Distinguished Service Cross for the action at Nijmegen the previous September. Left to right: Col Rueben H. Tucker, Lt-Col J. A. Cook, Capt. Wesley D. Harris, Lt John L. Foley, 1-Lt Lloyd L. Polette and S/Sgt. Shelton W. Dustin. (US Army)

continued to scout ahead of the group for the remainder of the journey, moving mainly at night. Finally after numerous encounters with enemy groups, he led his men through the German lines to regain his own side. This feat won him the Silver Star.

During the Nijmegen operations in September he led a three-man patrol against a German 20mm flak battery firing on gliders attempting to land. He drove off the defenders of the guns before leading an assault that killed 20 crew members and wounded many more. The guns were out of action before they could come to bear on the gliders. The Army awarded him the Distinguished Service Cross for 'courageous and heroic action'.

Finally he was involved in an incident during the Battle of the Bulge which was more than any other to demonstrate his fighting spirit. A group of around 80 German prisoners was being escorted to the rear when the few guards were approached by four 'troopers' in snow suits. At least one of their number was English speaking and the prisoners were duly left in their care whilst the original escort hastened to rejoin their unit.

As it transpired the 'troopers' were German paras who began to re-arm the others with the intention of attacking their erstwhile captors. At this point Sergeant Funk came upon the scene together with some other troopers. Once again the similarity of both sides' snow suits aided the Germans who used the resulting few seconds' hesitation to close on the Americans. Sergeant Funk suddenly found a machine pistol pressed into his ribs by the triumphant German officer who ordered him to surrender.

Funk, whose Thompson was slung barrel-up at his shoulder, stepped back and made as if to comply. Then with one swift movement and a shout of 'surrender hell!' swung the gun into his hand and riddled the German. Still standing in the middle of the road he then led the brief fire-fight that erupted, dispatching the others and regaining control of the situation.

Sergeant Funk survived the war to be presented with his Medal of Honor by President Truman in person, a truly remarkable soldier, even by the standards of the 82nd.

Left: 10 August 1944. This Change-of-Command Review in England was the occasion Ike made his 'I owe you a lot' address. A beaming Eisenhower is flanked by Gavin (with his trademark Airborne helmet) and Ridgway. Nearest the camera is Louis Brereton, who planned the D-Day drops. (US Army)

COMMANDING OFFICERS

World War I

Major General Eben Swift	25 August 1917 to 23 November 1917
Brigadier General James Erwin	24 November 1917 to 16 December 1917
Brigadier General William P. Burnham	27 December 1917 to 3 October 1918
Major General George B. Duncan	4 October 1918 to 21 May 1919

World War II

Major General Omar N. Bradley	23 March 1942 to 25 June 1942
Major General Mathew B. Ridgeway	26 June 1942 to 27 August 1944
Major General James M. Gavin	28 August 1944 to 26 March 1948

Major General Omar N. Bradley

Whilst Bradley only commanded the 82nd for a few months before going on to greater things, it was he who set it on the road to greatness. Had he not been so determined to get the division to a high standard it might not have become the nucleus of the Airborne. Bradley's deputy, Ridgway, proved to be an inspired choice, demonstrating that an élite formation will attract the best officers and soldiers. Both officers believed in not asking soldiers to do anything they would not do themselves and were to be seen on the assault course to prove it. Once in Europe the division had in Bradley an officer in the high command who recognised its capabilities and championed its cause. His influence on the 82nd was felt long after he had relinquished direct command.

Major General Matthew B. Ridgway

Matthew Ridgway was born on 3 March 1895 and graduated from the US Military Academy in 1917. After varied assignments and study in the service schools, he went to the Philippines, where he served as Technical Advisor to the Governor General in 1932–33. In the next few years he served in various staff posts and studied at the Army's Command and General Staff school and the War College.

In Memoriam

As well as the many memorials to the 82nd (see page 92), the dead of the division lie in US military cemeteries all over the world including those in:

Ardennes, Belgium
Cambridge, England
Florence, Italy
Henri-Chapelle, Belgium
Luxembourg
Netherlands
Normandy, France
North Africa, Tunisia
Rhone, France
Sicily-Rome, Italy

http://www.geocities.com/pentagon/5340/wmmain1.htm
This website provides more information and links to the American Battle Monument Commission which helps those seeking information on any individual interned or memorialized at these sites.

In September 1939 Major Ridgway joined the War Plans Division in the War Department General Staff. Ridgway became Assistant Division Commander of the 82nd when the 82nd Infantry Division was reactivated on 25 March 1942 at Camp Claiborne, Louisiana. He succeeded to the command on 26 June 1942.

Under the wise leadership and skillful handling of its new commander, the 82nd soon developed into the most promising among the new units being quickly whipped into shape. On 15 August its designation was changed to 82nd Airborne Division, Major General Ridgway commanding. Half of its strength was subtracted to form the 101st Airborne Division. Ground training in new techniques commenced at Camp Claiborne. In early October the division had a foretaste of the future by shifting to Fort Bragg in the largest airborne troop movement ever attempted by the Army. Advanced ground training in alternation with flight exercises by both troop transport and parachute and by troop transport and gliders was pushed rigorously.

In the short space of eight months Major General Ridgway changed the 82nd from a brave dream into a deadly fighting machine. This amazing transformation was due entirely to the imagination, initiative and will power of a leader who was resolved that his command should become the premier airborne division of the Army, the first overseas and the first into battle. On 20 April 1943, the troopers left Fort Bragg en route for the combat zone.

In July 1943 the first major use of the Airborne was nearly a disaster, The destiny of the Airborne hung in the balance for many weeks thereafter until General Ridgway's convictions prevailed. Then General Clark called for help at Salerno. Eight hours later General Ridgway's troopers were on the DZ, and there was no doubting the value of the Airborne after that.

Ridgeway led the 82nd through the greatest invasion in history at Normandy. His planning and leadership resulted in the success of his division in that campaign despite the terrible losses it suffered during the initial drop. It was at this point, with the Germans 400 yards from his CP, that he made his famous signal: 'Short 60 percent infantry, 90 percent artillery, combat efficiency excellent.' The division fought on without relief for over a month in some of the war's hardest fighting, to take every objective assigned.

Following Normandy the division returned to the UK for re-fitting. In less than a month it was back to full strength and on 10 August 1944 Major General Ridgway assembled his reorganised division for a review by General Eisenhower. It was during this review that Eisenhower made his famous speech about how much he owed the 82nd.

Later that month, the XVIII Corps (Airborne) was born and General Ridgway became its commander, handing the command of the 82nd to Jim Gavin.

Major General James M. Gavin

> 'To the troopers of the 82d Airborne Division, who with courage and determination in their hearts, carried the fight to the enemy from Africa to Berlin. It has been a great privilege to have served in your ranks.' James M. Gavin.

Right: Major General M. D. Ridgway, CG XVIIIth Airborne Corps, and Major General J. H. Gavin (right), CG 82nd Airborne, talk somewhere in Belgium. Note Ridgway's trademark hand grenades and Gavin's 82nd Airborne Divisional patch. (via Real War Photos)

James M. Gavin was born in New York, New York, on 22 March 1907. At the age of seventeen, with some slight exaggeration about his age, he enlisted to begin a career as one of the best military minds the US has ever produced. He served as private, private first class and corporal in the 16th and 2nd Coast Artillery

Above: Official portrait of Gavin. (82nd Airborne Museum)

Regiments in 1925 but his ambition was always to reach the US Military Academy, West Point. This he did, graduating from there with a Bachelor of Science degree and a commission as a 2nd Lieutenant, Infantry, on 13 June 1929.

In August 1941 Gavin attended the Parachute School and upon graduation was assigned to the 503rd Parachute Battalion. In December 1941 he was made Plans and Training Officer of the Provisional Parachute Group at Fort Benning, Georgia. In September 1942 he attended the Command and General Staff School at Fort Leavenworth, Kansas, and upon graduation was assigned to the Airborne Command at Fort Bragg, North Carolina, as G-3.

Gavin became Commanding Officer of the 505th Parachute Infantry in July 1942 and remained in that command when the regiment was assigned to the 82nd Airborne Division in January 1943. The 82nd Airborne Division went overseas in April and the 505th Parachute Combat Team under the command of Colonel Gavin spearheaded the assault of Sicily on the night of 9 July 1943. He commanded the regiment in the parachute landing at Salerno Bay on the night of 14 September 1943 and the following month was made Assistant Division Commander of the 82nd Airborne Division.

In November 1943 he was placed on Temporary Duty with COSSAC in England as Airborne Advisor to the Supreme Commander, remaining on that assignment until about 1 February 1944 when he returned to duty with the division which had now arrived at Leicester.

In the Normandy invasion on the night of 5/6 June 1944 he commanded the parachute assault echelon of the 82nd Airborne Division, consisting of the 505th, 507th, and 508th Infantries. Upon being relieved from the Normandy front, the division returned to England in July 1944 and on 28 August General Gavin assumed command of the division, the youngest divisional general in the Army.

As division commander he led the division in the airborne operation at Nijmegen, in the Battle of the Bulge the following winter, and the spring offensive of 1945, until the surrender of the German Army. The division was assigned to duty in Berlin in July 1945 where Gavin served as American representative on the City Kommandantura until the division left that city in October 1945.

Known universally to his men as 'Slim Jim', Gavin was a natural leader, always first to jump. Dressed and armed exactly as they were, he led from the front. In

Holland he suffered cracked vertebrae during the jump (a terribly painful injury) and not once did it appear to slow him down. His chief of staff at the time, Colonel Weinecke once commented 'We have a wonderful system worked out, I stay home with the telephones, and my general goes out and fights with the troops.' His troops loved him, more so that he had a fine tactical mind which was able to apply fully the skills the Airborne possessed. The success of the 82nd owed more to Gavin than almost anything else.

Major General William C. Lee

Known with good reason as 'the Father of the Airborne' Bill Lee's career was cut short by a heart attack in February 1944. His contribution to the development of the Airborne, however, was immense.

Born in March 1895, Lee was commissioned into the US Army in the spring of 1917 as a 2nd lieutenant. He served some 18 months in Europe, first as an infantry platoon commander and then as company commander, rising to the rank of captain.

After the war he graduated from North Carolina State in 1920 and from the US Army's Officer School at Fort Benning in 1922. His various assignments between then and 1940 included observation of the burgeoning German airborne force. By now Major Lee, he returned to a staff job in Washington convinced that the US, too, should have paratroops. His enthusiasm and position earned him the command of the Test Platoon which so ably proved the concept of airborne soldiers.

By March 1941 Lee had been promoted to lieutenant colonel and was in command of the Provisional Parachute Group at Fort Benning and busily honing the skills and equipment an airborne force would need. As was to become essential for all Airborne officers Lee underwent the same training and jump qualifications as his men, despite being more than twice the age of the average trooper.

With the expansion of the Airborne came further responsibility and promotion. By mid 1942 Lee was a brigadier general in command of the Airborne Command Headquarters, re-located at Camp MacKall. With full activation of the Army's first airborne divisions in August 1942 came command of the 101st and the rank of major general.

Ironically, having built the Airborne from scratch, Bill Lee was denied the chance of leading his men into combat when, on 5 February 1944, his soldiers in England and ready to go, he suffered a heart attack. Invalided out of the Army in October that year he nevertheless continued to work for the Airborne, serving as the UN's first airborne advisor until his death in 1948.

Brigadier General William Yarborough

No look at the personalities of the 82nd would be complete without mention of Yarborough. One of the early pioneers, he contributed hugely to the Airborne. As a lieutenant in the 501st he designed the Airborne Brevet, the special uniforms with large cargo pockets, and most treasured of all, the Airborne jump boots.

By the time of Operation Husky he had risen to lieutenant colonel commanding the 2nd/ 504th. No mean soldier either, he and two troopers took over 100 Italian prisoners whilst supposedly on a recce mission during that operation. Later, as commander of the 509th, he instituted the wearing of small silver stars to indicate combat jumps, a practice taken up throughout the Airborne.

Postwar his interest in uniform and equipment continued, in the sixties as a brigadier general he was instrumental in the adoption of the green beret by Special Forces. He was also involved in designing jungle clothing suitable for South-East Asia.

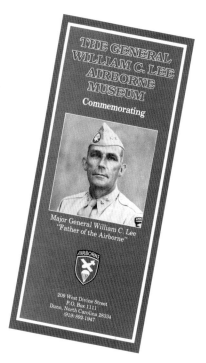

Above: The 'Father of Airborne' has his own museum in his home at Dunn, NC.

POSTWAR

The first post-war task the 82nd faced, even as its Honor Guard impressed the great and the good who visited Berlin, was to stay in existence. With officialdom's usual disregard for military achievement once a war is over, the 82nd was due for disbandment. Gavin used the opportunity presented by the hordes of important visitors to lobby for a permanent place in the Army's plans for the future.

During its time in Berlin the division received many honours, the most famous and unique of these being two presented to the entire division by grateful countries it had been instrumental in liberating. By royal order the Belgian Minister of National Defence presented the Belgian Fourragère to the division whilst the Dutch granted the 82nd the Willems-Orde orange lanyard. Soldiers of the division wear both decorations with pride to this day.

The division had won much respect in high places and was kept alive as part of the strategic reserve, becoming part of the regular Army in 1948 and thus assuring its future. During this time, the new atomic era, much debate raged about how to use airborne forces. The positions ranged from 'do we need them at all?' all the way to 'train the whole Army to be airborne'. Gavin, as ever years ahead of his time, continued to be the principal advocate and theorist of airborne tactics and predicted most of the modern developments.

'Developments' is the appropriate word. Sound tactics remain just that, it is equipment that changes. Thus when Colonel Jay Vanderpool's men at Fort Rucker were developing 'Airmobile' forces in the late 1950s, the mobility offered by the helicopter was combined with tactics from an 1898 manual for horse soldiers!

The division therefore remained combat ready. Ironically its high state of training kept it out of the Korean War for fear of a Russian or Chinese attack elsewhere. This meant that less capable divisions went to Korea with a consequent lengthening of the conflict.

Through the 1950s the 82nd trained for any contingency. Although primarily expecting to fight in Europe, if anywhere, it trained for territories from the Arctic to the jungle. The equipment continued to improve. The gliders were gradually phased out as new aircraft

Below: President Harry S. Truman and Secretary of the Army Frank Pace Jr in the Rose Garden behind the White House with men of the 82nd Airborne Division who toured the capital in February 1951. (via Real War Photos)

such as the C-119 Boxcar were introduced. At the end of the decade the classic C-130 Hercules arrived and continues to serve in updated form to this day. At the height of the Cold War in 1962 came the Cuban Missile Crisis. The level of brinkmanship was such that the 82nd was actually 'chuted up and ready to drop at the point when the Soviets finally backed down.

There were a number of structural re-organisations during this period, but the division's first actual (non exercise) deployment since 1945 came in 1965 when the USA intervened in the Dominican Republic's civil war. Elements of the 82nd remained there for some 17 months.

By this time the USA was involved in Vietnam. Once more the 82nd was held in reserve but as protests about this unpopular war grew so did civil unrest and rioting on the streets of America. In 1967 it was decided to use the Airborne to restore law and order. This, of course, was a controversial decision—rather like the British use of paratroops in Northern Ireland it could have led to even greater provocation. In the American case, however, the reverse proved to be true. Thanks to the efforts of the 555th and Gavin's early foresight, the 82nd by now contained large numbers of black soldiers at all levels. Seeing these men patrolling the ghettos proudly wearing the uniform of the nation's finest division made it hard for those intent on fomenting trouble to claim racist oppression. It was not a duty the troopers relished but their discipline remained unshaken and they carried it out professionally.

Meanwhile the 3rd Brigade was rushed to Vietnam to counter the Tet Offensive in 1968. This left the division very thinly stretched indeed and a 4th Brigade was formed to bring it back to strength.

During the 1970s the 82nd continued to train. Maintaining the standards it strove for was difficult in the post-Vietnam era but the division, probably because of its élite status, suffered less than other parts of the Army. Two major alerts brought the division's ready elements to within hours of deployment during this period. May 1978 saw the 82nd preparing for a jump on Kolwezi in Zaire to rescue civilians. In the event political prevarication meant that the French Foreign Legion went instead. Their successful combat jump was, however, to provide a powerful illustration of what could be achieved.

In November 1979 the fall of the Shah of Iran and the seizure of hostages in Teheran again saw the 82nd ready to go. Again it was not deployed on political grounds. Fort Bragg, however, was more than somewhat involved in the failed rescue mission that was mounted. Debacle though it was, valuable lessons were learnt and changes made for the benefit of the Army in the long run.

A new decade saw the 82nd serving as peacekeepers in that most volatile part of the world the Gaza Strip. For six months in 1982 the troopers of the 82nd kept the peace and worked (fortuitously as it later turned out) on their desert training. The following year the Airborne teamed with the Marines to restore the rightful government in Grenada. Operation Urgent Fury saw the first combat use of the new Kevlar

Below: 82nd Airborne train for combat in Saudi Arabia during 'Desert Shield'. (82nd Airborne)

helmet, and the UH-60 Blackhawk helicopter which was just beginning to replace the ubiquitous UH-1 Huey.

In March 1988 following an incursion by Nicaragua, the 82nd was deployed to Honduras. The mere presence of the paras was sufficient to ensure withdrawal, nobody now doubting that they meant business. By this time the shape of the division had changed, too, with better aircraft and equipment now on line, and increasingly, a true night capability. This capability was tested in December 1989 when the 82nd was instrumental in Operation Just Cause, the arrest of General Noriega in Panama. Panama also saw the first combat deployment of the awesome AH-64 Apache second generation attack helicopter.

The 82nd's biggest deployment since WWII came when Saddam Hussein invaded Kuwait in August 1990. As ever the Airborne went first. The 3rd/504th was for some time the only real force the Alliance could muster in theatre, though the troopers considered it lucky for Saddam that he did not attack them. When the shooting did eventually start it was, unsurprisingly, the Airborne who went further into Iraq than any other American force.

Since Desert Storm the division has not been idle either. Members of the division help keep the peace in the Balkans, whilst the development of new equipment and the relentless training keep them at the cutting edge. Nowadays, too, women troopers jump alongside the men—whilst they are still excluded from front line combat, most other specialities within the Army are open to women. That means that there are plenty of them in the 82nd, and that in turn means they have to jump. When the 82nd goes everyone goes, from the CG to the lowliest private soldier.

In the post Cold War age of defence cuts and 'drawdown' there are once again voices questioning the validity of airborne troops. It is to be hoped that those who criticise realise that they are free to do so because airborne soldiers gave their lives defending that right.

Below: Another sign of the times—a woman MP of 82nd Airborne in Panama. Note the Blackhawk in the background and the .50 cal Browning in the front. (82nd Airborne)

ASSESSMENT

Any discussion of how a unit performed can easily get bogged down in statistics. Perhaps the most important one in this case is how many good men died to achieve what the Airborne did. A better measure, if it could be made, would be how many did not die because of what the 82nd achieved.

There is no question that Airborne forces shortened the war, and that they were unable to shorten it further due to the failure of Market Garden was not of their making.

Right from the first operations they proved effective far beyond the numbers committed. Kurt Student, founder of Germany's much vaunted *Fallschirmjäger*, stated that had not the 82nd prevented a Panzer division reaching the beaches, the Allies would have been repulsed from Sicily. The Normandy invasion for all the air and sea power, for all the men hurled ashore, could well have had a different outcome without the Airborne, and for all that is written about Arnhem the fact remains that Airborne forces caused the Germans irreparable attrition. In the Ardennes, amidst indescribable conditions and having been caught by surprise, the Airborne took on and defeated the finest divisions the Germans had, preventing Hitler from splitting the Allies both politically and militarily.

In this last campaign of course they fought as infantry, without using their special Airborne capabilities—they just happened to be the available reserve. The point of course is that, unlike almost any other formation that could have been there, they were the ones with the skill, the determination, the tenacity and the confidence that being part of the Airborne had given them. Compared to 'ordinary' infantry Airborne soldiers were more motivated, better trained and better led. It is those three qualities that mark out élite units.

The men of the Airborne also built something this author has only come across in one other formation in the US military. Those who have served in the armed forces mostly speak generically about being 'in the Navy 'or 'in the Air Force'. The bonds formed in close knit élite forces, however, remain for life. In much the same way that anyone who has served in the USMC 'is a Marine' so the 82nd's veterans are 'Airborne'. This ésprit de corps extends across generations and remains as strong today as ever. That is a good sign for a society in an age of increasing selfishness and insecurity.

Above: After the problems of Sicily, US airborne troops—and 82nd in particular—performed with great skill and tenacity in attack and defence. Here, men of the 1st Battalion, 505th Regiment track down the enemy in winter conditions, January 1945. (via Real War photos)

Right: There are many memorials to the 82nd Airborne Division, such as the famous obelisk at Fort Bragg. This is the Memorial to the US Army Parachute Test Platoon—'We led the way'—at the Airborne and Special Operations Museum, Fayetteville. (Mike Verier)

Below and Below left: The original 'Iron Mike' Memorial is the work of Leah Herbert—he now has a replica at the La Fière bridge in France. (Mike Verier)

Below centre: Airborne memorial at Grave bridge. (Mike Verier)

Below right: Exhibit in the Ste-Mère-Église Airborne Museum commemorating the 5 June 1944 airborne landings. (Mike Verier)

During 422 days of combat in six countries the 82nd established a record quite unsurpassed in the US Army, its high casualty rate testimony to the way its masters threw it at the most difficult jobs. The 82nd alone could not of course win wars, what it did better than anybody else, was spearhead, breaching defences and taking on the most difficult opponents so that those who followed could complete the task.

What it also achieved was to influence the Army for a generation. The 82nd produced more generals and senior officers in WWII than any other division, proving that the best officers were indeed attracted to the Airborne. Post-war many other famous commanders would have their roots in service with the Airborne. The division also did more than any other to break down racial barriers and prejudice within the Army. The title 'All Americans' is one it is justly proud of.

REFERENCE

MUSEUMS

82nd Airborne & Special Operations Museum Foundation
PO Box 89, Fayetteville, NC 28302.
A brand new and very impressive museum sited just outside Fort Bragg in Fayetteville itself. The standard of the exhibits is extremely high. Covering the whole Airborne field it has one of (if not the) best restored CG-4As as well as more modern equipment. Website: www.asomf.org/

82nd Airborne Division War Memorial Museum Fort Bragg, North Carolina.
The division's own museum is sited in the heart of Fort Bragg. It has an impressive collection of equipment and memorabilia. There are also extensive archives for the serious student and a shop. Displayed outside are some artillery pieces and aircraft used by the division ranging from the C-46 to the Huey helicopter. Website: www.bragg.army.mil/rbc/training/82mus

JFK Special Warfare Museum Fort Bragg, North Carolina.
Also sited on Fort Bragg the JFK focuses on special operations from WWII to the present.

General William C. Lee Airborne Museum
209 West Divine Street, PO Box 1111, Dunn, NC 28334
Housed in the former home of General Lee, the museum charts the life and achievements of the man often referred to as the 'Father' of the Airborne.

Museum of Army Flying
Middle Wallop, Hampshire, England
Sited on an operational British Army airfield this museum has a fascinating collection of aircraft, including many rare prototypes and all the gliders used by the Allies. A complete CG-4 and Horsa are on display as is the fuselage and one wing of the world's only surviving Hamilcar. An extensive library is also maintained. At the time of writing restoration of a Hotspur glider is also underway.

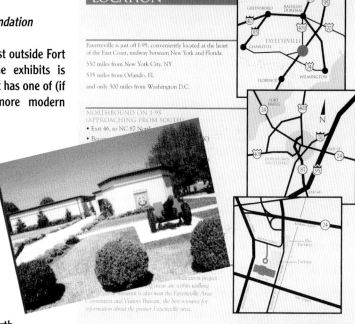

INTERNET SITES

www.bragg.army.mil/www-82dv/
82nd Airborne home page with history and individual unit links.

www.army.mil/cmh-pg/
US Army Center of Military History: large section on the 82nd.

www.fayettevillenc.com/airborne82dassn/
Official site of the 82nd Airborne Division Association which is chartered by Congress. It has chapters around the US—such as that in Washington, www.sy-dc.com/82nd/

www.quorndon-mag.org.uk/82nd-airborne/
Friends of the 82nd Airborne Division Association who help people trying to trace information on any servicemen from the 82nd Airborne Division who went through Quorn (Quorndon), prior to D-Day.

www.thedropzone.org/misc/mission.html
On-line virtual museum of airborne subjects.

There are many reenactment sites linked to the division and its units— eg the site of the 82nd Living History Association or that of 2nd Platoon, Fox Company, 505th PIR or D Company 505th PIR (www.mypage.onemain.com/db1014476/db1014476.html, www.foxcompany.org/ and www.dco505pir.fsnet.co.uk/index.html).

www.normandyallies.org/index.htm
Organisation to remember and teach about the US side of D-Day, includes histories of units.

www.army.mil/cmh-pg/matrix/82ABD/82ABD-Decs.htm
82nd Airborne Division Unit Decorations.

www.geocities.com/Pentagon/5340/
504th PIR homepage. Really good site with loads of info and links.

www.csupomona.edu/~rosenkrantz/paratroop/sgtdave.htm
Poignant website to the memory of S/Sgt Dave 'Rosie' Rosenkrantz of the 504th PIR who died in Holland 28 September 1944.

www.nijmegenweb.myweb.nl/
Tribute to the liberators of Nijmegen.

www.marketgarden.f2s.com
The story of Operation Market Garden including details of units and the battles at Nijmegen and Arnhem.

www.triplenickle.com
The excellent website of the 555th Parachute Infantry Association, with photos and historical data on this remarkable unit.

BIBLIOGRAPHY

Ambrose, Stephen E.: *Band of Brothers*; Touchstone, 1992.
A personal account from the perspective of a member of the 506th/101st Division. Again much useful detail on life in the Airborne.

Dawson, Buck: *Saga of the All American*; 82nd Airborne Division Association, 1946.
Published immediately after the war this is an invaluable source. Although the reproduction of the pictures is poor, the content more than makes up. Original reports from soldiers and war correspondents abound and the book covers every campaign in which the 82nd served.

Goldstein, Dilon and Wenger: *Nuts! The Battle of the Bulge*; Brasseys, 1994.
Original pictures are used to illustrate the terrible fighting in the Ardennes. The text is detailed and informative, offering details of the protagonists, the actual fighting and a comparison of the weapons used by the opposing sides.

HQ 52nd Troop Carrier Wing: Secret report 'Operation Market Garden'; USAAF, 1944
A time capsule that details the vast logistic effort needed to get the troops and their supplies to the battlefield.

Kershaw, Robert: *D-Day—Piercing the Atlantic Wall*; Ian Allan Publishing, 1993.
Excellent all-round examination of the invasion of France and the German defence.

McKenzie, John: *The All Americans. The 82nd Airborne*; David & Charles, 1998.
A personal account of one man's war with the 82nd's artillery. It is written with considerable skill and observation, both of the individual events affecting the author directly, and the overall narrative of the division's progress. Descriptions of both glider-borne and parachute combats are vivid, while a good deal of more personal detail of the men and conditions of the day adds substance to the whole. As a senior NCO the author was ideally placed between officers and other ranks to observe and record a very balanced account of life in the Airborne.

Thompson, Leroy: *On time, on target*; Presidio, 2000.
This book offers a detailed overview of the 82nd from its inception to the late eighties. As such it is thorough if a little brief in some areas, but on the whole this is a very readable and workmanlike account written by a noted authority on the subject.

Arnold, James R.: *Campaign 5—Ardennes*; Osprey, 1990.
Badsey, Stephen: *Campaign 24—Arnhem*; Osprey, 1993.
Kemp, Anthony: *Allied Commanders of WWII*; Osprey, 1982.
Quarrie, Bruce: *Order of Battle 5—The Ardennes Offensive V & XVIII US Corps*; Osprey, 1999, 2000.
Rottman and Volstad: *Elite 31—US Army Airborne 1940–90*; Osprey, 1990.
Smith, Carl: *Warrior 26—US Paratrooper 1941–45*; Osprey, 2000.
Osprey's handy guides to uniforms, equipment and organisation are invariably worth examination, and this collection makes a fine starting point for a more detailed examination of the division.

Abbreviations

AA	Anti-aircraft
AA(A)	Anti-aircraft artillery
AB	Airborne
ADC	Aide de camp
Amb	Ambulance
Arty	Artillery
asst	Assistant
A/Tk	Anti-tank
ATRL	Anti-tank rocket launcher (M6 Bazooka)
Bn	Battalion
BR/Br	British
Brig	Brigade
Bty	Battery
camo	Camouflage
Cav	Cavalry
CC	Combat Command
C-in-C	Commander-in-Chief
Cml	Chemical
Col	Column
Coy	Company
Det	Detachment
DZ	Dropzone
ea	each
Engr	Engineer
ETO	European Theatre of Operations
FA	Field Artillery
FJR	Fallschirmjäger-Regiment (parachute regiment). This may be followed by the number of the regiment, thus FJR 2. The individual battalion, where indicated, takes the form of a Roman numeral, thus II./FJR 2, indicating 2nd Battalion, 2nd Parachute Regiment
FJD	Fallschirmjäger-Division (parachute division). The divisional number takes the form of a prefix. Thus 4. FJD for 4th Parachute Division
FlaRegt	Flak Regiment
FPzD 'HG'	Fallschirm-Panzer-Division 'Herman Goring'
GIR	Glider Infantry Regiment
gren	Grenade
HMG	Heavy machine gun
Hy	Heavy
Inf	Infantry
LLStR	Luftland-Sturm-Regiment (air-landing assault regiment), with a battalion prefix as before, thus II./LLStR
LMG	Light machine gun
LST	Landing Ship Tank
Lt	light or Lieutenant
(1-/2-)Lt	(First/Second) Lieutenant
LZ	Landing zone
Maint	Maintenance
MC	Motorcycle
Med	Medium or Medical
MG	Machine gun
Mor	Mortar
Mot Inf	Motorised infantry
MP	Military Police
Mtrel	Materiel
QM	Quartermaster
Pfc/Pvt	Private (first class)
PIR	Parachute infantry regiment
Pl	Platoon
PzJg	Panzerjäger (anti-tank)
Recce	Reconnaissance
RA	Royal Artillery
RCT	Regimental Combat Team
RHQ	Regimental Headquarters
RZ	as in RZ20 parachute—*Rückenpackung Zwanglaulosung*, Lit backpack delivery System
Sect	Section
(T or S) Sgt	(Technical or Staff/) Sergeant
SHAEF	Supreme HQ Allied Powers in Europe
Sig	Signals
SP	Self-propelled
Tac	Tactical
Tk	Tank
USAAF	United States Army Air Force
USMC	US Marine Corps
Veh	Vehicle

Dates

20/07/54	20 July 1954

INDEX